Illinois
Off the Beaten Path®

"If you're a typical tourist, you won't need the book. But if you look for something different when traveling around the state, this guide . . . describes, county by county, unusual museums, country inns, festivals and other unusual places and activities."
—*Outdoor Highlights*

"*Illinois: Off the Beaten Path* lives up to its ambitious goals. The listings are comprehensive, readable and idiosyncratic. . . . Belongs on the bookshelf—or better, in the glove compartment—of anyone with a serious itch to explore Illinois."
—*State Journal-Register,* Springfield, Ill.

Help Us Keep This Guide Up to Date

Every effort has been made by the author and editors to make this guide as accurate and useful as possible. However, many things can change after a guide is published—establishments close, phone numbers change, facilities come under new management, etc.

We would love to hear from you concerning your experiences with this guide and how you feel it could be improved and kept up to date. While we may not be able to respond to all comments and suggestions, we'll take them to heart and we'll also make certain to share them with the author. Please send your comments and suggestions to the following address:

The Globe Pequot Press
Reader Response/Editorial Department
P.O. Box 480
Guilford, CT 06437

Or you may e-mail us at:

editorial@globe-pequot.com

Thanks for your input, and happy travels!

OFF THE BEATEN PATH® SERIES

Illinois

SIXTH EDITION

Off the Beaten Path®

by Bob Puhala

The Globe Pequot Press

Guilford, Connecticut

Cover and text design by Laura Augustine
Cover photo by Tom Deitrich © Index Stock Photography
Maps created by Equator Graphics © The Globe Pequot Press
Illustrations by Carole Drong

Library of Congress Cataloging-in-Publication Data

Puhala, Bob.
    Illinois : off the beaten path / Bob Puhala. —6th ed.
        p. cm. —(Off the beaten path series)
    Includes index.
    ISBN 0-7627-0795-X
    1. Illinois—Guidebooks. I. Title. II Series.
    F539.3 .F46 2001
    917.7304´44—dc21   00-046256
                                                        CIP

Manufactured in the United States of America
Sixth Edition/First Printing

For my Pa,
who made Illinois my backyard,
and my girls,
who make it heaven.

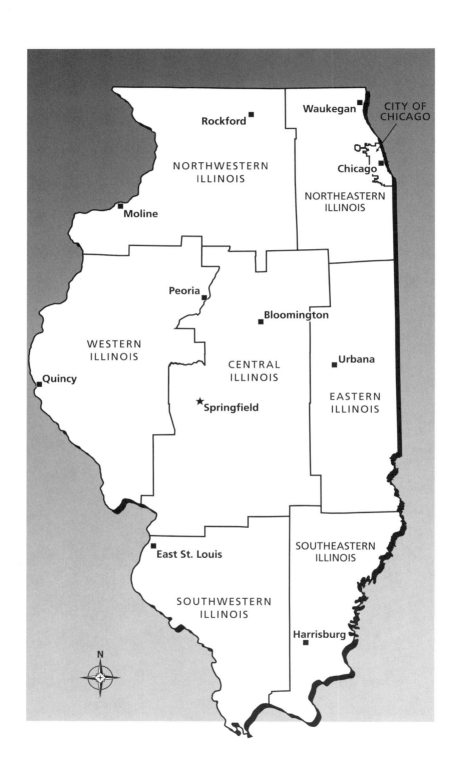

Contents

Introduction

Why would people want to spend their free time puttering around the backroads of Illinois?

Good question.

Maybe it's because the little discoveries that you make when wandering the Land of Lincoln—you know, the old French colonial forts that speak to another age in Illinois, the covered bridge spanning a little creek, the river bluffs hugging the Mississippi, the 200-million-year-old rock formations that look like something out of *The X-Files*, even the French restaurant located in the heart of the state's Amish country that doubles as a bowling alley—take you back to a simpler time.

That's what it does for me. I can remember my first off-the-beaten-path wanderings in Illinois, taken mostly with my dad when I was a little kid. Every Saturday morning, he'd come and wake me up at around 6:00 A.M. with a kiss on the cheek, fix me a breakfast of bacon and eggs. Then we'd kiss mom good-bye (she was never one for long car trips), point the Chevy in any direction, and take off.

Where did we go? Just about everywhere and anywhere.

We'd visit Galena and talk about the old lead mining days, maybe even take a tour of one of the old mines. We'd antique hunt in Frankfort and Richmond and anywhere anyone had a garage sale sign on the lawn. We followed the Lincoln Trail until we became close friends with Ole Abe. And we'd overnight on trips to southern Illinois, where the hiking in the Shawnee National Forest and among eons-old rock formations was almost beyond belief.

Could this all be Illinois?

All this—and more. Read on as I take you on a journey, crisscrossing the state to discover off-the-beaten-path Illinois. The real Illinois. Where people are friendly, the pace slows, and the beauty startles.

Enough talking. Let's go!

Illinois Facts

Tourism Contact
Illinois Bureau of Tourism: (800) 2–CONNECT;
www.enjoyillinois.com

Major Daily Newspapers
Chicago Sun-Times; Chicago Tribune; Daily Herald, Arlington
Heights; *Wall Street Journal,* Midwest Edition, Naperville; *Journal Star,* Peoria; *Register Star,* Rockford; *State Journal-Register,*
Springfield; *News-Gazette,* Champaign; *The Daily Chronicle,* De
Kalb; *Clinton Daily Journal,* Clinton; *Effingham Democrat-News,*
Effingham; *Southern Illinoian,* Carbondale; *The Beacon News,*
Aurora; *The Register Mail,* Galesburg; *The Daily Journal,*
Kankakee; *LaSalle News-Tribune,* LaSalle; *The Pantagraph,*
Bloomington; *Herald & Review,* Decatur; *The Telegraph,* Alton;
Daily Dispatch, Moline; *Belleville News-Democrat,* Belleville;
Freeport Journal-Standard, Freeport; *Commercial-News,*
Danville; *Herald-News,* Joliet.

Reading
Somewhere Over the Dan Ryan, Joanne Y. Cleaver, Chicago Review
Press; *52 Illinois Weekends,* Bob Puhala, Country Roads Press,
Castine, Maine; *Illinois State Parks,* Bill Bailey, Glovebox Guidebooks of America, Saginaw, Michigan; *Metro Chicago Almanac,*
Don Hayner and Tom McNamee, Bonus Books, Chicago.

Reading for Kids
Kids Explore Chicago, Susan D. Moffat, Adams Publications,
Holbrook, Massachusetts.

Public Transportation
Chicago: Chicago Transit Authority (bus, subway, and elevated
trains), (312) 836–7000, CTA buses require exact change ($1.00
as of this writing); Metra commuter train service to Chicago and
suburbs, (312) 322–6900; Amtrak train service to various parts
of the state, (800) 872–7245; O'Hare International Airport, (773)
686–2200.

Climate Overview
If you don't like the weather, just wait a minute and it'll change.
Chicago's weather can be quite mercurial, and the rest of the
state can offer dramatic changes almost overnight, too. Remember that the state's length is equal to that of an area stretching

from New England to Virginia, so geography explains some of the variation.

Count on cold, snowy winters and hot, humid summers, with some major temperature differences when comparing the northern and southern portions of the state. In the north, mean winter temperature is 22 degrees, summer 74 degrees; in the south, mean winter temperature is 37 degrees, summer 80 degrees.

The southern portion of the state also gets, on average, more precipitation than the north, with means of 46 inches and 34 inches, respectively. And tornadoes can occur frequently in the spring.

Population

Illinois (state)—12 million

Chicago—3 million

Chicago and its Metropolitan Statistical Area—8.5 million

Famous People

Carl Sandburg, poet

Everett M. Dirksen, senator

Wyatt Earp, lawman

Ronald Reagan, President

Wild Bill Hickok, lawman

Ernest Hemingway, writer

Edgar Lee Masters, writer

Studs Terkel, writer

Nelson Algren, writer

Charlton Heston, actor

Chris Chelios, hockey player

Jesse Jackson, civil rights leader

Jack Benny, comedian

William Jennings Bryan, politician and lawyer

Clarence Darrow, lawyer

Mahalia Jackson, gospel singer

John Hope Franklin, historian

Bill Murray, comedian

Quick Fun Facts on Illinois's State Web Site

• The name "Illinois" comes from a Native American word meaning "tribe of superior men."

• Illinois became a state on December 3, 1818. Illinois was the twenty-first state to enter the Union.

• When Illinois became a state in 1818, it had a population of 34,620 people. Illinois is now the sixth most populous state in the country, with almost 12 million people.

• Illinois's favorite son is Abraham Lincoln. The Lincoln sites in Springfield are among the best known tourist sites in the world.

• The state slogan, "Land of Lincoln," was adopted by the General Assembly in 1955. The State of Illinois has a copyright for the exclusive use of the slogan.

• The Sears Tower, located in Chicago, was the world's tallest building from 1973 until 1996. The Sears Tower is still the tallest building in North America. It covers two city blocks and rises one-quarter mile above the ground.

• Illinois ranks third in the nation in the number of interstate highway miles.

• Illinois was the home of President Ulysses S. Grant, whose home is preserved in Galena.

The prices and rates listed in this guidebook were confirmed at press time. We recommend, however, that you call establishments before traveling to obtain current information.

Chicago

hy not start your Illinois off-the-beaten-path adventures in Chicago? Okay, I can hear you saying, "What is he talking about? I'm in search of the undiscovered gems lurking in the Land of Lincoln, and he's sending me to the Windy City—second-largest (or third, depending on which government statistics sheet you use) city in the country."

Are you loopy?

Funny you should say that. Because the "Loop" and its environs in the downtown Chicago area is a great place to begin looking for "off-the-beaten-path" Chicago.

In fact, there's lots more to Chicago than Michael Jordan, the Sears Tower, and Wrigley Field. For example . . .

To set the tone for undiscovered Chicago, head to the *International Museum of Surgical Science and Hall of Fame,* 1516 North Lake Shore Drive, Chicago 60610–6502. While you take a time-travel tour through the history of surgical science (more than thirty "rooms"), you'll see everything from ancient medical instruments dating back to Roman times to true oddities.

Like the postmortem plaster cast of the right (writing) hand of English novelist William Makepeace Thackeray, encased in a red Moroccan leather folding case, with the original label on the collectible, reading, "A superb Thackeray memento"; (312) 642–6502.

Get the idea?

> **Chicago Trivia**
>
> *The site of Mrs. O'Leary's barn, where legend says the Chicago Fire started, is now occupied by the Chicago Fire Academy— the city's training school for new firefighters!*

Now that I've pointed the finger at one of Chicago's less traveled but quite interesting sidetrips, let's wander the city for some more off-the-beaten-path pleasures. These can be either places that are brand new to you or familiar favorites that hold some kind of lesser known enticement.

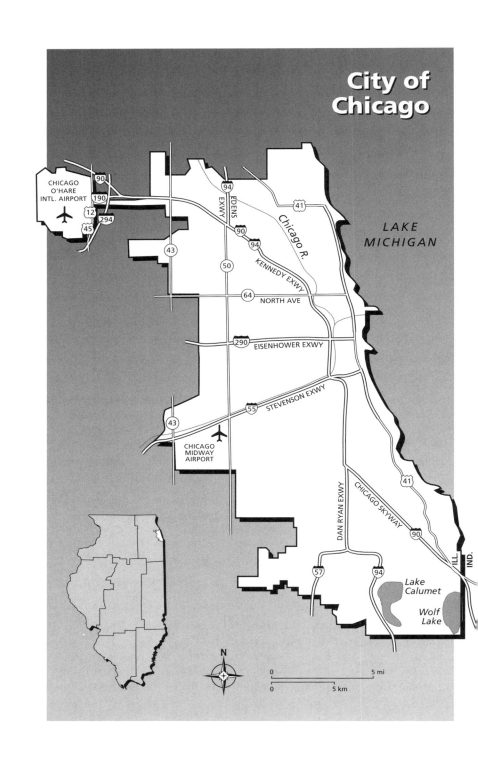

City of Chicago

CHICAGO
O'HARE
INTL. AIRPORT

90

190

12

294

45

EDENS EXWY

94

90

94

41

Chicago R.

LAKE
MICHIGAN

43

50

KENNEDY EXWY

64

NORTH AVE

290

EISENHOWER EXWY

55

STEVENSON EXWY

43

CHICAGO
MIDWAY
AIRPORT

DAN RYAN EXWY

CHICAGO SKYWAY

41

90

ILL.

IND.

57

94

Lake
Calumet

Wolf
Lake

N

0   5 mi

0   5 km

The Magnificent Seven

Perhaps we'll start at the north end of Michigan Avenue, dubbed the *"Magnificent Mile,"* to see what we can see. This portion of the "mile" is home to some of the swankiest downtown hotels and haute couture stores in the world. In fact, this strip of unbridled capitalism has been compared to New York's Madison Avenue (there's that Second City thing again) and even Rodeo Drive in Beverly Hills.

Nike Town Chicago, near Michigan and Erie, is certainly not one of those locations unknown to Chicagoans or out-of-towners. This paean to the "house that Jordan built" is 68,000 square feet of shoes, shoes, and more shoes. Okay, so there's authentic sports memorabilia, archival displays, inspirational video theater, and more. Bet you didn't know that you can try out those shoes on the second-floor basketball half-court to see if they'll really help you be more like Mike; (312) 642–6363.

Continuing south, the John Hancock Center plays second fiddle to its skyscraping, bigger, more tourist-popular brother, the **Sears Tower.** But that doesn't mean you should pass by a chance to take the tower elevators up to the observation deck. You'll travel at a speed of 1,800 feet per minute and, before your ears can finish popping, be more than 1,000 feet above the ground. It's said that on a clear day, you can see four states from up here; (312) 875–9696.

If you're still proud as a peacock to watch "Saturday Night Live," you can purchase a T-shirt bearing the show's logo at the NBC Tower, located off Michigan Avenue almost directly behind Tribune Tower. (312) 836–5555.

At the **Tribune Tower,** walk to the side of the building (I think they call it Pioneer Court these days). Here you'll see an interesting collection of stones cemented into the walls of the main building edifice, labeled as parts of the Alamo, Great Wall of China, Pompeii Baths, Hamlet's castle, and so on. They could be authentic; then again, at least they're a great conversation starter.

You'll have to take the stairs down from Michigan Avenue to Rush Street and on to Hubbard for lunch at the **Billy Goat Tavern.** Remember this is the place made famous by John Belushi of "Saturday Night Live," who as cook barked out the orders, "Cheezborger, cheezborger, no Pepsi, Coke." You can sample your own Billy Goat cheezborger, then get hip to Billy Goat's curse that has gotten the goat of the Chicago Cubs for more than fifty years.

At Michigan and Wacker, note the lines on the pavement signifying the structure that stood here until August 15, 1812—Fort Dearborn, which gave name to the Fort Dearborn Massacre. More than 500 British-leaning Pottawatomie Indians attacked U.S. soldiers and civilians inhabiting the fort, killing thirty-six men, women, and children while taking some hostages. (It is said that the wife of the fort's commander, one of those taken in the attack, was later bought back from the Indians for a mule and ten bottles of whiskey.)

Continue far south on Michigan Avenue to Grant Park. The object of your attention here is **Buckingham Fountain,** built in 1927 to resemble the Latona Basin at Louis XIV's Versailles palace. The massive fountain shoots water nearly 150 feet into the air, and for an hour before its 10:00 P.M. summertime shutdown boasts a fantastical color-and-water dis-

Be Like Mike!

*E*ven though I wrote that Chicago is more than Michael Jordan, lots of visitors—even off-the-beaten-path wanderers—would like to be like Mike, or at least visit some Mike sites. Okay. You might have already visited Nike Town Chicago on North Michigan Avenue, where you can try out the newest styles of those Mike-like $150 gym shoes on their own wooden half-court basketball floor. Then head to the city's near West Side, where a giant statue of Mike sits in front of the "house that Mike built"—the United Center, 1901 West Madison, home of the Chicago Bulls.

Other Mike activities can include everything from browsing the Michael Jordan Golf Stores (one is located in Water Tower Place on North Michigan Avenue) to teeing off on some golf balls at the Michael Jordan Golf Center, 4523 Michael Jordan Drive, in west suburban Aurora, 60504. Kids can play miniature golf there, too.

Of course, if you really want to be like Mike nowdays, you actually have to travel to our nation's capital; Jordan is now the head honcho of the NBA's woeful Washington Wizards, and he plies his CEO skills from a fancy office in Washington, D.C. When he's not on the golf course, of course. And though his Airness may not be as big a draw as he once was in the Windy City (his Michael Jordan restaurant on North LaSalle closed, and he's defected to the East Coast) he's still remembered for the unbelievable thrills (and the six NBA championships) that he brought to the city and the Bulls.

play. Watch the fountain, feel its cooling spray, stare at the stars, walk across Lake Shore Drive and gaze at the boats harbored in Lake Michigan as the blue waters stretch to the night horizon and disappear into a silky blackness

It won't feel like Chicago. It'll feel like paradise.

State Street/The Loop

State Street, the onetime Great Street that's making a comeback, is the heart of Chicago's Loop—named for the elevated train that encircles this area. You can browse the street and its environs yourself to conjure up the latest discoveries. But note that on the far south end, 1717 South State Street, rests the American Police Center and Museum, a well-deserved testament to the brave men and women who give their lives for our security and well-being; (312) 431–0005.

Open-Air Sculptures

I have always said that walking around Chicago's *Loop* is like visiting a museum without walls. That's because when it comes to open air sculptures by the greatest artists of the twentieth century, the Second City is in first place all by itself—a factoid little realized by visitors to the City of Big Shoulders.

To glimpse the grandeur of five of these magnificent works, some of which are often overlooked by the public, let's start with "the Picasso," located on the plaza grounds of the Richard J. Daley Civic Center, 50 West Washington, in the heart of downtown Chicago. When it was unveiled here in 1967, the untitled monumental contemporary by famed artist Pablo Picasso caused quite a stir—and lots of head scratching, too. What was it? A giant bird with wings? The profile of the late mayor?

Off the Beaten Path

Chicago Trivia

Chicago, nicknamed the "Windy City" for its blowhard politicians rather than lake breezes, actually ranks sixteenth in terms of windiest U.S. cities, with an average wind speed of a little over ten m.p.h.; Great Falls, Montana, is number one.

Picasso never revealed just what his piece represented. We do know that it is a 50-foot-high work of Cor-Ten steel. It kind of looks like a double exposure of one of Picasso's famous depictions of women, a head with an akimbo body. What do you think?

Marc Chagall's *The Four Seasons* often can be overlooked because of its location in a busy sunken deck of the First National Plaza at the crazed intersection of Dearborn and Monroe. Made of thousands of pastel-hued chips of more than 250 colors, the work (also adorned with hand-chipped stone and glass) depicts Chagall's images of flowers, birds, suns, lovers, and so on.

Much less viewed by visitors is a controversial sculpture by Frank Stella called *The Town Ho's Story.* Located at 77 West Jackson Boulevard, in front of the Ralph H. Metcalfe Federal Building, it has been denigrated for both its name (which refers to a chapter in Herman Melville's *Moby Dick*) and its aesthetic. In fact, some critics simply called it a pile of junk.

Whatever, the 18-foot-high amalgam composed of several smaller structures made of steel and aluminum evokes Stella's abstract bent.

Another overlooked work is *Reading Cones* by Richard Serra, resting in Grant Park on Monroe Street between Columbus Drive and Lake Shore Drive. Two austere, solid steel cups sit like ancient monuments, with a slight opening between them that only one person can squeeze through at a time. The minimalist work is worth a peek.

You have to go inside the Brunswick Building Plaza at 69 West Washington to see Joan Miro's *Mystical Force of a Great Earth Mother.* It was cast in the artist's hometown of Barcelona, then shipped and finished here. It stands 39 feet tall and is made of steel, wire mesh, concrete, bronze, and ceramic tiles.

Neighborhood Discoveries

One of Chicago's most intriguing characteristics is its neighborhoods. It might even be said that the city more resembles a "city of neighborhoods" than a typical metropolitan area. So let's head out of the downtown area and explore some of Chicago's less trod neighborhoods while revisiting a few favorites.

Little Village is the heart of the Mexican community in Chicago and maybe the entire Midwest. You can experience a little bit of "old Mexico" in the area around 26th Street and Kedzie Avenue, with all the sights, sounds, and aromas of the old country mixing here in a festive atmosphere. (In this neighborhood, 26th Street actually goes by the name "Avenida-Mexicana.") Note the handpainted murals on neighborhood walls depicting Mexican heroes (like Emiliano Zapata), history, culture, politics and religion, especially between 18th and 26th streets.

There may be no finer Hispanic museum in the Midwest than the often overlooked **Mexican Fine Arts Center,** 1852 West 19th Street, Chicago 60608-2797. Showcasing the finest of Mexico from both sides of the border, the museum boasts more than 1,000 objects in its permanent collection by such Mexican masters as Orozco, Siqueiros, Linares family folk art, and contemporary works by the likes of Carmen Lomas Garza; (312) 738–1503.

And if you're looking to sample an authentic Mexican meal, try **Los Dos Laredos,** 3120 West 26th Street, Chicago 60623-4144. Steak gorditas and fajitas are among the sumptuous traditional dishes; (773) 376–3218.

Walk through the colorful gate into **Chinatown,** which arches across Wentworth Avenue just south of Cermak Road, and you'll be entering

Don't Forget to Say Grace

*D*id you ever think of combining attendance at Sunday morning service with a good meal?

It's not a sacrilege at Chicago's House of Blues, located at the foot of downtown's futuristic Marina Towers, huddled against the Chicago River at State Street. Sacred music combines with exotic Sunday brunch at this eye-popping music venue, whose decor alone (a mixture of American folk art, African-American and Caribbean influences, and exuberant colors and textures) causes heads to shake with amazement and wonder.

More than a dozen serving tables provide all kinds of brunch specialties: smoked turkey, jambalaya, smoked catfish, peanut noodle salad—even brandy-laced Bananas Foster, flambéed in front of your eyes.

Then music begins, music that has been called "the best gospel this side of heaven." You'll be raising the roof in no time. And if the heavenly strains so inspire you, saunter up to the front of the stage where a handheld microphone allows you to join in with the morning's featured choir, selected from some of the finest African-American local and regional church choirs in the Midwest. Call (312) 923–2000.

The Best Laid Plans . . .

*O*n one of my first dates as a high school senior, I took my girl to a Friday night viewing of Buckingham Fountain. It was an extremely warm night and the thought of the cooling spray from the fountain was as appealing as possibly sneaking off to one of the park benches within sight of the water and exchanging smooches with her.

Of course, as a high school senior, being "James Bond cool" was the uppermost thing on my mind during all these maneuvers.

Unfortunately, the evening did not go as I had planned. The "spray" from the fountain was caught up in a mighty Chicago-style gale and nearly soaked us. My date began shivering uncontrollably. Nevertheless, I deftly guided us to the aforementioned park bench with romance in mind; but on my way I clonked my noggin on the low branch of a tree, scratched my forehead, and started bleeding. Then I tipped over the bench and we both muddied our already wet clothes.

James Bond? Nope, more like Woody Allen.

an exotic world of Asian culture and history. Forget the shops that cater to tourists; venture inside some of the smaller neighborhood stores that residents frequent (keep your eyes open). You can get your fortune told at tea shops, buy cures for what ails you at herbal shops, purchase rare Chinese silks and other arts, eat treats at authentic Chinese bakeries, and sample Chinese cuisine.

The best dim sum, served daily until 3:00 P.M., might be tasted at **Hong Min,** 221 West Cermak Road, Chicago 60616, located in a very plain storefront that belies its superstar cuisine status; (312) 842–5026. Another dim sum notable is the **Original Three Happiness,** 209 West Cermak, Chicago 60616, feted for its Cantonese/Szechwan specialties; (312) 842–1964.

Greektown, on Halsted between Adams and Van Buren, is all that remains of what was once among the largest Hellenic communities in the country. So populous was this ethnic neighborhood that the area was called "Delta" (the triangular letter in the Greek alphabet). Today, it's mainly a gourmet's delight, with restaurants such as Athena, Greek Islands, Pegasus, the Parthenon, and Rodity's serving up authentic Greek favorites such as saganaki, Greek sausage, roast lamb—and all washed down with generous swallows of ouzo. And you must try the flaming cheese appetizer—concocted not in Greece but here in Chicago.

More overlooked is the specialty shopping here. For example, **Athens**

Grocery offers those plump Greek olives; and baklava is the treat at the Pan Hellenic Bakery.

Taylor Street is the epicenter for one of my favorite neighborhoods, *Little Italy*, located just west of the University of Illinois–Chicago near Racine and Harrison. It's a tiny slice of Italy mixed into a spaghetti-bowl mixture of tall university buildings, expensive new townhomes, and old ethnic enclaves.

One comes here for the ambience, starting with "A Touch of Italy" posters hanging from area lampposts. And, of course, the food. Not many people realize that the *Vernon Park Tap,* on Harrison Street right across the street from the university's Behavioral Science Building (the one that looks as if it's been disassembled by a recent earthquake), was a favorite of Frank Sinatra. It's also a hangout for Chicago Blackhawk hockey players, who often grab a bite to eat before or after games.

Gennaro's, 1352 West Taylor Street, Chicago 60607, serves up homemade gnocchi, eggplant, veal dishes, and more. *The Rosebud Cafe,* 1500 West Taylor Street, Chicago 60607, has offered some of the best Italian food for almost a quarter century; in fact, it was named one of the fifteen best pasta restaurants in the country. You often can spot Hollywood stars eating here as they pass through town.

For a more casual approach to dining, try *Al's No. 1 Italian Beef,* another Taylor Street eatery, offering a mammoth sandwich of steaming hot beef smothered in hot and sweet peppers. And there's no better place for old-fashioned Italian ice than Taylor Street's *Mario's Italian Lemonade.*

Popcorn

*N*o trip to downtown Chicago is complete without a stop at one of the five Garrett Popcorn Shops sprinkled throughout the Magnificent Mile and the Loop. This heavenly concoction of freshly made gourmet popcorn has been a Chicago favorite since 1949.

It's good at any time. But when you're waiting in line for a bag of goodies, and the CaramelCrisp corn is piping hot, just popping out of the roaster,

and the counter person scoops it into your waxed-paper bag, and you reach down inside and pull out some of those caramel-drenched hot kernels . . . umm, umm, it is heavenly.

For a special treat, try Garrett's "Downtown Mix"—a combination of CaramelCrisp and CheeseCorn. It has been called "addictive"; it also has been rated "the best in the world" by food critics.

Chicago Trivia

One of the city's "newest" neighborhoods is *Printer's Row,* just south of the Loop. A once-dilapidated area, the region's renaissance (spearheaded by urban pioneers—stores, and lots of yuppies) includes a plethora of landmark buildings, expensive lofts, condominiums and townhomes, art galleries, bookstores, and jazz and blues clubs. Even Mayor Daley moved near here a few years ago from his family's historic enclave in Bridgeport.

Chicago's Official Visitors Guide says that "if you loved San Francisco's North Beach in the 1960s, you're going to feel right at home in Chicago's hottest new neighborhood"—*Bucktown/Wicker Park.* I have always loved it. But maybe that's because this is where I grew up.

Of course, back in my kid days, Bucktown was filled with mostly Polish (and German) ethnics who kept clean houses, well-scrubbed families,

Go Wild in the City

*O*kay, so the Lincoln Park neighborhood may be one of the best-known sections of the city, with its beautiful Lake Michigan shorefront parks, tony high-rises, and bikes paths galore. But I couldn't write a book about Illinois without a mention of my favorite zoo in the world—Lincoln Park Zoo.

And it's not just because entrance is free—remarkable in this day—but because this is one of the most accessible wildlife retreats in the country, with spectacular animal displays in natural habitats that put you almost face-to-face with these beautiful creatures.

The zoo got its start back in 1868, when New York's Central Park Zoo gave the Windy City two swans. Acreage was taken near the lakefront for these animals, and the collection continued to grow. Today, Lincoln Park Zoo is the second oldest zoo in America, as well

as the smallest "major" zoo—covering little more than 35 acres but including more than 1,600 animals.

It boasts a spectacular Great Ape House, where you can watch 400-pound gorillas swing on heavy ropes from station to station. There also is a Lion House, Reptile House (look, Steve-O, an alligator . . . isn't she a beauty!), Sea Lion Pool (these guys are real hams), Penguin and Seabird House (it's cold in here and a great spot for summer cool downs), walk-through Rookery, Children's Zoo, and more.

One of my favorite zoo spots remains Farm-in-the-Zoo, a mini-farm where you can pet a horse, tend to sheep, see chicks being hatched, watch cows being milked, and more. All in all, a real moo-ving experience. The zoo entrance is on Webster and Stockton; for hours, call (312) 742–2000.

Chicago Trivia

Baggage tags for Chicago's O'Hare International Airport are marked "ORD" because the airport was originally named Orchard Field.

and even washed the sidewalks in front of their home daily. When their children moved to the suburbs, the neighborhood fell into disrepair.

But it has risen like a phoenix, becoming "the place" for artists, actors, and other free-spirited types. Most visitors don't make it to Bucktown during a Chicago visit. You must. The coffeehouses, jazz clubs, poetry slams, performance art, galleries, and restaurants are cutting edge. Be sure to visit my favorite eatery in Bucktown—*Club Lucky,* 1824 West Wabansia, Chicago 60622. Not only is the food really good, but also the waitstaff are ultra hip. And people-watching here is a fascinating delight.

Other neighborhoods worth checking out on your own include the tony *DePaul/Halsted area,* just off the Loop; *Heart of Italy,* one of the oldest sections of the city, where most of the residents come from Tuscany, located ten minutes west of the Loop; *River North,* an art lover's delight; and *Andersonville,* filled with bakeries, stores, shops, and restaurants featuring Scandinavian crafts and food.

Mary

"*R*esurrection Mary" is perhaps Chicago's most enduring (and endearing) apparition. For decades the tales of encounters with this ghost, a beautiful young woman with blue eyes and flaxen hair, haven't changed.

She takes her name from her ultimate destination, **Resurrection Cemetery,** 7200 South Archer Road in nearby suburban Justice. Is Mary her real name? No one knows for sure, but there is a girl of Polish descent named Mary about the same age interred in the cemetery, according to burial records there.

Mary is always seen wearing a long, off-white ballroom gown and dancing shoes . . . in which she died in 1934.

Legend says she met her end upon returning from the O. Henry Ballroom (now called the Willowbrook).

How do appearances occur? She is most often seen coatless and in her gown on the side of a road (especially in bad weather) near Resurrection. A kindly Good Samaritan, most often a male driver, pulls over to give the beautiful lady in distress a ride to her home. She gets in and drivers note that the car suddenly seems icy cold inside. Then as the car passes the cemetery, she either simply disappears from inside the car . . . or asks the driver to pull over in front of the cemetery, jumps out of the car, and runs right through the cemetery's closed gates!

Tour Tales

It seems like everyone who comes to the Windy City takes some kind of tour to get a better feel for the area. But why sign up for a bus tour that will take you to all the usual haunts when you could do some tours that are much more fun—and unusual.

Take Me Out to the . . .

Finally, let's not forget one of Chicago's most famous neighborhoods, at least during the April through October baseball season—Wrigleyville. This upscale enclave owes most of its joie de vivre to Wrigley Field, the venerable home ballyard of the Chicago Cubs, which is located at Clark and Addison. It is a happening that should be experienced even by non-baseball fans.

The excitement builds outside the ballpark as crowds swirl around the Harry Caray statue (a tribute to the Hall of Fame Cubs' broadcaster who passed on a few years ago), look for scalpers hawking hard-to-get tickets, and stock up on bargain peanuts before going inside.

As you make your way through the bowels of the old stadium and finally emerge to the playing field, you'll be overcome by a sense of nostalgia. This is the way baseball should be played—on a sea of green grass, with brick outfield walls covered with ivy (which occasionally turn a triple into a ground-rule double when the ball disappears into the vines), and seating right on top of the action. You could literally touch Sammy Sosa when he practices his mighty swing in the on-deck circle (but don't try— you'll immediately be ejected from the park!).

Night baseball is another twist to the Wrigley Field experience. Though it seems no big deal elsewhere, remember that the Cubs only started playing night home games at Wrigley in the late 1980s. So the atmosphere for these nearly impossible-to-get-tickets-for games more resembles Mardi Gras than an ordinary baseball game.

If you are lucky enough to get Cubs tickets for any game, make sure to look over the outfield walls, past the bleachers (home of the Cubs' infamous Bleacher Bums, who yell all kinds of quaint names at opposing ball players, in addition to throwing back opponents' home runs onto the field). You'll notice tall three-flat apartment buildings across the street (Waveland Avenue on the left field side, Sheffield on the right field side) from Wrigley. Note that several of these buildings have built their own bleachers on their roofs, so that residents can view the action without ever having to set foot inside the ballpark. A few apartments even sell "season tickets" to their "bleachers."

All in all, you haven't really seen a baseball game until you've seen the Cubs in action (or inaction) at Wrigley Field. For more information about Wrigley Field, contact the Chicago Cubs at (773) 404-2827.

Like hopping aboard the *"Supernatural Tour,"* which leaves in darkness and searches for things that go bump in the night. Led by Chicago's most notable professional ghostbusters, who claim to have seen all kinds of spooky spirits, you will visit some of the allegedly most haunted sights in Chicago—including creepy cemeteries and doppelganger-filled houses. You might even see "Resurrection Mary," one of the city's most famous ghosts; (708) 499–0300.

For more of the city's ghoulish history, take the *"Untouchables" Tour,* which centers on the gangster-related historic sites made famous during the city's Prohibition Era; (773) 881–1195.

If you have kids, note that the **Pirate Bob** cruise ship, which leaves from the Wendella boat docks off Michigan and Wacker, will have him or her yearning to swash buckles sometime soon. The retrofitted "pirate schooner" sails on the Chicago River and out to the breakwater of Lake Michigan while regaling kids with pirate tales from costumed crew members.

Maybe you would rather see the splendor of Chicago from the air. You should know that Allegra's Aircraft and Helicopter Tours can make it happen for you; (312) 735–4440.

Chicago's Ethnic Museums

If some cities are a melting pot for nationalities, Chicago is a thick ethnic stew. And it seems each ethnic group boasts its own museums that are often well off the beaten path. More than 1,000 years of Lithuanian art is featured at the *Balzekas Museum of Lithuanian Culture,* 6500 South Pulaski Road, Chicago 60629. Antiquities and artifacts include suits of medieval armor, crossbows, rare books, and maps; there's also an extensive collection of ornamental designed clothing, weaving, and even Easter eggs; (773) 582–6500.

Home to the largest population of ethnic Poles outside of Warsaw, Chicago's residents of Polish descent can point proudly to the *Copernicus Cultural and Civic Center,* 5216 West Lawrence Avenue, Chicago 60630. It features artifacts, tapestries, paintings, and hosts cultural events, plays, exhibits—and a huge annual summer Polish festival; (773) 777–8898.

You also can visit the *Polish Museum of America,* 984 North Milwaukee Avenue, Chicago 60622, which claims to be one of the largest and oldest ethnic museums in the country—but because of its location, it remains largely a best-kept secret; (773) 384–3352.

The *DuSable Museum of African American History,* 740 East 56th Place, Chicago 60637, has become one of the country's finest depositories of black history and culture; (773) 947–0600. More than 3,000 artifacts covering nearly 3,500 years of Jewish history can be viewed at the *Spertus Museum of Judaica,* 618 South Michigan Avenue, Chicago 60605; (312) 922–9012.

Greeks have the *Hellenic Museum and Cultural Center,* 168 North Michigan Avenue, Chicago 60601; (312) 726–1234; Irish herald the *Irish American Heritage Center,* 4626 North Knox, Chicago 60630, which has undergone an extensive renovation (including a depiction of designs from the ancient Book of Kells stenciled on walls throughout the center) and hosts a massive annual St. Patrick's Day bash complete with live bands, Irish step dancers, and Guinness on tap.

Two more worth noting: the *Swedish American Museum Center,* 5211 North Clark, Chicago 60640, which features an annual traditional family Christmas dinner; (773) 728–8111; and the *Ukrainian National Museum,* 721 North Oakley, Chicago 60612, with beadwork, costumes, dolls, jewelry, and Easter eggs from twenty-six different Ukrainian regions; (312) 421–8020.

Shopping and Nightlife

I am always very hesitant to recommend any off-the-beaten-path shops or clubs because of the nature of those businesses—more than 90 percent of them fail within the first year. But there are a precious few of these kinds of discoveries I can note, ones that have shown at least some staying power.

One of Chicago's most unusual and least frequented (at least by visitors) stores is *Augustine's Spiritual Goods,* 3114 South Halsted Street, Chicago 60608. It's a place to get your Mojo working—as in voodoo. Called Chicago's "best voodoo shop," Augustine's offers everything from love potions and candle spells to curse removers and money charms; (312) 326–5467.

The *Abraham Lincoln Book Shop,* 357 West Chicago Avenue, Chicago 60610, is a gem specializing in Civil War history and Lincoln memorabilia; (312) 944–3085. *Joy of Ireland,* 700 North Michigan Avenue, Chicago 60611, seventh floor in the Water Tower Complex, is an unlikely location for this bastion of all things Irish, from handknit Aran wool sweaters and traditional grandfather's shirts to Claddagh jewelry and Irish christening gowns; (312) 664–7290. *Gigi's Dolls and Sherry's Teddy Bears,* 6029 North Northwest Highway, Chicago 60631, has one of Chicago's finest selections of antique and collectible dolls, bears, miniatures, and more; (773) 594–1540.

For nightlife fans, hear authentic Chicago blues at the *Checker Board Lounge,* 423 East 43rd Street, Chicago 60653 (Grand Boulevard), practically a living museum of Chicago blues; (773) 624–3240. *Rosa's,* in the out-of-the-way Humboldt Park area (3240 West Armitage Avenue, Chicago 60647), offers all kinds of topflight (and adventuresome) bookings; (773) 342–0452. *The Wild Hare,* 3530 North Clark Street, Chicago 60657, is a great place to see Afro-Caribbean acts; (773) 327–4273. And the *Abbey Pub,* 3420 West Grace, Chicago 60618, is an authentic Irish haven that regularly books acts from the Auld Sod; (773) 478–4408.

PLACES TO STAY
IN CHICAGO

Allerton,
701 North Michigan
Avenue, 60611
(800) 621–8311 or
(312) 440–1500

Chicago Hilton and Towers,
720 South Michigan
Avenue, 60605
(312) 922–4400

Chicago Marriott,
540 North Michigan
Avenue, 60611
(312) 836–0100

Comfort Inn Lincoln Park,
601 West Diversey
Parkway, 60614
(773) 348–2810

The Fairmont,
200 North Columbus
Drive, 60601
(800) 527–4727

Four Seasons Hotel,
120 East Delaware
Place, 60611
(312) 280–8800

Holiday Inn Chicago City
Centre,
300 East Ohio Street, 60611
(312) 787–6100

Hotel Inter-Continental
Chicago,
505 North Michigan
Avenue, 60611
(312) 944–4100

Hyatt on Printer's Row,
500 South Dearborn
Street, 60605
(312) 663–3200

Hyatt Regency Chicago,
151 East Wacker
Drive, 60601
(312) 565–1234

The Inn at University
Village,
625 South Ashland
Avenue, 60607
(312) 243–7200

Chicago Palmer House,
17 East Monroe
Street, 60603
(800) 445–8667

Park Brompton Hotel,
528 West Brompton
Avenue, 60657
(773) 404–3499

Radisson Hotel and Suites
Chicago,
160 East Huron
Street, 60611
(312) 787–2900

The Raphael,
201 East Delaware
Place, 60611
(800) 821–5343
or (312) 943–5000

Ritz-Carlton Chicago,
160 East Pearson
Street, 60611
(312) 266–1000

Sutton Place,
21 East Bellevue
Place, 60611
(800) 810–6888
or (312) 266–2100

Swissotel,
323 East Wacker
Drive, 60601
(312) 565–0565

The Tremont,
100 East Chestnut
Street, 60611
(800) 621–8133
or (312) 751–1800

The Westin Hotel,
909 North Michigan
Avenue, 60611
(312) 943–7200

**PLACES TO EAT
IN CHICAGO**

Ambria,
2300 North Lincoln
Park West, 60614
(773) 472–5959

Ann Sather's,
929 West Belmont
Avenue, 60657
(312) 348–2378

Avanzare,
161 East Huron
Street, 60611
(312) 337–8056

Berghoff's,
17 West Adams
Street, 60603
(312) 427–3170

Blackhawk Lodge,
41 East Superior
Street, 60611
(312) 280–4080

Busy Bee,
1550 North Damen
Avenue, 60622
(773) 772–4433

Carlucci,
2215 North Halsted
Street, 60614
(312) 281–1220

Charlie Trotter's,
816 West Armitage
Avenue, 60614
(773) 248–6228

Ed Debevic's,
640 North Wells
Street, 60610
(312) 664–1707

Eli's the Place for Steak,
215 East Chicago
Avenue, 60611
(312) 642–1393

Frontera Grill,
445 North Clark
Street, 60610
(312) 661–1434

Gibson's Steak House,
1028 North Rush
Street, 60611
(312) 266–8999

Gino's East,
633 N. Wells Street, 60611
(312) 943–1124

Goose Island
Brewing Company,
1800 North Clybourn
Avenue, 60614
(312) 915–0071

Green Door Tavern,
678 North Orleans, 60610
(312) 664–5496

Selected Visitors Bureaus and Chambers of Commerce

Chicago Office of Tourism,
Michigan Avenue and Randolph Street, 60616
(312) 744–2400

Chicago Convention and Tourism Bureau,
2301 South Lake Shore Drive, 60616
(312) 567–8500

Mayor's Office of Special Events Hotline,
(312) 744–3370

Chicago Fine Arts Hotline,
(312) 346–3278

Illinois Bureau of Tourism—Travel Information,
(800) 2–CONNECT

Web Sites

Illinois Tourism,
www.enjoyillinois.com

Chicago Convention and Tourism Bureau,
www.chicago.il.org

Harry Caray's,
33 West Kinzie
Street, 60610
(312) 828–0966

Hat Dance,
325 West Huron
Street, 60610
(312) 649–0066

Heartland Cafe,
7000 North Glenwood
Avenue, 60626
(773) 465–8005

Lou Mitchell's,
565 West Jackson
Boulevard, 60661
(312) 939–3111

Orbit Restaurant,
2954 North Milwaukee
Avenue, 60618
(773) 276–1355

Pump Room,
1301 North State
Parkway, 60610
(312) 266–0360

Schulien's Restaurant
and Saloon,
2100 West Irving Park
Road, 60618
(773) 478–2100

The Signature Room
at the 95th,
875 North Michigan
Avenue, 60611
(312) 787–9596

Tucci Benucch,
900 North Michigan
Avenue, 60611
(312) 266–2500

OTHER ATTRACTIONS WORTH SEEING IN CHICAGO

Art Institute

Field Museum of
Natural History

Sears Tower

Chicago Board of Trade

John G. Shedd Aquarium
and Oceanarium

Terra Museum of
American Art

Museum of
Contemporary Art

Museum of Science
and Industry

Anita Dee

Disney Quest Cruise

Navy Pier

Dave & Buster's

Water Tower Place

Adler Planetarium
and Astronomy Museum

Chicago Academy
of Sciences

Chicago Historical Society

Chicago's Children
Museum

Museum of Broadcast
Communications

Peace Museum

Pullman Historic District

University of Chicago

University of Illinois
at Chicago

Robie House

Chicago Fire Academy

Lincoln Park and Garfield
Park Conservatories

Bergen Garden

Navy Pier North Pier

Northeastern Illinois

North Suburban Chicagoland

ake County seems to possess the best of both worlds, at least in the eyes of those who live there—and the rest of us from the outside looking in. At its lower edge are some of the Chicago area's most affluent suburbs, such as Lake Bluff, Lake Forest, Kenilworth, Glencoe, and Winnetka. The county even claims the second greatest buying power in the United States at $34,428 per household average. At its northern border lies Wisconsin, and to the east, Lake Michigan. Other lakes, too, are never far away; there are more than 120 fishing and boating lakes in the county, including **Chain O'Lakes State Park.** Open year-round, the park has 220 campsites—some with electric hookup—showers, boat rental, fishing, and a playground. Go horseback riding from May 1 to October; snowmobiling and cross-country skiing are popular during the winter months. At 39947 North State Park Road, Spring Grove 60081; (847) 587–5512.

Illinois Beach State Park, only 20 miles east of Chain O'Lakes on Lake Michigan at Zion, is a 7-mile stretch of beach with Illinois's last and best natural lakeshore dunes area.

Appropriate to its name, Zion hosts the **Zion Passion Play** each year at the Christian Arts Auditorium. Performances are scheduled in April and May and on Good Friday. (847) 746–2221.

In Libertyville is a very special place called **The Lambs** (Route 176, east of I–94), a nonprofit organization dedicated to helping mentally handicapped adults. The Lambs is both a residence and a workplace where vocational training and employment are provided. More than 155 residents work here in the ten businesses at the sixty-three-acre farm. Each year, a quarter of a million

> ### Strange But True
>
> *Those Golden Arches seem to be everywhere, right? Yep, even on the water. Seems that McDonald's of Fox Lake is one of the only Mickey D's in the country with "drive-up" service for boats. That's right—you can motor your boat right up to the pier and order to go some of that famous McDonald's grub—a Big Mac, fries, Coke. Hey, let's supersize this one. We've got a long stretch of road . . . er, water ahead of us.*

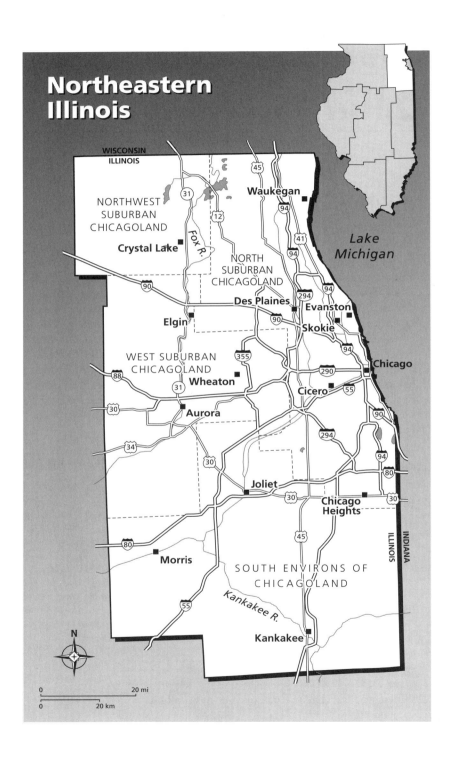

Northeastern Illinois

WISCONSIN
ILLINOIS

NORTHWEST
SUBURBAN
CHICAGOLAND

Crystal Lake

Fox R.

Waukegan

NORTH
SUBURBAN
CHICAGOLAND

Lake
Michigan

Des Plaines

Evanston

Elgin

Skokie

WEST SUBURBAN
CHICAGOLAND

Wheaton

Chicago

Cicero

Aurora

Joliet

Chicago
Heights

Morris

SOUTH ENVIRONS OF
CHICAGOLAND

Kankakee R.

ILLINOIS
INDIANA

Kankakee

N

0   20 mi

0   20 km

NORTHEASTERN ILLINOIS

people visit Lambs Farm for special events and to sample the products made by residents. Shop at the pet shop housed in a turn-of-the-century barn for some cuddly puppies or furry cats; the thrift shop, country store, the silk screen shop; or indulge your sweet tooth at Grandma's Bakery. Younger visitors can entertain themselves at the petting farm (do feed the animals) or the minigolf course. The possibilities for fun are endless: an ice cream parlor, carousel, pony rides, miniature train rides, and antique fire truck rides. One of the most popular of The Lambs's offerings is **The Country Inn,** a wonderful old-fashioned restaurant with hearty home cooking. Open daily for lunch at 11:00 A.M. On Sunday, brunch is served 10:00 A.M. Dinners range from $5.00 to $12.00. For reservations call (847) 362–5050.

Also in Libertyville is the **Dave Adler Cultural Center** at 1700 North Milwaukee 60048; (847) 367– 0707. Adler, an architect, built this twenty-three-room house around 1920, and it is now home to art exhibits and occasional concerts, storytelling, and barn dances. The family's private dining room has been restored with original furnishings. Open year-round, Monday through Friday 9:00 A.M. to 4:00 P.M. and Saturday 9:30 A.M. to 4:00 P.M. Admission is free.

What was formerly the farm of Illinois's most political family, the Adlai Stevensons, is here in Libertyville as well, now part of the **Lake County Forest Preserve.**

Bigger than the herd at Vienna's famous Spanish Riding School, the stable of the handsome Lipizzan stallions at **Tempel Farms** is the country's largest, right here in Wadsworth, Illinois. Catch a rare demonstration of equine talent at the 6,000-acre farm. Performances are held from early July to late August. Dates and times vary, so call for information. Performances last an hour and fifteen minutes and are held regardless of the weather. Stick around after the show for a tour of the stables, a "can't miss" delight. No reserved seating, adults, $16.00; seniors, $13.00; children four to fourteen, $6.00; under 4, free. At 15280 Wadsworth Road, 60083; (847) 623–7272.

AUTHOR'S TOP TEN PICKS

1. **Goose Lake Prairie State Park,** Morris, (815) 942–2899
2. **Six Flags Great America,** Gurnee, (847) 249–1776
3. **Garfield Farm Museum,** LaFox, (630) 584–8485
4. **Morton Arboretum,** Lisle, (630) 968–0074
5. **St. Charles (the village),** (630) 377–6161 or (800) 777–4373
6. **Wauconda Orchards,** Wauconda, (847) 526–8553
7. **Fermi National Accelerator Laboratory,** Batavia, (630) 840–3351
8. **Illinois and Michigan Canal National Corridor (State Trail)** (815) 942–0796
9. **Old Volo Village Auto Museum,** Volo, (815) 385–3644
10. **Waukegan Coho Charter Fishing,** Waukegan, (847) BIG–FISH

For nature lovers, the **Des Plaines River Wetlands Demonstration Project** in Wadsworth is a show of its own. A joint undertaking of the Lake County Forest Preserve District and the conservation organization, Open Lands Project, it's 450 acres of marshes that have been restored or created. Project Director Donald Hey calls it a "living laboratory" where botanists, water quality experts, and environmental engineers from universities across the country come to conduct research. It's open to the public as well for hiking, bird-watching, and nature study. Watch for beaver, muskrat, and the rare yellow-head blackbird, in addition to migrating waterfowl. The project is at U.S. Highway 41 at Wadsworth Road.

Cleopatra's ghost! Also in Wadsworth is the unique and kind of downright weird **Gold Pyramid House.** Built by contractor James Onan, the 55-foot, 24K gold-plated pyramid is probably one of the most unusual residences in the country. With a 200-ton statue of Ramses II standing guard, the structure is protected, too, by a spring-fed moat. It's oriented to true north, as is its model, the Great Pyramid of Cheops in Egypt. It's open to the public by reservation only April through October. Call (847) 662–6666 for information. Take I–94 north to Route 132, exit eastbound to Dilley's Road, turn left.

Another family entertainment spot—one with plenty of "show biz"— is **Six Flags Great America** in Gurnee, the most popular amusement theme park in Illinois. Bugs Bunny, musical stage reviews, and the American Eagle, the world's biggest and fastest double racing wooden roller coaster, featuring a 147-foot drop on its first hill that speeds pas-

The Gold Pyramid House

sengers to thrills at more than 67 mph, bring families by the thousands each summer. Theme villages, 150 attractions, and plenty of entertainment and food make it a sure bet for a Lake County outing. Open weekends only from the end of April, then daily mid-May through Labor Day and on weekends only through mid-October. Opens 10:00 A.M., closes at varying times. Guests 48" and taller, $42.99; under 48" pay $21.49; two and under, free. At Gurnee, on Grand Avenue (Route 132), 1 mile east of I–94. Just west of Great America is bargain central, **Gurnee Mills,** one of the country's largest outlet malls. Bring your walking shoes to this behemoth.

Long Grove (at Route 83 and Route 53 in the southern part of the county) invites you to turn your watch back to yesteryear. The historic village was settled in the 1840s by a group of German farmers who found it much like their own Alsatian homeland. Even after World War I, they continued to speak Plattdeutsch and tend their farms. The village grew up as a place for farmers to buy their supplies, weigh their milk, make their cheese at the cooperative, and have their horses shod. In 1847 they built a tiny church on a hill near town, where services are still held today.

Antiques seem to be everywhere you look in Long Grove now, with one of the better collections of shops anywhere. The **Long Grove Apple Haus** (847–634–0730) presses its own cider, makes heavenly apple butter and jam, and should be a definite stop. **Long Grove Confectionery** (847–634–0080), on the other hand, is famous for hand-dipped chocolates. Try a fat (the size of a child's fist), juicy, chocolate-covered strawberry on for size.

Each summer, the acclaimed Chicago Symphony Orchestra migrates north to Highland Park, taking up residence in their summer home, **Ravinia Park.** Since 1916 its outdoor music festival has featured a wide variety of classical and popular programs—even soft rock like James Taylor and Jackson Browne as well as renowned guest artists, ballet, and chamber music. For a more relaxed atmosphere, forsake seats under the roofed pavilion, take a picnic and lie on the lawn for music

Top Annual Events

Lilac Time, Lombard, early May, (630) 953–6000

Kane County Flea Market, St. Charles, first weekend of every month, (630) 377–2252

Swedish Days Festival, Geneva, late May, (630) 232–6060

Ernest Hemingway Birthday Week, Oak Park, mid-July, (708) 848–2222

DuPage County Fair, Wheaton, late-July, (630) 668–6636

Momence Gladiolus Festival, Momence, mid-August, (815) 472–6730

Garfield Farm Heirloom Garden Days, LaFox, mid-August, (630) 584–8485

Wauconda Orchards Family Harvest Weekends, Wauconda, late August/September, (847) 526–8533

Fright Fest, Gurnee, mid/late October, (847) 249–1776

Polar Express Santa Train, Lisle, mid-December, (800) 733–9811

under the stars. Call (847) 266–5100 for reservations and prices. Late June through mid-September.

Settled in 1835, Waukegan has a rich history well worth exploring. Originally an Indian village and then a French trading post, its name means "Little Fort" in the local Indian dialect. In 1860 Lincoln, interrupted by fire, delivered what came to be known as his "unfinished speech" here. Today a bit of that past remains in *Old Waukegan,* a designated Historic District along North Avenue and Franklin Street. For more history the *Waukegan Historical Society,* 1917 North Sheridan Road, 60087, is open 8:00 A.M. to 4:00 P.M. Monday, Wednesday, Thursday, Friday (with tours from 1:00 to 3:00 P.M.), and Tuesday 10:00 A.M. to 6:00 P.M. (with tours from 4:00 to 6:00 P.M.); (847) 336–1859.

At 414 North Sheridan Road, the white-pillared Greek Revival structure is home to the *Lake County Chamber of Commerce.* Built in 1847 by carriage maker John Swartout, the house is on the National Register of Historic Places.

If fishing is more to your taste, Waukegan is one of the two main Illinois ports for charter boats. (The massive $51 million, 2,000-boat marina at Winthrop Harbor, just to the north, is the other.) Call (708) BIG–FISH for information on day trips for chinook and coho salmon. In June the city sponsors a *Coho Fishing Derby* with daily prizes. Just south of Waukegan and North Chicago is the *Great Lakes Naval Training Center,* Sheridan Road at Route 137. This 1,600-acre installation is the Navy's largest train-

Very Punny

*G*urnee is home to one of the most charming bed and breakfasts in the Midwest—**Sweet Basil Hill Farm.** *My wife and daughters spent a fall weekend here not too many years ago, and besides beautiful fall colors on this seven-and-one-half-acre sheep farm, there were lots of interesting happenings.*

Like a guided tour of the farm by Bob Jones, who with wife, Teri, operates this little gem. Bob introduced the kids to all the sheep by name, including

Johann Sebastian Baa. And he even intimated how Half Jack got his name.

Sweet Basil Hill Farm also is home to two llamas—Fernando and Dali. They love to rub noses, Eskimo-style, with guests. So if you haven't kissed a llama mama lately, here's your chance. And there's even a "hugging tree" on the grounds. Bob says all tree-huggers get seven years good luck. And if you feel silly hugging that old barkmeister, you'll get eleven years!

ing center, even though it's 1,000 miles from saltwater. There are no tours, but most Fridays a public and colorful graduation ceremony for recruits is held. Guests begin arriving at 8:30 A.M. Call (847) 688–2201.

In the Lakewood Forest Preserve, at Route 176 and Fairfield Road, you'll find the **Lake County Museum,** a "small gem" of a place, according to the *Pioneer Press,* with a surprising postcard collection. Numbering 1.5 million pieces from 1878 to 1975, the collection documents a century's worth of popular American history. Some years in June the museum also stages a Civil War reenactment. Call for details. Open 11:00 A.M. to 4:30 P.M. Monday through Saturday and 1:00 to 4:30 P.M. Sunday. Admission is $2.00 for adults and $1.00 for ages four to seventeen. Mondays are free. Call (847) 526–7878.

At the western edge of the county, in the little town of Volo, U.S. Highway 12 and Route 120, the **Antique Auto Museum** has on display more than 150 classic motor cars. And if you're souvenir-minded, the showroom has mint condition, classic autos for sale; I'm partial to the big-finned 1965 Cadillac convertible myself; (815) 385–3644. Hours are 10:00 A.M. to 5:00 P.M. daily. Admission is $4.95 for adults, $3.00 for seniors, and $2.50 for children.

One of the area's best pick-your-own fruit farms is **Wauconda Orchards** at 1201 Gossell Road in Wauconda, 60084, just east of U.S. Highway 12. During the late spring and summer, you might find black raspberries, red raspberries, strawberries, or a handful of apple varieties just waiting to be picked; but come autumn and the orchard nearly bursts with trees bearing Red and Golden Delicious, Jonathan, McIntosh, and other apple varieties. And try their country store for souvenirs such as cider, cheese, and sausage or their gadget that peels and cores apples almost magically. It really does! Call (847) 526–8553. The orchards are open 9:00 A.M. to 5:00 P.M. weekdays as well as weekends; 7:00 A.M. to 5:00 P.M. May through December.

Northwest Suburban Chicagoland

The lucky people of Union—all 600 or so—have more to see and do than many in much larger towns. Fairly close to almost nothing, Union boasts three major museums, each with a busy calendar of special events, and a collection of antiques shops to suit every taste.

To start with, the **McHenry County Historical Museum** is on Main Street (6422 Main Street) 60050, in the middle of town. The log cabin in the front yard makes it even more difficult to miss. The 1847 structure was built by Luke Gannon on a site 5 miles northeast of Huntley, in the southern part of the county, and donated to the museum in 1964 by the family. Pioneer exhibitions are held here during the season. The museum also houses a collection of nineteenth-century musical instruments, ladies' fashions and handiwork, a quilt collection, farm equipment, and Civil War memorabilia. An 1895 school building is part of the museum complex. Open May through October Tuesday through Friday from 1:00 to 4:00 P.M. and Sunday from 1:00 to 4:00 P.M. Admission, adults $3.00; seniors and children, $2.00. Call for information on specially scheduled events; (815) 923–2267.

Just around the corner and a bit east of town on Olson Road in the middle of cornfields is one of our most-recommended museums in northern Illinois, the ***Illinois Railway Museum.*** Here you can touch the solid, worn seats as you sit back and enjoy a short train ride. Feel the tingle of excitement as the train bell rings and the whistle blows. And watch with loving affection as the old steam engine comes puffing into the station. The Railway Museum is a nonprofit organization run by volunteers, train buffs who love the thrill of classic locomotives as much as we do. And most important, the exhibit is someplace the whole family can find fun. It's open air, with plenty of places to go—fifty-six acres worth—cars to ride, noises to hear, and even a spot for picnics.

When is a train more than a train? Well, when it's one of the museum's 200 cars and locomotives, which include electric interurbans, streetcars,

"You Call This Prairie?"

*M*iles *of lakeshore, sand dunes, marsh meadows, scores of lakes, and even soggy bogs make up some of the landscape of northeastern Illinois. It's not what lots of people expect from the Prairie State.*

In the east, the magnificent shoreline of Lake Michigan dominates all geography. Up north, near the Wisconsin border, you can find the last great sand dunes of the Chicagoland area that haven't been destroyed by the progress of man. There are also wooded ravines and narrow winding roads through

tree-filled towns that are some of the toniest in the country.

Move farther west and you'll find yourself in the winding hills of the Fox River Valley. It's a place to explore graceful historic towns that took advantage of the riverways. But as you travel southward, you'll start to discover lands more open—patches of prairie here, grassland there— really a kind of gateway to the great Midwest prairie everyone really expects to find in the Land of Lincoln.

trolleys, diesels, Chicago elevated cars, and even a complete silver Burlington Zephyr streamliner. It's one of only two places in the state you can ride a steam engine. (The other's in Monticello.) One of the most exotic stars of the show is the Russian Decapod from the Frisco Railroad, built in 1917 by Baldwin for the czarist Russian government, but, due to a revolution, never delivered.

Dating from 1851, the depot originally served as the station in Marengo. Behind it are the gift shop and bookstore with a mountain of railroad lore. Throughout the summer are special events, such as the July 4th Trolley Pageant, Railroad Day, and Diesel Day. From Memorial Day to Labor Day, the museum is open daily 10:30 A.M. to 5:00 P.M. In May, September, and October, it's open weekends only; in April openings are limited to Sundays. For a ride on the steam train, plan to visit on a summer weekend when the trains run hourly. Admission varies but includes unlimited rides; call (815) 923–2488.

South of town, at 8512 South Union, is **Donley's Wild West Town.** It's like someone's attic—someone who collected almost everything. One of the country's largest antique phonograph collections can be found along with records, cylinders, and needles.

A nickelodeon shows movies throughout the day right around the corner from the "Street of Yesteryear," a collection of old-time shops. Outside, the town has its own saloon, blacksmith shop, and pioneer cabin. Desperadoes shoot it out daily during the summer months in a flashy Wild West gunfight show. And conveniently nearby is the gallows, a real Chicago version, from the old Cook County jail on Hubbard Street, still waiting for "Terrible Tommy" O'Connor, who escaped on December 11, 1921, four days before his scheduled execution, the last one by hanging in the state. To record your day in the past, make a date with the photography studio, where you can get dressed up in Victorian garb or Wild West attire and have a sepia-toned souvenir in a matter of minutes. But certainly the favorite activity for kids is panning for gold (pyrite, that is). Try it—strike it rich! And afterward celebrate with a scoop at the ice cream parlor. Open daily May through August and weekends only in April, September, and October. Call for hours; (815) 923–2214. Admission is $10.00 for everyone over three.

In the center of the county is Woodstock, the quaint Victorian county seat, named after the Vermont town from which many of its early citizens came. In the center of the town is the square, not with a courthouse (which is off to one side), but with a handsome park complete with bandstand, spring house, and a statue dedicated to "the soldiers of 1861–65, in honor of our nation's defenders."

On one side of the brick-paved square is the **Woodstock Opera House,** an 1890 structure listed in the National Register of Historic Places (121 Van Buren) 60098. With its tall tower and ornate interior, its style has been called "Steamboat Gothic." Paul Newman and Orson Welles, who attended school in Woodstock, began their careers here. A seasonal schedule of performances is offered; (815) 338–5300.

On the other side of the square is the former courthouse and jail where a number of Chicago characters, including Eugene Debs, were once held. A stone on the side of the courthouse tells us that all this is only 954 feet above sea level.

Driving north from the brick-paved square at Woodstock, take Route 47 to Hebron, where even the perennial optimism of the Chicago Cubs fans is outdone by the Hebron water tower, painted to resemble a basketball with the notice that this is the home of the 1952 State Champions.

Just east of Hebron on Route 173 is Richmond, only blocks south of the Wisconsin state line. The legendary antique village is chockablock with antiques shops of every description. Most shops in town are closed on Monday. Whatever your weakness, chances are it will find you here—from oak furniture to primitives, from china dolls to Mrs. Anderson's heavenly homemade chocolates.

Since 1919 **Anderson's Homemade Candies,** 10301 Main Street, 60071, has been bringing them in for hand-dipped English toffees, meltaway fudge, and old-fashioned "candy bars" that are really chocolate-covered apricot, orange peel, pudding, or "krispy" rice. This is a must visit for any candy lover—these homemade sweets might be the best in the state! Open daily 9:00 A.M. to 5:00 P.M., Sunday noon to 5:00 P.M. Closed Monday and two weeks in January.

The town holds special exhibits, such as a quilt show and an art glass exhibit, throughout the summer months. The last weekend in August is "Richmond Round-Up Days," where local service clubs, aided by the village, put on a do over at the Community Church. Fill up on a bratwurst, roasted ears of corn fresh from the field, and slabs of roast beef. Call the Richmond Memorial Hall for more information; (815) 678–4040.

A moraine, according to Webster, is "a mass of rocks, gravel, sand . . . carried or deposited by a glacier." And that's exactly what you'll find at

Moraine Hills State Park, 3 miles south of McHenry. *Lake Defiance,* in the park, was created by a chunk of glacier left to melt there. Unusual natural features include a leatherleaf bog—120 acres of floating sphagnum moss and leatherleaf surrounded by a moat of open water. The pike marsh contains the largest-known colony of pitcher plants in Illinois along with cattails and bullrushes. It's a protected nature preserve and, as such, attracts a rich variety of wildlife as well. Visitors will want to stop at the interpretive center, which explains the park's natural resources. The Pike Marsh Nature Trail features a floating boardwalk perfect for exploration of park plant life. All state parks are open year-round except Christmas and New Year's Day. Contact the Site Superintendent, 914 South River Road, McHenry 60050; (815) 385–1624.

West Suburban Chicagoland

O f what are euphemistically known as the collar counties—those surrounding Cook—Du Page County is surely the white collar enclosing the beefy neck of Chicago—buttoned-down, starched, of oxford cloth. It's conservative, Republican, a place of manicured lawns and solid brick homes (a drive through one of the county's prettiest towns, Elmhurst, will convince you of that).

On its northeast corner Du Page County slices through O'Hare International Airport; on the south it encloses the Argonne National Laboratory; and on the west it bisects the grounds of the Fermi National Accelerator Laboratory, one of the world's largest particle accelerators, where scientists from around the world come to study quirks and quarks. There's a lot going on in the county.

The *Morton Arboretum* offers a spectacular year-round escape to nature for harried city dwellers. One mile north of Lisle, at the Route 53 exit of the East-West Tollway (I–88), the garden encompasses 1,500 acres of lush plants and trees and shrubs. Thirteen miles of footpaths and interpretive trails provide an up-close look at nature. Hours are 7:00 A.M. to 7:00 P.M. during daylight saving time, 7:00 A.M. to dusk or 5:00 P.M. after October 29. There is a $7.00 charge per car ($3.00 on Wednesday). The arboretum has a delightful restaurant, *The Gingko,* open for lunch and tea daily (lunch ranges from $5.00 to $7.00), and a gift shop; (630) 968–0074.

For history buffs (and kids), visiting the *Old Naper Settlement,* at 201 West Porter in Naperville 60540 (630–420–6010) makes an ideal afternoon. Here, twenty historic buildings on a twelve-acre site re-create a nineteenth-century village. Costumed guides lead visitors through an assortment of structures: a windmill, barn, print shop, blacksmith shop, post office, smokehouse, and the tiny gothic **Century Memorial Chapel.** The **Caroline Martin-Mitchell Mansion,** built in 1883, is listed in the National Register of Historic Places. Open May through October, 10:00 A.M. to 4:00 P.M. Tuesday through Saturday and 1:00 to 4:00 P.M. Sunday. During July & August, hours are 10:00 A.M. to 8:00 P.M. Admission is $6.50 for adults, $5.50 for seniors, $4.00 for children ages six to seventeen.

The **Old Graue Mill** at York and Spring Roads in Oak Brook is grist for a nostalgic afternoon. It's the only operating waterwheel in the state, and a white-aproned miller turns out stone-ground cornmeal for sale in the country store. At five pounds for $6.00, it's a bargain. Upstairs are a Victorian drawing room, kitchen, and children's room with antique dolls and toys, plus exhibits of spinning and weaving. Visit the new exhibit commemorating this stop on the historic Underground Railroad. Open 10:00 A.M. to 4:30 P.M. daily (closed Monday except holiday weekends) mid-April through mid-November; (630) 655–2090. Admission, $3.75 adults, $1.50 children, and $3.00 seniors.

Wheaton, the county seat, is home to **Wheaton College,** founded in 1853, and the headquarters of a number of religious publishing houses and organizations. Wheaton College is Billy Graham's alma mater and the site of the **Billy Graham Center Museum** with its Walk Through the

Naperville

*T**he village of Naperville has blossomed into an off-the-beaten-path wanderer's delight.*

Its Riverwalk, a linear park nestled along the shoreline of the Du Page River, offers an opportunity for romantic strolls through covered bridges, past bubbling fountains, and along red brick pathways meandering through landscaped finery.

There's even a Riverwalk Art gallery where you can ponder paintings done by local and regional artists, an amphitheater where summertime

concerts are held, and paddleboats for rent in the nearby Riverwalk Quarries.

Don't forget to visit the boutiques, artsy shops, and eateries near Chicago Avenue and Washington Streets, an epicenter for browsers. And a Farmers' Market is offered Saturdays, May through October.

Kids win out in Naperville, too. Besides the Naper Settlement, the village boasts Centennial Beach, billed as the "world's third-largest chlorinated body of water."

Gospel and scenes from American evangelism since 1702. Temporary exhibits change quarterly. Open Monday through Saturday, 9:30 A.M. to 5:30 P.M., Sunday 1:00 to 5:00 P.M.; (630) 752–5909.

Not every county has its own mastodon, but at Armerding Hall on campus, a skeleton of the giant **Perry Mastodon,** which was found locally, is on exhibit; (630) 752–5010.

One of Wheaton's most famous sons is football hero Red Grange. At the **Red Grange Museum/Heritage Gallery,** 421 County Farm Road, 60187, displays and films tell the story of his life. Open Monday through Friday 8:00 A.M. to 4:30 P.M.

Also in Wheaton is **Cantigny,** the former estate of the late Colonel Robert R. McCormick, celebrated publisher of the Chicago *Tribune.* Today the 500-acre grounds are open to the public from 9:00 A.M. to sunset daily. Picnicking and walks through the formal gardens are popular pastimes. On Sunday at 3:00 P.M. from May through August, outdoor concerts are held. The **First Infantry Division Museum** here commemorates the division in which the colonel served in World War I. At 1 South, 151 Winfield Road, 60187; (630) 668–5161. Admission is free, but there is a $5.00 parking fee; guided tours of the mansion are available. Open 10:00 A.M. to sunset daily except Monday during the summer months; 10:00 A.M. to 4:00 P.M. after Labor Day. The museum is closed during the month of January.

Another free and worthwhile Wheaton attraction is the **Du Page County Historical Museum,** located in an 1891 Romanesque-style limestone building. Visit the special interactive gallery (popular with families), the Victorian period room, and the permanent collection of Du Page history. Little girls who "dress up" will love the historical costume gallery. Here, too, is almost a half mile of model railroad track. Watch trains chug along each third Saturday of the month from 1:30 to 3:30 P.M. At 102 East Wesley Street, 60187; (630) 682–7343. Its hours are 10:00 A.M. to 4:00 P.M. on Monday, Wednesday, Friday, and Saturday and 1:00 to 4:00 P.M. on Sunday. Du Page County, in fact, has no shortage of museums—over a dozen in all.

Equally numerous are golf courses, if history's not your game. Du Page boasts twenty-four public courses, plus a handful of private courses, making it one of the most golf-accessible counties in the state. This mania is no recent phenomenon. The Chicago Golf Club, a private club in Wheaton, claims to have been the first eighteen-hole course in the United States, having opened in 1892.

Colonial Romance

*O*ne summer day on the way back to Chicago from Cantigny, my wife and I were taking a leisurely drive through the Wheaton area when we came to an intersection boasting a building that looked like something out of Colonial Williamsburg. Of course, we just had to go inside and take a peek.

It turns out that this historic-looking building was brand new—the Wheaton Inn had just opened its doors a few weeks prior to our discovery. The manager of the elegant sixteen-room inn took us on a brief tour—and after what we saw, we booked a room immediately for that night. (This was before the kids came along, of course, when spontaneity was still doable.)

All the rooms are named for Wheaton notables—we opted for the Rice Room, where its Jacuzzi tub sits languidly in the middle of the bedchamber, directly in front of a large fireplace, with two skylights overhead to allow coosome twosomes to gaze up into the stars. A real romantic find, and only a short drive from the Windy City, too.

Plenty of other outdoor activities are available in Du Page County, as well. For example, if your interests are somewhat patrician, there are polo matches each Sunday afternoon at 1:00 and 3:00 P.M. during the summer and fall at the **Oak Brook Polo Club,** York Road at Thirty-first Street in Oak Brook; (630) 990–2394.

During mid-May Lombard is abloom for the annual **Lilac Festival,** making it one of the best-smelling towns in the county. Parades are scheduled and a Lilac Queen is named. Call (630) 629–3799 for more information.

Especially pleasant is the **Illinois Prairie Path,** beginning in Elmhurst at York Road south of North Avenue. This 55-mile-long biking and hiking trail follows an old railroad right-of-way, where wildflowers, prairie grasses, tiny parks, and rest stops are plentiful. Call the highway department at (630) 682–7318 for a free map.

At Glen Ellyn, the **Willowbrook Wildlife Haven,** 525 South Park Boulevard, 60137, is always popular with children. Here, wounded, lost, and captured native wildlife are cared for. Take a self-guided tour and visit the **Touch & Feel Museum.** The haven's hours are from 9:00 A.M. to 5:00 P.M. daily; (630) 942–6200. Admission is free.

The county's forest preserves are among the finest in the area, with thirty preserves encompassing 17,500 acres. At various locations you'll find dog training fields, model airplane runs, bird-watching facilities, cross-country skiing, ice skating, hiking, and equestrian fields.

Oak Brook Center, Twenty-second Street and Route 83, is one of the Chicago area's outstanding regional shopping centers with Marshall Field's, Saks Fifth Avenue, Nordstrom, and Neiman-Marcus as major tenants. More than a hundred shops and restaurants are laid out around a landscaped courtyard.

One man could be credited almost solely with the settlement of the Fox River Valley, although that was certainly not his intention. Chief Black Hawk of the Sauk Indians was among the least friendly of the Indian leaders in the area that is now Illinois. In the War of 1812, he sided with the British against the Americans. The encroachment of the white settlers on his traditional lands led to the tragic Black Hawk War of 1832 in which the Sauk and Fox tribes were virtually exterminated.

Soldiers returning east from this frontier battle spoke highly of the fertile land along the river. Thus communities sprang up beside the waterway, notably Geneva in 1833, as supply centers for area farms and pioneers traveling farther west.

For the weekend traveler on nothing more than a sightseeing excursion, a trip through the Kane County towns of the Fox River is richly rewarding. Follow Route 31 along the eastern edge of the county as it meanders along next to the Fox River. In the south begin with Aurora, one of the first major cities in the nation to light its streets with electricity (1881).

Here the best show in town is the ***Paramount Arts Centre,*** 23 East Galena Boulevard, 60506. On an island in the Fox River, the opulently stylish and historic art deco movie and vaudeville palace was built in 1931 by noted theater architects Rapp and Rapp as a romanticized version of Venice. A 70-foot cascade light marquee adorns the red-brick and terra-cotta exterior. The Paramount was restored in 1978 and protected in the National Register of Historic Places two years later. In the theater's early days, Charlie Chaplin and the Marx Brothers were headliners. Today there's a varied schedule of visiting entertainers. Call (630) 896–6666 for program information.

West of town on Galena Boulevard (and about $2^1/_2$ miles west of Randall Road) is the Fox Valley Park District's ***Blackberry Historical Farm-Village.*** From what was once a dairy farm has been fashioned a unique park with a collection of rides and historic exhibits. It receives high marks as an ideal spot for family outings.

Pony rides and an antique carousel vie for junior riders. A miniature steam train, Old Engine #9, takes visitors around the sixty-acre park and Lake Gregory to an 1840 *Pioneer Farm.* A petting barn with barnyard animals, hay wagon rides, and a pioneer log cabin where craftspeople demonstrate frontier skills are among the attractions.

Museums on the property exhibit early carriages, a one-room schoolhouse, and Victorian women's furnishings. Throughout the season special events, such as *Antique Auto Day, Chautauqua Sunday, Smithing Day,* and *Indian Summer Day,* are scheduled. Open daily 10:00 A.M. to 4:30 P.M. May to Labor Day; Friday, Saturday, and Sunday 10:00 A.M. to 4:00 P.M. Labor Day to mid-October. Admission, which includes all rides, is $7.50 for adults, $6.50 for seniors and children; free for children ages two and under. Call (630) 892–1550.

Back in Aurora one of the most unusual museums in the Fox Valley is the *Grand Army of the Republic Hall and Museum,* 23 East Downer, 60506; (630) 897–7221. The castellated limestone building with a statue of a Civil War soldier on top was built in 1877 and is listed in the National Register of Historic Places. Cannons line the front yard of the museum, which looks something like a church. Inside, Civil War memorabilia are the focus of the collection. Open 1:00 to 4:00 P.M. Monday, Wednesday, and Friday.

Between North Aurora and Batavia on Route 31 lies one of the most unusual communities in the entire state. *Mooseheart* is a wonderful, warm place you're certain to want to visit. An orphanage for 270 boys and girls, it's also a self-contained community run entirely by the Loyal Order of Moose. On 1,300 acres are a dairy farm and garden, a post office and bank, a school, field house, and even a furniture shop for supplying the needs of the residents. Tours are offered by student guides seven days a week, 9:00 A.M. to 2:00 P.M.; (630) 859–2000.

North of Aurora in Batavia is *Fermilab,* one of the world's largest particle accelerators. A free self-guided tour is offered seven days a week from 8:30 A.M. to 5:00 P.M. for groups of ten or fewer; (630) 840–3000. Included is a fascinating eighteen-minute video that explains the working of the research center. The tour begins on the fifteenth floor of the Robert Rathbun Wilson Hall, with a view out over the entire complex. Complete the tour in your car, driving through the Fermilab facility (no public access to buildings in this area). Keep an eye out for the center's buffalo herd, some sixty strong, a historical counterpoint to the high-tech activities of the laboratory.

Just down the road, at 14 North Washington Avenue in Batavia, 60510, is the 1885 Alexander Grimes farmhouse. The lovely old Victorian is home to **The Savery Shops,** a collection of five dealers and artists. Open daily from 10:00 A.M. to 5:00 P.M. and Sunday from noon to 5:00 P.M.; (630) 879–6825.

Continuing north on Route 31, **Geneva** is the next stop. Its historic district is a bonanza of period architecture with more than 200 structures listed in the National Register of Historic Places. Geneva is the county seat, and the 1891 **Kane County Courthouse** is historically significant, with unique wrought-iron balconies gracing the first to the fourth interior floors. Also be sure to see the WPA mural in the post office at 26 South Third Street, 60134. Founded as a trading center, Geneva is still that, with dozens of charming shops.

One of the oldest annual festivals in the state, Geneva's **Swedish Days** is held each June to commemorate the area's Swedish heritage. Quilts, crafts, *rosemaling* (Swedish painted flower decoration on furniture), and an unforgettable Swedish buffet are part of the fun.

Although it might not be fair to the other towns along the way, we think **St. Charles** is the jewel of the Fox River. Here pretty wooded slopes fall away to the slow-running river where the **Fox River Trail** (a premier bicycle and walking path from St. Charles to Aurora and north to Elgin) hugs the water. It's the perfect walking town, bisected by a river, with plenty of quaint shops, boutiques, and side streets to explore. It's nice to see a small town where things are going well, business is thriving, the economy healthy. You come away with an almost Disney-like impression of a town where clean streets and smiling faces are part of the package.

Holy Cow! . . . er, Cougars

*I*f you're a fan of baseball, then you must take in a game at Elfstom Stadium—home to the Kane County Cougars. The Cougars are the Class A affiliate of the Florida Marlins who play in their quaint stadium from April through September.

But it's not just the love of the game that brings fans to this picturesque ballyard. The stadium boasts great up-close looks at up-and-coming ballplayers for as little as a few dollars. Or you can opt for the cheaper alternative: lawn seats—just plop down on the grass and enjoy the rhythms of the game.

Better yet, why not rent out the hot tub just over the left field wall. It's a great way to watch baseball, seated in your jet-streamed water pod, while sipping on a cool drink and witnessing some great all-out hustle from these young ballplayers. Let's face it: Some major leaguers could learn a thing or two about the love of the game from these guys.

Make sure to schedule a visit to St. Charles during August for the town's Living History Month, put on by the St. Charles Heritage Center. Over three weekends, it's a potluck of military events. There are Revolutionary War and Civil War reenactment/encampments, each with costumed participants, demonstrations, two battles daily, period music, and a living, working camp with tents and supplies. Call (630) 584–6967 for dates and information. Or, during the rest of the year, stop by the museum at 304 East Eader Avenue, 60174.

St. Charles's claim to fame is antiquing. **Giant Antique Markets I, II, and III** are dealer cooperatives with a remarkable collection of stuff under each roof.

On the first Sunday of each month and the Saturday afternoon preceding it, the massive **Kane County Flea Market** takes over the County Fairgrounds with 1,400 dealers on twenty-five acres, attracting fifteen to twenty thousand or so shoppers. It has been called the largest flea market in the world, perhaps rightly so. The market ignores the weather and never cancels. Its success is the work of Helen Robinson, a seventy-something grandmother who actively supervises the monthly operation, including three kitchens and eight food trailers to feed the bargain hunters. Located on Randall Road just south of Route 64; (630) 377–2252. Open 1:00 to 5:00 P.M. on Saturday and 7:00 A.M. to 4:00 P.M. on Sunday. Admission is $5.00; children under twelve are free. Free parking.

Shoppers, too, will enjoy the three restored areas in town—**Old St. Charles, Century Corners,** and **Fox Island Square,** designed around the original Howell factory brick chimney. Lunch is a welcome respite, and the choices of restaurants are numerous.

In the handsome old 1928 **Baker Hotel,** a National Register building, the oval Rainbow Room has a back-lit colored glass floor and a view of the river. The Moorish stucco interiors lead out onto a terrace with a gazebo that's perfect for photographing the waterfalls behind the hotel. At 100 West Main Street, 60174; (630) 584–2100.

But to *really* get the feel of the river, you have to get out on it. And the best way to do that is a ride on the **St. Charles Belle** or the **Fox River Queen,** 132-passenger paddlewheelers. Adults, $5.00; children, $3.50. Mid-May through mid-October, the excursion boats leave from Potawatomie Park at 3:30 P.M. on weekdays and at 2:00, 3:00, and 4:00 P.M. on Saturdays and Sundays; also at 5:00 P.M. on Sunday. Call (630) 584–2334. Also in this hilly, tidy park north of downtown are a swimming pool, a miniature golf course, and tennis courts. Note that there is a parking fee for the park.

Professional entertainment in St. Charles is offered at the *Dellora A. Norris Cultural Arts Center,* 1040 Dunham Road, 60174, (630) 584–7200, and at *Pheasant Run,* a resort complex with dinner theater, a comedy club, and children's theater east of town on Route 64, (630) 584–6300. Both feature name entertainers and shows.

Just west of St. Charles in La Fox is the *Garfield Farm Museum,* a living history farm of the 1840s. Roosters wander in and out of the weathered barns. Herbs and flowers grow in the curator's garden. In 1841 Timothy and Harriet Frost Garfield brought their eight children from Vermont to the prairie lands of Illinois. In 1977 the third-generation owner, Elva Ruth Garfield, donated the farm as a museum; one of the most intact historical sites in the country, it is used for ongoing archaeological studies. It's the

> ### Northeastern Illinois Trivia
>
> *In 1900, the Chicago River became the first river in the world to have its course altered, engineered to flow westward into a canal system rather than eastward into Lake Michigan.*

largest Illinois farm in the National Register of Historic Places, and it gives the visitor an excellent idea of just how a farm family of the 1840s must have lived. Walk through the grounds and the interior of the brick (made locally) home and teamster tavern (inn) with curator Jerome Johnson and his wife, Holly. In August, come to the farm's Heirloom Garden Show, where you'll see pioneer veggies like purple tomatoes, blue potatoes, and an 1800s carrot more than a foot-and-a-half long. In October its three-day *Fall Festival* features historical music, a storyteller, blacksmithing, craft demonstrations, and hearty farm cooking appropriate to the period. Open 1:00 to 4:00 P.M. on Wednesday and Sunday, June through September or by appointment. Adults, $3.00; children, $1.00. Call (630) 584–8485 for a schedule of seasonal events.

Farther north on Route 31, in South Elgin, is the *Fox River Trolley Museum,* where you can take a 3-mile, 30-minute ride along the Fox River on this electric railway. Vintage railway cars are on display. Open Sunday 11:00 A.M. to 5:00 P.M. May through early November; Saturday 11:00 A.M. to 5:00 P.M. in July and August; (847) 697–4676. The museum is on Route 31 in South Elgin, 3 blocks south of State Street. Adults, $2.50; children, $1.50.

In Elgin don't go looking for the Elgin Watch Factory, from 1866 the manufacturer of America's best-known timepieces. It closed in 1965. What you can explore, however, is the *Elgin Historic District.* The National Register district includes 667 structures, many of noteworthy architecture—Greek Revival, Queen Anne, Shingle style, and brick row houses. Walking tour or bicycle tour maps are available from the Elgin Visitors Bureau; (847) 695–7540.

Another important industry for Elgin was the dairy business, and it was here that Gail Borden invented his process for condensing milk in 1856. Have lunch at *Focaccia's,* a restaurant located in the old Borden library on Spring Street in the heart of Elgin.

The *Dundee area,* just north of Elgin, claims its famous sons as well. Allan Pinkerton, famous detective and head of the Union Army's spy service in the Civil War, lived here from 1844 to 1850. A historical marker indicates the site on Third Street in West Dundee. Evangelist Billy Sunday owned the farm on which his wife was born in Sleepy Hollow, just west on Route 72.

In Dundee tour the family-owned *Haeger Potteries Factory* at 7 Maiden Lane, 60118. From the banks of the Fox River, the company founder took clay to use in his Dundee Brickyards in 1871 to make bricks that were used to rebuild Chicago after the Great Chicago Fire; (847) 426–3033. Factory outlet open Monday through Friday, 8:30 A.M. to 6:00 P.M.; Saturday and Sunday, 11:00 A.M. to 5:00 P.M.

Santa's Village, Route 25 and Route 72 in East Dundee, is a popular amusement park for children, with more than forty rides, shows, and attractions—and live shows at the Evergreen Theater. Here kids can visit Santa (and Mrs. Claus), then ride a roller coaster, and finally cling to the always frozen and ice-covered "North Pole" marker that's a park landmark. Open daily mid-June to Labor Day, weekends mid-May through September. September through April family skating's the thing at the *Polar Dome Ice Rink* ($4.75 per person). Hours are 10:00 A.M. to 6:00 P.M. weekdays, 11:00 A.M. to 6:00 P.M. weekends. Admission, on Monday and Tuesday, $15.95, Wednesday through Saturday, $18.95, free for children two and under.

One of the Fox Valley's most popular restaurants, *The Milk Pail,* is also located in East Dundee. The fifty-year-old family favorite features country cooking with specialties such as breast of pheasant, trout, duck, and fresh-baked goods. But its delectable chicken dinners might be its claim to fame. Dinners range from $7.95 to $16.95. At Route 25, open seven days a week; (847) 742–5040.

In the northwest corner of the county is the town of Hampshire, home of *Eberly's Honey Hill Apiaries*—with 1,600 hives, the largest in Kane County. The retail shop sells clover, buckwheat, and wildflower honey in addition to beekeeping supplies and homemade beeswax candles. If you're not afraid of being stung, out back is abuzz with the busy little creatures. The apiary is located on U.S. Highway 20 in Hampshire; (847) 464–5165. Open 9:00 A.M. to 5:00 P.M., seven days a week.

South Environs of Chicagoland

Will County's seat, Joliet, may call to mind only the Blues Brothers (part of the movie was set here) and an infamous state prison. But this community of 78,000, 40 miles southwest of Chicago, has other, more pleasant features. For example, it's known as the City of Spires, for the 122 houses of worship that dot the area.

The temple of art, however, that attracts the cultural faithful from miles around is the historic ***Rialto Square Theatre,*** "The Jewel of Joliet." Built in 1926 by the renowned theater designers Rapp and Rapp, this masterpiece is a remarkable example of theater baroque. Restored in 1981, it is in the National Register of Historic Places. Here, where Fanny Brice and Al Jolson once performed, a list of modern-day luminaries headlines the bill at the new performing arts center—Broadway shows, orchestras, singers, and comedians.

But in this palace for the people, the real show's before the show. You enter a block-long lobby lined with mirrors, its splendor compared to that of the Hall of Mirrors at Versailles. This lobby leads into the domed rotunda with bas-relief sculptures by Eugene Romeo. From the dome hangs the largest hand-cut chandelier in the United States, "The Duchess," 20 feet long with eight arms of copper and bronze and more than 250 lights. Beyond the rotunda is the auditorium, no less impressive. The twenty-one-rank Barton Grande Theatre Pipe Organ is a prized instrument that is used in occasional recitals at the Rialto. Tours are scheduled each Tuesday at 12:45 P.M. or by appointment; (815) 726–7171. Admission is $4.00. For performance information and tickets, call (815) 726–6600.

The city's historic districts are also worth inspection. The ***South East Neighborhood Historic District,*** south and east of downtown, is a Registered National Landmark District. The feature home is the opulent ***Victorian Manor,*** a three-story, forty-room Italian Renaissance mansion (at 20 South Eastern Avenue, 60433, tours available). Just west of the Des Plaines River, on North Broadway and Hickory Streets, are splendid Second Empire-style homes and authentic examples of original Joliet limestone residences. Up the hill from downtown Joliet, west along Western Avenue, are turn-of-the-century Victorian mansions in all of their ornate glory.

Northeastern Illinois Trivia

Oak Park, one of Chicago-land's most historic nearby suburbs, is said to have been called a place with "neat lawns and narrow minds" by hometown boy Ernest Hemingway.

Another reminder of this river city's historic past is the **Empress River Casino**. And while the idea is old-fashioned, the boat is sparklingly new—a "contemporary mega-yacht" as the promotional material says. Try your hand at blackjack, roulette, craps, or the slots (for as little as 25 cents). There are snack shops on the boat and restaurants in the land-based pavilion. Call (815) 744–9400 for information. On the Des Plaines River, 3 miles southwest of downtown on Route 6.

Completed for the nation's bicentennial year for a lasting memorial, the **Bicentennial Park Theater and Bandshell** complex at Jefferson and Bluff Streets is home to an outdoor concert season and a beautiful 300-seat formal theater. Free weekly lawn concerts are offered each Thursday in June, July, and August. Call (815) 740–2216 for more information.

Joliet, named for French explorer Louis Joliet, who explored the area with Father Marquette in the 1600s, is home to the county's first junior college. The castellated stone structure, designed in 1902 by noted architects Daniel Burnham and F.S. Allen, is today the central campus of **Joliet Township High School** at 201 East Jefferson Street, 60432.

In the city's Highland Park is the **Greenhouse,** repository for an exceptional collection of exotic flora. Featured are cacti more than a hundred years old and seasonal flower shows.

An essential part of Joliet, as well as Will County as a whole (and Cook, La Salle, and Grundy counties), is the Illinois and Michigan Canal. In 1984 it became the newest member of the National Park System, the **Illinois and Michigan Canal National Heritage Corridor,** running from Chicago to Peru, Illinois. It contains historic sites, residential neighborhoods, forest preserves for picnicking, fishing, hiking, canoeing, and camping, plus thirty-nine rare natural areas, remnants of the ancient Illinois landscape. Among them is the **Lockport Prairie** at Route 53 and Division Street, south of Route 7, across from Stateville Correctional Center. Some of the best examples of native prairie grasses and wildflowers still may be found there.

Now obsolete, the canal was once the principal transportation link connecting the Chicago and Illinois Rivers, providing a continuous waterway from the Atlantic Ocean through the Erie Canal, Great Lakes, and the Mississippi to the Gulf of Mexico. The I&M Canal, dug over 96 miles by hand between 1836 and 1848, made possible the settling of the northern part of the state and the growth of the city of Chicago.

Over it traveled immigrants from Sweden, Germany, and Ireland; cattle and goods; and the tools of settlement of the American westward movement. Settlement and industry followed the opening of the water-way, and with that, the growth of canal towns characterized by distinc-tive architecture.

One of the most picturesque is Lockport. History in Lockport is every-where. The town was platted in 1836 by the I&M commissioners to serve as the headquarters for the canal. The headquarters building—in the National Register and part of the Lockport National Register Historic District—is now the **Will County Historical Society Museum**—crammed with artifacts of the canal period—at 803 South State Street, 60441; (815) 838–5080. Free. Open daily 1:00 to 4:30 P.M. year-round.

Adjacent to the museum is the **Pioneer Settlement,** located along the banks of the canal at Eighth Street. In an open area once used by farm-ers to load their cargo onto canal boats, the historical society has cre-ated an open-air museum with historic buildings brought to the site from around the county. Included are a one-room schoolhouse, a black-smith shop, an 1860s farmhouse, a jail, and an 1830s log cabin, the old-est building in the county. Open mid-April to early October. Free.

A 2½-mile trail follows the east bank of the canal through Lockport. Accessible year-round by hikers, joggers, bicyclists, and cross-country skiers, the trail is marked with interpretive signs explaining the history of the waterway. It crosses over old **Lock Number One,** where locally quarried stone walls remain. The trail terminates in **Dellwood Park,** originally built in the early 1900s by the Chicago Interurban Railroad as an amusement park. Today it boasts tennis courts, a swimming pool, floral gardens, ball fields, and a summer program of free concerts at the performing arts center.

A side note: Some of the county's earliest steel plows were first fash-ioned in Lockport by inventor John Lane in 1835. His plows, which shaped the face of Illinois agriculture, were manufactured at a site near Gougar Road and Seventh Street.

After an afternoon of history, a delightful counterpoint is **Tallgrass,** a decidedly gourmet restaurant, 1006 South State Street, 60441, a place that's even been acclaimed by tough Chicago restaurant reviewers. Housed in what was once a barn used for I&M canal workers, the mood is elegant, the food epicurean, the prices steep.

Frankfort, forty-five minutes south of Chicago at U.S. Highway 30 and U.S. Highway 45, is known as the "town with 1890 charm." Listed on the

Illinois Historic Landmark survey, the **Frankfort Historic District** contains many restored shops and homes typical of a nineteenth-century crossroads village. Today antique-hunters come from miles around for the village's growing collection of antiques stores. Most shops are closed on Monday. The Chamber of Commerce has further information, including walking maps and tours; (815) 469–3356. An annual fall festival is scheduled over Labor Day weekend. Visit, too, the **Frankfort Area Historical Society Museum** at Kansas and Hickory Streets, open Sunday 1:00 to 4:00 P.M.

In the southern part of the county, Wilmington is one of northern Illinois's most unusual towns. On the Kankakee River, it's known as the "Island City" because the river runs through downtown, forming an island home to two city parks, **North and South Island Parks.**

Architecturally significant is the **Schutten-Aldrich House,** 600 Water Street, 60481, a landmark octagonal residence built in 1856. The 1836 **Peter Stewart House,** at Kankakee and the Outer Drive, was an important stop on the Underground Railway in the years before the Civil War.

During most of the year, visitors come to Wilmington for the dozens of antiques shops in the area.

The little village of New Lenox is home to a historically important building—the **Gougar residence** at Gougar Road and U.S. Highway 30, home of the first county postmaster. On the last Saturday in June, the village holds its **Old Campground Festival.**

Perhaps nothing demonstrates quite as eloquently the changes in our society as the juxtaposition of the historic and the futuristic. In Morris, the seat of Grundy County, the towering shapes of the Dresden Nuclear Power Station form a striking contrast to the waters of the old Illinois and Michigan (I&M) Canal, which flow past town and through **Gebhard Woods State Park.**

The thirty-acre park, named after its donor, Fred Gebhard, is situated off Route 47 at the southwest edge of Morris on the north bank of the I&M Canal. The park has four ponds for children's fishing plus adult fishing in the canal and in **Nettle Creek,** which form the north and east boundaries of the park. Largemouth bass, bluegill, sunfish, and catfish are caught. With an impressive collection of shade trees—walnut, oak, cottonwood, ash, and maple—picnicking is a popular activity here. Gebhard Woods is part of the **I&M Canal State Trail** and the **I&M Canal National Heritage Corridor.** For further information contact the Site Superintendent, Gebhard Woods State Park, P.O. Box 272, Morris 60450; (815) 942–0796.

The Schutten-Aldrich House

East of Morris, in *Evergreen Cemetery,* lies the grave of Shabbona (1775–1859), the chief of the Potawatomi tribe, who sided with the settlers during the Black Hawk War of 1832. Even though a proven friend, Shabbona and his tribe were forced to move to a reservation in Kansas in 1836. He later returned to Illinois. The city of Morris honors the Indian hero with one of the last working steam pump fire engines in the country. *Old Shab-a-nee,* in use from 1868 to 1922, still appears today in parades.

The last weekend in September, Morris hosts the *Grundy County Corn Festival,* one of the largest county agricultural festivals in the state. Parades, exhibits, musical concerts, and boat excursions on the Illinois River make it a perfect family outing. Call (815) 942–CORN for information.

About 8 miles southeast of Morris and south of the Illinois River is one of my favorite Illinois natural preserves, *Goose Lake Prairie State Park,* one of the last remnants of prairie left in this, the Prairie State, and one of the largest preserves in the tall grass region of North America. As such it has national significance. Of its 2,357 acres, 1,513 are dedicated as an Illinois Nature Preserve.

There is, however, no lake at Goose Lake, having been drained at the end of the last century for farming and for the clay deposits under it. Instead, the grasses and flowers are much like what the state's earliest settlers would have encountered. The palette of wildflowers changes in hue throughout the seasons: in spring the violet shooting star and blue-eyed grass; in summer false indigo and blazing star; and in fall aster and goldenrod.

The park's *Tallgrass Nature Trail* offers a fascinating walk through 1½ miles of prairie and across potholes, marshes, and a unique floating bridge.

A two-story replica of the 1834–35 *John Cragg cabin,* nicknamed the Palace, stands in the park. The original was a station on the Underground Railroad.

An interpretive program is offered year-round except winter weekends. The visitors center is open 10:00 A.M. to 4:00 P.M. The park's address, on Jug Town Road, comes from an early settlement here. Dating from 1853 Jug Town was a small community whose inhabitants made drain tiles, water jugs, and pottery from the region's clay. For information on the park, contact the Site Superintendent, 5010 North Jug Town Road, Morris 60450; (815) 942–2899.

The Kankakee River, the namesake of the county and city, offers more than just scenic beauty. Six miles northwest of Kankakee on Route 102, along the river's banks, is the *Kankakee River State Park,* 2,780 wooded acres spread out along 11 miles of the river. The first European to travel down that river was Rene Robert Cavalier, Sieur de la Salle, who, with a party of fourteen men, traveled from the headwaters of the Kankakee down to the Illinois River in 1679.

Modern explorers make the trip downstream daily throughout the summer on one of the cleanest waterways in the state. *Reed's Canoe Trips,* 907 North Indiana Avenue, Kankakee 60901, books canoe trips from two hours to six hours and overnight, as well. Canoes, paddles, life jackets, and return transportation are provided. The service operates daily from April 1 to October 15; (815) 932–2663.

An Empty Jug (Town)

*T*he tiny settlement of Jug Town began in 1853 and eventually grew to more than fifty families who fashioned drain tiles and pottery claimed from clay mined on the edge of Goose Prairie. In fact, the tiny town had pottery factories, homes, two boarding houses, a school, blacksmith shop, general store, kilns—and a saloon.

Most townies were from New York, as well as immigrants from England and Ireland. It remained prosperous for a short time, but then suddenly "gave out." Historians aren't quite sure why Jug Town suddenly was deserted. But all that remains of Jug Town is an old drying shed, kilns, and part of a school building. Yep, it's a real mystery on the prairie.

The state park's **Rock Creek Canyon** is especially pretty with its picturesque waterfall and gnarled cedars growing from its steep limestone walls. Hiking, equestrian, and snowmobile trails are laced throughout the park's forested acres. Picnic facilities and camping (with electric hookup) are available. In the summer the park rangers present an informative interpretive program. For information contact the Park Ranger, R.R. 1, Bourbonnais 60914; (815) 933–1383.

Each July, anglers from around the Midwest gather to try their luck in the annual **Kankakee River Valley Fishing Derby.** More than $100,000 is awarded in prizes to those who land the tagged fish. For more information call (800) 747–4837 in Illinois, (815) 935–7390 outside the state.

Golf, too, has its proponents, and Kankakee County has the courses to satisfy even the most avid. There are seven courses, including the **Bon Vivant Country Club** (815–935–0403), ranked second in the district only after Butler National by the Chicago District Golf Association.

During Labor Day weekend, the **Kankakee River Valley Regatta** brings powerboats to the river from miles around for fast and wonderful racing championships.

In the southwest part of Kankakee, at Eighth Avenue and Water Street, is the boyhood home of Len Small, twenty-eighth governor of Illinois. Situated on a twenty-two-acre park, the home is part of the **Kankakee Historical Society Museum.** The 1855 Italianate limestone building has been restored and rooms furnished in period style. On the grounds visitors can tour a historic one-room schoolhouse. Admission is free. Open year-round 10:00 A.M. to 4:00 P.M. Monday through Thursday and 1:00 to 4:00 P.M. on Saturday and Sunday. Call (815) 932–5279.

Kankakee's **Bradley House,** at Harrison and the river, was designed by Frank Lloyd Wright as a private residence, the first in his famous "Prairie style." The 1901 structure is true to form with long, low lines and overhanging eaves. Set in a grove of trees on the Kankakee River, the effect is a natural, harmonious one. Wright also designed the original furnishings, china, and rugs for the home. In 1953 the architectural showplace became a charming inn, run by two army cooks. It's private now and no longer open as a restaurant. Call the visitor's bureau for details: (800) 747– 4837 in Illinois; (815) 935– 7390 out of state.

Bourbonnais, just north of Kankakee, was one of the earliest settlements on the Kankakee, dating from the founding of a French trading post here in 1832. An influx of French Canadians followed, giving the region its French flavor. In Bourbonnais is the **Olivet Nazarene University**

The Bradley House

(formerly the Catholic St. Viator College), with its renowned ***Strickler Planetarium;*** (815) 939–5395. More than 4,800 stars are projected onto a 30-foot dome in a series of seasonal programs. Call for schedules and times. Admission is $1.00 for adults and children.

Momence, too, is a historic community, once known as the Old Border Town (between wilderness and civilization), situated on the Hubbard Trail linking Fort Dearborn (Chicago) to Vincennes, Indiana. The road, also known as the Vincennes Trail, was designated a state road, later Illinois 1.

Momence today boasts a number of historic homes. The ***Momence Historic House,*** 11 North Dixie Highway, 60954, is a furnished home that lets the visitor see what life was like in the period 1870–1900. The kitchen, with its dry sink and pump, pie safe, and butter churn, speaks of a time without modern appliances. Open May through September, Saturday and Sunday only, 2:00 to 4:00 P.M. Free.

A major industry in the area is the growing of gladioli—more than 150,000 are harvested annually. In early August, the ***Momence Gladiolus Festival*** draws thousands from across the country. In addition to lovely flowers, there are parades, antique car shows, a flea market, an antique tractor show, and a family fun run. Call (815) 472–4620 for more information.

**PLACES TO STAY IN
NORTHEASTERN ILLINOIS**

ELMHURST
Courtyard by Marriott,
370 North Route 83, 60126
(630) 941–9444

Holiday Inn,
624 North York
Road, 60126
(630) 279–1100

FRANKFORT
Abe Lincoln Motel,
10841 West Lincoln
Highway, 60423
(815) 469–5114

GENEVA
The Herrington,
15 South River Lane, 60134
(630) 208–7433

GURNEE
Sweet Basil Hill Farm,
15937 West Washington
Street, 60031
(847) 244–3333

LAKE FOREST
Deer Path Inn,
255 East Illinois, 60045
(847) 234–2280

LIBERTYVILLE
Best Western Hitch Inn
Post Motel,
1765 North Milwaukee
Avenue, 60048
(847) 362–8700

LINCOLNSHIRE
Marriott Lincolnshire
Resort,
10 Marriott Drive, 60069
(847) 634–0100

LISLE
Hyatt Lisle,
1400 Corporetum
Drive, 60532
(630) 852–1234

LOMBARD
Embassy Suites,
707 East Butterfield
Road, 60148
(630) 969–7500

NAPERVILLE
Days Inn,
1350 East Ogden
Avenue, 60563
(630) 369–3600

Hampton Inn,
1087 East Diehl
Road, 60563
(630) 505–1400

Wyndham Garden Hotel,
1837 Centre Point
Circle, 60563
(630) 505–3353

OAK PARK
Wright's Cheney House
Bed and Breakfast,
520 North East
Avenue, 60302
(708) 524–2067

ST. CHARLES
Hotel Baker,
100 West Main
Street, 60174
(630) 584–2100

Pheasant Run Resort,
4051 East Main
Street, 60174
(800) 999–3319

WAUKEGAN
Ramada Inn,
200 North Green Bay
Road, 60085
(847) 244–2400

WHEATON
The Wheaton Inn,
301 West Roosevelt
Road, 60187
(630) 690–2600

WINNETKA
Chateau des Fleurs,
552 Ridge Road, 60093
(847) 256–7272

**PLACES TO EAT IN
NORTHEASTERN ILLINOIS**

EVANSTON
Oceanique,
505 Main Street, 60202
(847) 864–3435

Pete Miller's Steakhouse,
1557 Sherman
Avenue, 60201
(847) 328–0399

Trio,
1625 Hinman
Avenue, 60201
(847) 733–8746

GENEVA
Mill Race Inn,
4 East State
Street, 60134
(630) 232–2030

JOLIET
White Fence Farm,
Joliet Road
(Romeoville), 60441
(815) 838–1500

LAKE FOREST
Egg Harbor Cafe,
512 North Western
Avenue, 60045
(847) 295–3449

English Room,
255 East Illinois, 60045
(847) 234–2280

South Gate Cafe,
665 Forest Avenue at
Market Square, 60045
(847) 234–8800

LIBERTYVILLE
The Lambs Country Inn,
I–94 and Ill. 176, 60048
(847) 362–5050

MCHENRY
LeVichyssois,
220 West Ill. 120
(Lakemoor), 60050
(815) 385–8221

MORRIS
Drake's Farm,
5595 East Pine Bluff
Road, 60450
(815) 942–5580

NAPERVILLE
Meson Sabika Tapas Bar &
Restaurant
1025 Aurora Avenue, 60540
(630) 983–3000

Montparnasse,
200 East 5th Avenue, 60563
(630) 961–8203

ST. CHARLES
Old Church Inn,
18 North 4th Street, 60174
(630) 584–7341

WAUKEGAN
Mathon's,
6 East Clayton Street, 60085
(847) 662–3610

WHEELING
Bob Chin's Crab House,
393 South Milwaukee
Avenue, 60090
(847) 520–3633

Don Roth's,
61 North Milwaukee
Avenue, 60090
(847) 537–5800

Harry Caray's,
933 North Milwaukee
Avenue, 60090
(847) 537–2827

Le Francais,
269 South Milwaukee
Avenue, 60090
(847) 541–7470

Weber Grill,
920 North Milwaukee
Avenue, 60090
(847) 215–0996

Selected Visitors Bureaus and Chambers of Commerce

Illinois Bureau of Tourism—Travel Information,
(800) 2-CONNECT (226–6328)

DuPage Area Convention and Visitors Bureau,
915 Harger Road, Oak Brook, 60523
(800) 232–0502

Elgin Area Convention and Visitors Bureau,
77 Riverside Drive, Elgin, 60128
(800) 217–5362

Heritage Corridor Convention and Visitors Bureau,
81 North Chicago Street, Joliet, 60432
(800) 926–2262

Lake County Convention and Visitors Bureau,
401 North Riverside Drive, Gurnee, 60031
(800) 525–3669

Oak Park Visitors Bureau,
158 North Forest Avenue, Oak Park, 60301
(888) 625–7275

Greater St. Charles Convention and Visitors Bureau,
311 North Second Street, St. Charles, 60174
(800) 777–4373

Helpful Web Sites

Illinois Bureau of Tourism,
www.enjoyillinois.com

WILMETTE
Walker Brothers
Original Pancake House,
153 Green Bay Road, 60091
(847) 251–6000

WINNETKA
Tanglewood,
566 Chestnut Street, 60093
(847) 441–4600

WORTH SEEING

Argonne National
Laboratory,
Argonne

Michael Jordan Golf Center,
Aurora

Villa Olivia Ski Area,
Bartlett

McDonald's Museum,
Des Plaines

Lizzadro Museum of
Lapidary Art,
Elmhurst

Northwestern University
Sculpture Garden and
Galleries,
Evanston

Chicago Botanic Garden,
Glencoe

Nordic Hills Resort,
Itasca

River Trail Nature Center,
Northbrook

Ernest Hemingway
Museum and Birthplace,
Oak Park

Medieval Times Dinner
Theater and Tournament,
Hemingway

Old Orchard Center,
Skokie

Kohl's Children Museum,
Wilmette

Kline Creek Farm,
Winfield

**MORE ATTRACTIONS WORTH
SEEING IN NORTHEASTERN
ILLINOIS**

Baha'i House of Worship,
Wilmette

Blackberry Historical
Farm/Village,
Aurora

Brookfield Zoo,
Brookfield

Cantigny,
Wheaton

Chicago Botanic Garden,
Glencoe

Cuneo Museum and
Gardens,
Vernon Hills

Frank Lloyd Wright Home
and Studio,
Oak Park

Gross Point Light House
and Lakefront,
Evanston

Harrah's Casino Joliet,
Joliet

Hawthorne Racecourse
Suburban Downs,
Stickney

JFK Health World,
Barrington

Kemper Lakes Golf and
Tennis Club,
Long Grove

Marytown/St. Maximillan
Kolbe Shrine,
Libertyville

Manilow Outdoor
Sculpture Park,
University Park

Seven Bridges Ice Arena,
Woodridge

The Grove,
Glenview

Woodfield Shopping
Center,
Schaumburg

Northwestern Illinois

Mississippi River Banks

The scenery along the Mississippi River, down into the Mississippi River Palisades State Park, is one of the prettiest and hilliest terrains in the state. Beginning at the northwestern corner of the state is the historic lead-mining town of Galena, the third-largest tourist attraction in Illinois (after Chicago and Springfield). Although it wouldn't quite be considered "off the beaten path," so many small-town charms are here that it would be a mistake to overlook it.

Galena's life as a tourist attraction began about thirty years ago as a spot to spend the day, browse through quaint shops, hunt for antiques, and visit the home of General Ulysses S. Grant.

Galena Nuggets

The recorded history of Illinois began just north of present-day Galena. On June 20, 1673, explorers Père Jacques Marquette and Louis Joliet paddled their canoe along the Mississippi River and put ashore on its sandy banks, thereby becoming the first Europeans to have ever set foot in what would become known as Illinois.

To explorers, Illinois was a wilderness to be tamed. The missionary priest and his companion were followed by French fur traders and trappers, who plied the state's inland waterways and carved out a crude but vast river transportation system. These men also struck up trading relationships with native Illinois peoples, like the Illiwek, Sauk, and Fox. Eventually trading posts were established, many of which turned into towns.

However, the French influence in Illinois came to an end largely because of the results of the French and Indian War (1756-1763), which pitted France against England for control of the vast resources of North America's interior regions. England won, the French were forced out (though you can still see some remnants of their occupation, especially in southwestern Illinois), and English and Irish pioneers poured in.

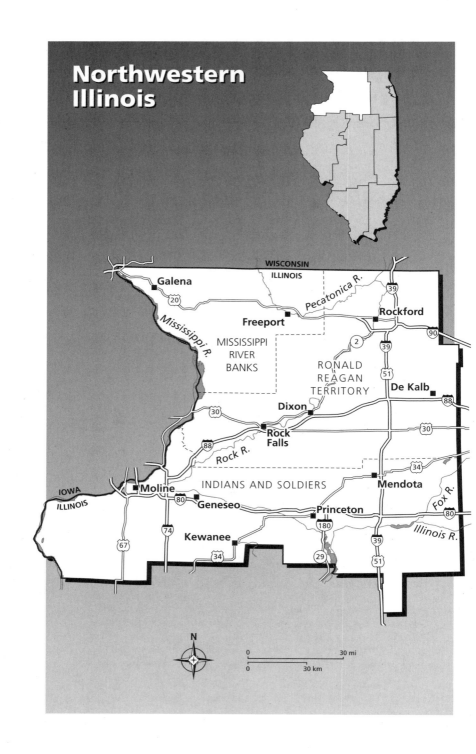

Northwestern Illinois

WISCONSIN
ILLINOIS

Galena

Pecatonica R.

39

Rockford

20

Freeport

90

Mississippi R.

MISSISSIPPI
RIVER
BANKS

2

39

RONALD
REAGAN
TERRITORY

51

De Kalb

88

Dixon

30

30

Rock
Falls

88

Rock R.

34

IOWA
ILLINOIS

Moline

80

INDIANS AND SOLDIERS

Mendota

Fox R.

80

Geneseo

Princeton

Illinois R.

74

180

39

67

Kewanee

34

29

51

N

0   30 mi

0   30 km

NORTHWESTERN ILLINOIS

As an introduction to the town, the *Galena/Jo Daviess County History Museum,* 211 South Bench Street, 61036, offers two thirty-minute self-guided walking tours. This is an excellent way to get your bearings and to decide at which places you will want to spend more time. The tours begin at the Chamber of Commerce office in the railroad depot at 101 Bouthillier Street, where you can pick up a map that takes you through the business and shopping district, about 6 blocks long.

There are a half dozen other guided tours available in Galena. Contact the Galena/Jo Daviess County Convention and Visitors Bureau, (800) 747–9377, 101 Bouthillier Street, Galena 61036, for a listing.

Galena's main attraction is the *Ulysses S. Grant Home.* It's not on the walking tour but is within walking distance from the Chamber of Commerce. Instead of heading west across the bridge, go east along Bouthillier Street and you'll run right into it, on the corner of Bouthillier and Fourth Streets. The house is open daily from 9:00 A.M. to 5:00 P.M., and admission is free.

There is also the guided *Galena History Tour,* which begins at the Galena/Jo Daviess County History Museum on Bench Street. See a slide-tape presentation and tour the museum. Next visit the General Store Museum, the historic downtown district, and Grant's home. The tour then travels through Grant Park, with its statue of the general, and recrosses the bridge to end at the 1845 Market House, where you see a slide presentation on Galena's architecture. For tour information contact the Galena/Jo Daviess County History Museum, P.O. Box 18, Galena 61036; (815) 777–9129. The museum is open daily 9:00 A.M. to 5:00 P.M. year-round.

The *Belvedere Tour Home,* Park Avenue, built in 1857, is one of Galena's largest mansions and has been meticulously restored and furnished with antiques. Other restored homes that are open to the public are the *John Dowling Stone House,* Diagonal Street, and the *Turney House,* U.S. Highway 20 West, 61036. The homes are open 10:00 A.M. to 5:00 P.M. daily.

Galena also has two *House Tours weekends,* the last full weekend in September and again in June, when you can view privately owned, restored homes, mansions, and cottages not usually available to the public.

The *Old Market House* is open 9:00 A.M. to noon, 1:00 to 5:00 P.M. daily, and admission is free. Inside its Main Hall are wall panel photos, diagrams, and a short narrated slide show about architecture. The South Wing has a commerce and mining exhibit, and the basement has a mural collection of photos and printed documents of the Market House.

Grant Hills Antique Auto Museum has antique, classic, and special-interest automobiles of yesteryear on display. Hours are 10:00 A.M. to 5:00 P.M. daily during the summer and weekends 10:00 A.M. to 5:00 P.M. from November through May 15. No set schedule for the rest of the year, so call (815) 777–2115 for hours.

Galena Cellars Winery, 515 South Main Street, 61036, (815) 777–3330, is

Boom . . . and Bust

*G*alena's lead-mining history would make a good television miniseries. How did it happen?

Since the last great glacier bypassed what we call northwestern Illinois, most of the landscape remained as it had developed naturally—with mineral deposits lying just beneath the surface of the ground.

Fox and Sac Indians had mined the abundant lead and used it for trade with other tribes. In fact, they operated small lead mines and smelters even before the French came here in the 1720s, the first Europeans to mine this area who used 200 of their own men and slaves from San Domingo to get the lead out.

When this region became part of the United States, it was incorporated into a huge Federal Mining District. In 1822, the first mining lease was granted to a Col. James Johnson, who brought

twenty of his hardened Kentucky miners (and a number of slaves) to work the mines. (Even though laws prohibited the use of slaves in the old Northwest Territory, they were used in the mining industry here until the 1840s.)

The real lead boom began in the late 1820s with the arrival of the steamboats to Galena. Before the decade was over, more than 4,000 mining permits had been granted. By 1828, the tiny hamlet of Galena had grown to an important city of more than 5,000 people.

In 1845, 54 million pounds of lead (more than 80 percent of the nation's total) was mined here. But surface deposits quickly played out, and the discovery of gold in California in 1848 drew miners west. By the 1870s, Galena was reduced to a tiny hamlet again, filled with abandoned mines and abandoned houses.

just inside the Flood Gates on Galena's Main Street in a restored 1840s granary building. You'll enjoy watching the working of this operating winery. The family-owned business produces 8,000 cases a year, most sold at the winery. The forty-five-minute tour includes wine tasting. Admission is $1.00, and the winery is open daily except major holidays. Call for tour times.

Galena boasts plenty of places to stay, and that includes resorts, hotels, and more than forty bed and breakfasts. The Chamber of Commerce and the Visitors and Convention Bureau have listings. Many of the guest houses and bed and breakfasts are in restored historic homes and are a delightful way to spend time here in this "town that time forgot."

For additional information you can contact the Chamber of Commerce, 101 Bouthillier Street, Galena 61036, (815) 777–0203 or 800–747–9377, or the Convention and Visitors Bureau, 330 North Bench Street, Galena 61036, (815) 777–3357.

The *Galena Public Library & Historical Collection,* 529 South Bench Street, 61036; (815) 777–0200, includes a mosaic fireplace in a wisteria pattern, done in the style of Frank Lloyd Wright. Among its historic collections are Galena newspapers from 1834 to the present. Historical Collection hours are 1:00 to 8:30 P.M. Monday through Friday; 1:00 to 4:00 P.M. Saturday; or by appointment. Library hours are 1:00 to 6:00 P.M. Monday, Tuesday, Friday; 1:00 to 8:30 P.M. Wednesday; 9:00 A.M. to 6:00 P.M. Thursday and Saturday.

The *Old Stockade Refuge,* 208 Perry Street, 61036; (815) 777–1646, has Indian and pioneer history displays—and includes a spot where settlers hid from Indian braves during the 1832 Black Hawk War. Watch your head on the low timbers here! The tour runs about thirty-five minutes and admission is charged. Hours vary, so call ahead.

Galena also offers river cruises. The **Julia Belle Swain,** (815) 777–1660, is a 115-passenger steam-driven sternwheeler. A two-day cruise on the

Top Annual Events

Fulton Dutch Days Festival, Fulton, early May, (800) 995–2129

Annual Wildflower Pilgrimage, Starved Rock State Park, Utica, early May, (815) 667–4906

Civil War Days, Rockford, late June, (815) 397–9112

Annual Steam Threshing and Antique Show, Freeport, late July, (800) 369–2955

DeKalb Corn Festival, DeKalb, late August, (815) 748–CORN

Autumn Pioneer Festival, Belvidere, late September, (815) 547–7935

Sycamore Pumpkin Festival, Sycamore, late October, (815) 895–5161

Country Christmas, Galena, late Nov.–Dec., (815) 777–9050

Julmarknad, Bishop Hill, late Nov.–early Dec., (309) 927–3345

Eagle Watch, Rock Island, mid-Jan, (800) 747–7800

Room with a View

To be rewarded with some of the best vistas in Galena, book a room at the Hellman Guest House, built on Quality Hill with views of Horseshoe Mound. Especially noteworthy is the view from the 1895 merchant home's main tower, overlooking the "town that time forgot" and its many church spires and steeples, gingerbread houses, surrounding bluffs, and more.

Of course, the bed-and-breakfast guest rooms at this historic home are top quality, too. Victorian elegance sprinkled with authentic antiques, brass beds, and claw-foot tubs are part of the ambience that makes the Hellman House one of my favorite overnights in the Galena area.

Mississippi departs from LeClaire, Iowa, docks overnight near Galena, and returns to LeClaire. Reservations are required.

Nearby, ***Apple River Canyon State Park*** has 297 acres for picnicking, camping, fishing, hiking, and winter sport activities. Contact Apple River Canyon State Park, Apple River 61001; (815) 745–3302. From Warren drive 4 miles south on Route 78, then go 4 miles west on a county road.

The town of Hanover, about 30 miles from Apple River Canyon, boasts the ***Whistling Wings Duck Hatchery,*** which raises more than 200,000 mallards every year. This is the world center for mallard duck production. The hatchery is on Route 84, in the middle of town. Take home either the fresh or smoked variety for dinner in a handy shipping container; (815) 591–3512.

In October the town holds an ***Oktober Duck Festival.*** The festival is the first weekend in October and is similar to an old-fashioned Oktoberfest. Write to the Hanover Chamber of Commerce, P.O. Box 537, Hanover 61041, or call (815) 591–2201.

Mount Carroll is pure nineteenth-century Midwest America with its cobblestone courthouse square in the center of town, Victorian architecture, and 1870s-style storefronts lining Main Street. In fact, Mount Carroll was chosen from among seventy-six other Illinois towns as a "Main Street, Illinois" town based on the concept of "building on yesterday for tomorrow."

Mount Carroll, located in the northwest corner of the state, about 10 miles east of the Mississippi River, was named after Charles Carroll, a Maryland signer of the Declaration of Independence. The town was created by an Act of Legislature in 1839.

Appreciative of its architectural treasures, Mount Carroll has preserved many of its original buildings, and a major portion of them are listed in the National Register of Historic Places. A self-guided walking tour through the historical sites is available from the Chamber of Commerce, P.O. Box 94, Mount Carroll 61053.

Highlights of the tour include the ***Glenview Hotel,*** 116 East Market Street, 61053, built in 1886 at a cost of $20,000. The hotel remained open until 1976. The lobby is decorated with some of the original furniture and a large collection of antiques. The hotel is now an apartment building.

The **Owen P. Miles Home,** 107 West Broadway, 61053, has been turned into a museum. It is open Monday through Friday, 10:00 A.M. to 2:00 P.M., Saturday 10:00 A.M. to 3:00 P.M., and Sunday 12:00 to 3:00 P.M., or call (815) 244–3474 for an appointment. It is also open weekdays throughout the year when the curator is in the office.

The Main and Market Streets **Commercial Core** architecturally dates back to the 1850s, and a number of buildings were faced with galvanized sheet metal. These decorative facades are said to make up one of the finest collections in the United States.

Inside City Hall, 302 North Main, 60153, the United States Hissen brass bell, on loan from the Washington, D.C., Naval Historic Center, is on display.

In the center of the town square is the **War Memorial and Annex,** which is listed in *Ripley's Believe It or Not* as the only memorial with an annex. The annex is to accommodate the 1,284 names listed on the monument. The monument is crowned with a cavalryman designed and sculpted by Lorado Taft, a renowned Midwestern sculptor, lecturer, and author.

Mount Carroll holds an annual **Mayfest,** an arts festival and preservation fair, every Memorial Day weekend. Traditional artisans display their wares, showing examples of smithing, glass, pottery, and performing arts. For a program guide write Mayfest, P.O. Box 94, Mount Carroll 61053; or call (815) 244–9161.

Mount Carroll War Memorial and Annex

The ***Raven's Grin Inn,*** at 411 North Carroll Street, (815) 244–4746, 60153, is an out-of-body experience for those interested in local artist Jim Warfield's funhouse. Every room is packed with sensory and intellectual experiences. Warfield personally conducts the tours and no two of them are quite the same.

Northwestern Illinois Trivia

East Dubuque is the "northwesternmost" town in Illinois.

Abraham Lincoln served here as a company officer in the short-lived Black Hawk War of 1832.

The Campbell Center is a complex of Georgian Revival buildings previously occupied by Frances Shirmer College. The college was established at Mount Carroll in 1853 and closed in 1978. The center was purchased by the Restoration College Association after Shirmer College closed, and the campus now houses the ***Campbell Center for Historic Preservation.*** The center offers workshops in architectural and fine arts preservation, archaeology, and the educational, policy, and planning aspects of preservation. To contact the Campbell Center, call (815) 244–1173 or write Campbell Center for Historic Preservation, South College Street, Mount Carroll 61053.

The ***Oakville County School Museum Complex,*** 4 miles southeast of Mount Carroll, is also nostalgic of the nineteenth-century Midwest. A one-room country schoolhouse, a blacksmith shop, and two log cabins are on exhibition. The Carroll County Historical Society operates the complex, and it is open Monday through Friday 10:00 A.M. to 2:00 P.M., Saturday 10:00 A.M. to 3:00 P.M., and Sunday noon to 3:00 P.M. June 1 through Labor Day and by appointment. Contact the Mount Carroll Chamber of Commerce, P.O. Box 94, Mount Carroll 61053; (815) 244–3474 .

Four miles east of Mount Carroll is the ***Timber Lake Playhouse,*** a live, semiprofessional summer stock theater. The season runs from June 1 to Labor Day, and there are evening and matinee performances. New productions are offered every two weeks along with special children's shows. The 425-seat theater is air-conditioned. For information and tickets write Timber Lake Playhouse, P.O. Box 29, Mount Carroll 61053, or phone (815) 244–2035. Tickets should be purchased in advance. For overnight accommodations contact the Mount Carroll Chamber of Commerce; (815) 244–9161.

Farther south along the banks of the Mississippi River is Thomson, home of ***Melon Days,*** a yearly festival held on Labor Day in which watermelon is the star attraction. Thomson has recently restored its

Burlington Railroad Depot and turned it into a museum, which is open to the public. For information on festival dates and accommodations, contact the Thomson Chamber of Commerce; (815) 259–2847.

Mississippi Palisades State Park heads up the natural beauty in Carroll County. The 2,550-acre preserve is located 4 miles north of Savanna and is registered as a national landmark by the Department of the Interior. Its location near the confluence of the Apple and the Mississippi Rivers gives a breathtaking resemblance to tree-lined bluffs along the Hudson River in New York, thus the name palisades. Unusual rock formations have been sculpted by water and wind along the cliffs; among them are Indian Head and the Twin Sisters. There are 12 miles of heavily wooded trails for hiking (the back trails giving the best view of the Mississippi), 5 miles of snowmobile trails, and one hundred acres of open snow area. There are also facilities for picnicking, boating, and camping; a playground; and nature and equestrian trails. For information contact Mississippi Palisades State Park, 4577 U.S. Highway 84 North, Savanna 61074; (815) 273–2731. Hours are from sunup to sundown for the park and 7:30 A.M. to midnight for the campground.

In Lanark the *Standish House,* built in 1882, has been renovated into a bed-and-breakfast. The rooms are furnished with eighteenth- and nineteenth-century English antiques and reproductions. And yes, Puritan Miles Standish is part of the historic family tree. Contact the Standish House at (815) 493–2307 or 540 West Carroll Street, Lanark 61046.

William "Tutty" Baker, one of the early settlers in Freeport, is responsible for naming the town. Actually it was his wife who teased him about running a "free port" for everyone coming along the trail. Legend has it that one night a group of settlers were discussing a name for the town and Mrs. Baker suggested Freeport because of her husband's generosity.

Freeport is the site of the second Lincoln-Douglas debate, which is marked by a boulder at North State Avenue and East Douglas Street. The plaque is inscribed with words from both debaters: Lincoln's "This government cannot endure permanently half slave and half free," and Douglas's "I am not for the dissolution of the Union under any circumstances."

The county courthouse, at the junction of U.S. Highway 20 and Route 75, has a *Civil War Monument,* which was erected in 1869. On the four corners are life-size figures of a Civil War sailor, militiaman, cavalryman, and artilleryman. Engraved on the sides are the names of battles in which Stephenson County volunteers fought. Near the entrance of the courthouse is a plaque commemorating Col. Benjamin Stephenson, Illinois militiaman of 1812.

A bronze statue of Lincoln stands near the entrance to *Taylor's Park,* a mile east of the courthouse on Route 75. *Quality Gardens,* 871 West Stephenson Street, 61032, blooms in the latter part of May and early June and is worth a view.

The *Stephenson County Historical Museum* features memorabilia of early social worker Jane Addams, nineteenth-century furnishings, and an 1840s log cabin. Part of the museum is a farm exhibit, which displays a typical farm kitchen, a blacksmith shop, and many farm machines and tools. A furnished one-room schoolhouse dates from approximately 1910.

The museum is located at 1440 South Carroll Avenue, 61032, 4 blocks south of U.S. Highway 20 on Carroll Avenue between Jefferson and Pershing Streets. Admission is $3.00 for adults and $1.00 for children; hours are Wednesday through Sunday noon to 4:00 P.M.; (815) 232–8419. Closed on holidays.

The *Freeport Art Museum/Arts Council,* at 121 North Harlem Avenue, 61032, has a collection of primitive, Oriental, and American Indian art, European paintings and sculpture, old and new world antiques, plus a contemporary exhibit. It is open Tuesday through Sunday noon to 6:00 P.M., closed holidays. For exhibit information call (815) 235–9755.

Krape Park on Park Boulevard in Freeport is open year-round and has a merry-go-round, flower garden, duck pond, bandshell, boat rentals, tennis courts, miniature golf, and concessions. Open daily; admission is free. Call (815) 235–6114.

Lake Le-Aqua-Na State Park, 6 miles south of the Illinois-Wisconsin state line and 3 miles north of Lena off Route 73, got its name for the nearby town of Lena and *aqua,* the Latin word for water. Roadcuts near the park entrance and to the north contain excellent examples of glacial till with varieties of igneous rock foreign to Illinois. Hours are 6:00 A.M. to sunset from March 16 to November 14, and 8:00 A.M. to sunset from November 15 to March 15; (815) 396–4282. Camping, picnicking, fishing, boating, hiking, and winter sports are available.

The Second Battle of Black Hawk was fought near Kent, and a monument in Kent commemorates the event. The monument is listed in the National Register of Historic Places, and every year the town remembers the battle with a celebration. For information contact the County Clerk's Office, 15 North Galena Avenue, Freeport 61032; (815) 235–8289.

Ronald Reagan Territory

Dixon has gained new stature on the Illinois map as the ***President Ronald Reagan Boyhood Home.*** Reagan lived at 816 South Hennepin Avenue 61021, from 1920 to 1923, from his ninth to twelfth year. Dixonites consider these his formative years. This house is the only family home in Dixon mentioned in Reagan's autobiography. For hours call (815) 288–3404.

After the Republican National Convention in the summer of 1980, a local mailman noticed that the house was for sale. To preserve the house for future generations, he put down a $250 deposit and raised the remainder of the down payment through donations. A group of local businessmen signed a note to guarantee the mortgage. The house was purchased for $31,500. Fund-raising activities and donations paid off the balance of the mortgage by the winter of 1981.

The house and adjacent barn are restored to their 1920 condition; although the furnishings are not those of the Reagan family, they are typical of the time period. The refurbishing was completed in time for Reagan's birthday visit on February 6, 1984.

Listed in the National Register of Historic Places, the home is open to the public free of charge. Volunteers act as interpreters and tour guides. Hours are Monday through Saturday 10:00 A.M. to 4:00 P.M., Sunday 1:00 to 4:00 P.M.; (815) 288–3404.

Dixon is the petunia capital of the world, and to celebrate the city holds

Pigskin Play

The first time we visited the Ronald Reagan Boyhood Home, our two daughters were just toddlin' tots. As the tour guide, a lovely little lady who reminded me of my grandmother, led us through the home and explained the Reaganiana to us, the girls started getting a little antsy.

As the guide drew my attention to another relic of Reagan history, I caught some movement out of the corner of my eye. My five-year-old had crawled under the rope across the door of the President's boyhood room, picked up one of his actual footballs, and was tossing it in the air while lying on the floor.

I hurried over to scold her on such behavior when the tour guide interrupted me. "The President had so much fun in this house," she said. "I don't think he'd mind your lovely child having a toss with his football."

a *Petunia Festival* every Fourth of July weekend. The city boasts that more than 7¹/₂ miles of city streets are lined with petunias. The festival also includes a carnival, games, races, performances at the Dixon Theater, an arts and crafts show, parade, and fireworks. For more information and schedule of events, contact the Chamber of Commerce, 74 Galena Avenue, Dixon 61021; (815) 284–3361.

Dixon is rich in history as its many monuments to nineteenth-century pioneers testify. On the west bank of the Rock River is the site of *Fort Dixon,* built during the Black Hawk War. On May 13, 1832, a 23-year-old volunteer marched here from Sangamon County. That volunteer was Abraham Lincoln. The *Lincoln Statue,* a statue of Captain Abraham Lincoln when he served in the Black Hawk War of 1832, and the *Old Settler's Memorial Log Cabin* are located on Lincoln Statue Drive on the north bank of the Rock River between Abraham Lincoln Bridge and Ronald Reagan Bridge. The cabin is open only during the summer months.

A nearby granite boulder summarizes Lincoln's military service in the summer of 1832 on a bronze tablet in bas-relief. Another bas-relief shows founding father John Dixon with a picture of Fort Dixon and Dixon's ferry and tavern.

The *Nachusa Hotel,* 215 South Galena Avenue, 61021, is the hotel of the presidents. Five United States presidents have stayed there: Abraham Lincoln, Ulysses S. Grant, Theodore Roosevelt, William Howard Taft, and Ronald Reagan. The hotel was built in 1837 and is the oldest hotel in Illinois. It also claims to have had the first bathtub in Illinois. It is refurbished, and the Abraham Lincoln Room is decorated in authentic 1840 decor. The hotel is no longer operating and is not open to the public, but it's worth driving by.

Nachusa Grasslands on Lowden Road just east of Grand Detour is a privately held nature preserve comprised of sandstone buttes, rolling hills, oak savannahs, wetlands, and a sea of little bluestem grass. For information call (815) 456–2340.

Loveland Community House and Museum, 513 West Second Street, 61021; (815) 284–2741, exhibits local history. Pictures and personal items of John Dixon, a pioneer home, Indian artifacts, and a library with county books and records are part of the exhibit. There is also a Reagan memorabilia section. The curator, a classmate of the former president, has yearbooks and other souvenirs on display and some personal memories to share. Museum hours are Wednesday, Thursday, and Friday 8:00 A.M. to noon, and the first Saturday of the month 9:00 A.M. to 3:00 P.M.

Lowell Park, 3 miles north of Dixon, is a 205-acre park on the Rock River. Ronald Reagan served as a lifeguard here for seven years from 1926 to 1932. On display at *Loveland Community Museum* is a plaque, which at the time was affixed to a log on the beach. Reagan notched the log every time he saved a life.

The *Amboy Depot Museum* in Amboy was once the Illinois Central Railroad depot. The 106-year-old building is now a seventeen-room museum telling the history of Amboy. Museum hours are weekends and holidays only from 1:00 to 4:00 P.M., May 1 through November 1. Admission is free. No phone, but Amboy is a small community and the museum is easy to find on East Avenue.

Two memorials are near the Amboy depot. One is on the original site of the Carson Pirie Scott & Company department store, the other is a memorial to the early history of the Reorganized Church of Latter-Day Saints.

Grand Detour is an unincorporated area with about 400 inhabitants, but thousands of tourists visit each year because of a blacksmith named John Deere who opened a shop there in 1836. The shop was the beginning of Deere and Company, one of the largest manufacturers of plows in the world.

Grand Detour was named by the Indians because of the oxbow bend in the Rock River at this point. In 1834, pioneer Leonard Andres came to the Rock River Valley and made a claim to the land. He laid out the village of Grand Detour, but, unfortunately, the town was passed over by the railroad and never grew to its early promise of prosperity.

When Deere started farming here, he found that plowing the heavy soil was a difficult job and that most settlers gave up in despair. He experimented with different shapes and materials for plows, and in 1837 he developed a steel plow that worked. Deere and Company is now the oldest major manufacturing business in Illinois and the largest producer of farm implements in the world.

The John Deere Foundation maintains a brand new museum and exhibit center, original buildings, and other features of the original property in Grand Detour. An archaeological exhibition building covers the site of the original blacksmith shop and displays various machines and how they work. The *John Deere Historic Site* also includes Deere's house, authentically furnished from the 1830s, a visitors center, and a blacksmith shop reconstructed on the basis of archaeological findings. The shop has a working forge and equipment used by nineteenth-century iron craftsmen.

John Deere Historic Site

The John Deere Historic Site is open daily 9:00 A.M. to 5:00 P.M., April through October 31. Admission is $3.00 for ages twelve and older. For further information contact the John Deere Historic Site, R.R. 3, Grand Detour 61021; (815) 652–4551.

Another attraction in Ogle County is the Ogle County Courthouse in the center of Oregon. The building is listed in the National Register of Historic Places, and a Soldier's Monument designed by Lorado Taft adorns the lawn.

Lowden State Park, across the river from Oregon, is on a bluff overlooking the Rock River. *Black Hawk,* Lorado Taft's most famous statue, stands 50 feet high overlooking the area. Taft and a few artists retreated to this area every summer during the 1920s and created an artists' colony known as Eagle's Nest. The public library in Oregon has a collection of works by Taft on display in the second-floor gallery.

White Pines State Forest, (815) 946–3717, 8 miles west of Oregon, has 385 acres of recreation and forest area. The lodge has a restaurant, gift shop, and lounge. Best bet here is to reserve one of twenty-six cabins that the park offers to overnight visitors. The park is open from 8:00 A.M. to sundown year-round. For information concerning the lodge and restaurant, call (815) 946–3817.

Mount Morris, northwest of Oregon, has the *Freedom Bell* dedicated by Ronald Reagan in 1963. The bell was hung in the Illinois Pavilion in the

1964 World's Fair and again at a 1965 Cubs' game in Wrigley Field. It is a replica of the Liberty Bell in Philadelphia and is the focal point of the *Let Freedom Ring Festival* every Fourth of July in Mount Morris.

Fulton celebrates its Dutch heritage on the first weekend in May every year. **Dutch Days** are highlighted by *klompen* (wooden shoe) dancing in the the streets of the town. A parade is preceded by the *burgemeester* (mayor) and the town crier inspecting the streets to see if they are clean. When the mayor announces that "We must scrub the streets," costumed street cleaners come out with brooms and pails and scrub until the streets are declared clean.

One part of the parade is the "Parade of Provinces," where townspeople wear native costumes from each province of the Netherlands. Sinterclas, the Dutch version of Santa Claus, brings up the rear of the parade.

Delft jewelry and dishes, wooden shoes, and authentic costumes are on sale. Local stores offer tastes of Dutch cheese and pastry. Traditional Dutch meals, which include corned beef, potatoes and cabbage, pea soup, and currant buns, are served.

The townspeople plant more than 10,000 tulip bulbs every year, and windmills and tulips are in great profusion in Fulton. Even the information booth is housed in a windmill.

During Dutch Days the town crier walks the street announcing special events, and the library displays Dutch books and shows films of the Netherlands (no admission charged).

The festival ends Sunday afternoon with a traditional Dutch worship at a Fulton church. Men and women sit on opposite sides of the church, and part of the service is conducted in Dutch.

Artists' Aerie

*I*t's no coincidence that the magnificent statue of Chief Black Hawk (actually named Eternal Indian) stands on a high bluff overlooking the Rock River just across from the town of Oregon. Lorado Taft operated an artists' colony called Eagle's Nest on the site from 1898 until his death in 1936. And legend has it that he got the idea for the statue when observing some of his fellow artists standing on that very same bluff with their hands folded across their chests. By the way, it's a hollow statue of poured concrete fashioned with iron reinforcing rods and weighs about 100 tons.

For information contact Fulton Chamber of Commerce, P.O. Box 253, Fulton 61252; (815) 589–4545.

Prophetstown State Park, in Prophetstown, was once the site of the Winnebago Indian tribal village. The park derives its name from the Indian prophet Wa-bo-kie-shiek (White Cloud). The village was destroyed in the Black Hawk Indian War of 1832. The park borders the Rock River on the northeast side of Prophetstown. Picnicking, fishing, and camping are available, but with no lifeguards here, plan on swimming at the city park, just 4 blocks away. Call (815) 537–2926 for more information about Prophetstown State Park.

Sterling is the location of the ***P.W. Dillon Home Museum.*** The Italian Renaissance-style brick home at 1005 East Third Street, 61081, was built on the five-and-one-half-acre lot in 1857. Paul W. Dillon, owner of Northwestern Steel and Wire Company, lived there for ninety-six years from his birth in 1883 until his death in 1980. The home has antiques and artifacts on display, plus an Engine #73 steam locomotive and caboose. Hours are Tuesday, Thursday, and Saturday 10:00 A.M. to noon and 1:00 to 4:00 P.M., and Sunday 1:00 to 5:00 P.M.; (815) 622–6215.

The two ***Lincoln historical markers*** in Sterling are at 607 East Third Street, 61081, and at Sixth Avenue and Sixth Street. A ***founder's historical plaque*** is at Fourth Street and Broadway, the ***Grandon Civic Center*** is at Third Avenue, and a ***Civil War Monument and bandshell*** are at East Fourth Street.

Morrison-Rockwood State Park on Route 78 is located 2¹/₂ miles north of Morrison. Lake Carlton, at the center of the park, has a 38-foot-high, 1,800-foot-long dam with a road across it. Fishing, boating, camping, picnicking, and hiking are available. Call (815) 772–4708.

The ***Old Grist Mill*** in Morrison is no longer open to the public but can be seen from U.S. Highway 30 on the west side of Morrison.

Union Grove Cemetery, also on U.S. Highway 30 just outside Morrison, dates back to the early 1800s and is open to the public.

Route 84, running along the west edge of Whiteside County, is part of the ***Great River Road*** that parallels the Mississippi River and is one of the most scenic drives in Illinois.

Rockford has many museums for those who love browsing. The ***Midway Village and Museum Center,*** 6799 Guilford Road, 61107; (815) 397–9112, has a building featuring local history, an industrial building with thirty-two local industries represented, and Midway Village,

NORTHWESTERN ILLINOIS

a turn-of-the-century village complete with stagecoaches. The village has law offices, a black-smith shop, an old stone school, a town hall, lumber shops, a jail, a sheriff's office, and a bandstand. It also features an annual Civil War battle re-creation, complete with authentically dressed Blue and Gray troopers as well as soldiers' encampments that visitors can walk through to soak up some "living history." Admission fees are $5.00 for adults, $3.00 children under twelve. The center is open year-round.

The *Burpee Museum of Natural History,* 813 Main Street, 61103; (815) 965–3132, is housed in a Victorian mansion and is open Monday through Saturday 10:00 A.M. to 5:00 P.M., Sunday noon to 5:00 P.M. The *Rockford Art Museum,* 711 North Main Street, 61103; (815) 968–2787, is open Tuesday through Friday, 11:00 A.M. to 5:00 P.M., Saturday, 10:00 A.M. to 5:00 P.M., and Sunday noon to 5:00 P.M.

The *Discovery Center,* 711 South Main Street, 61101; (815) 963–6769, is a "hands-on" partici-patory museum where you can explore scientific and perceptual principles. The center is open Tuesday through Sunday 1:00 to 4:00 P.M. Sum-mer hours are daily 1:00 to 4:00 P.M.

For ethnic flavor, the *Erlander Home Museum,* operated by the Swedish Historical Society, has mementoes of Rockford's rich Swedish history. It is located at 404 South Third Street, 61104; (815) 963–5559. Hours are Sun-day 2:00 to 4:00 P.M.

The *Graham-Ginestra House,* 1115 South Main Street, 61101; (815) 968–6044, is an example of classic Greek Revival and Italianate archi-tecture. It has elaborately painted ceilings and authentic furnishings. It is open Sunday 2:00 to 4:00 P.M. and is listed in the National Register of Historic Places.

Victorian Village, Longwood Avenue, offers twenty neighborhood shops containing antiques and artwork. You'll find a restaurant, a needlework shop, and a tea room. The village is just off Business High-way 20 between Sixth and Ninth Streets.

Northwestern Illinois Trivia

The town of Aledo got its name by chance, with town founders picking letters out of a hat; the first pro-nounceable name spelled A-L-E-D-O.

In this town you can eat grub in the slammer just like the real criminals! Actually The Slammer is a three-story restaurant in the building that formerly served as a jail in 1909 and where former Mercer County Sheriff Dick May-nard and his wife Jennie lived from 1958 to 1962. Today, you'll eat in the jail cells, decorated with black and white prisoner-striped tablecloths and enjoy all kinds of food. You can even purchase a T-shirt that proclaims "I did time in the Slammer."

Another interesting architectural gem is the *Tinker Swiss Cottage,* built in the Swiss-chalet style after its owner, Robert Hall Tinker, visited Switzerland in 1862. The cottage's antique treasures include a 300-year-old painting, diamond-dust mirrors, Lincoln memorabilia, and dozens of family heirlooms. The cottage is open Tuesday through Sunday, with tours at 1:00 P.M., 2:00 P.M., and 3:00 P.M. Call (815) 964–2424 or write 411 Kent Street, Rockford 61102.

Cool off at *Magic Waters,* a wave pool that offers a playground beach, 40-inch-wide roller slide, and organized games, activities (including aerobics classes), and competitions. Magic Waters is located just off I–90 at the U.S. Highway 20/U.S. Highway 51 interchange near Rockford. Call (815) 332–3280 or write Magic Waters, 7820 CherryVale North Boulevard, Cherry Valley 61016.

Rock Cut State Park, off Route 173 about 6 miles northeast of Rockford, boasts picnicking, camping, trails, fishing, boating, ice skating, ice fishing, cross-country skiing, and snowmobiling. From Rockford take U.S. Highway 51 to Route 173. For information contact the Site Superintendent, 7318 Harlem Road, Caledonia 61011; (815) 885–3311.

One of the best ways to see this area is to follow the carefully mapped Boone County Historical Trail. Originally compiled by the Boone County Bicentennial Commission and the Boone County Conservation District in 1976, the guide to the trail is available by calling (815) 547–7935.

The trail follows four different routes: the South Pacific Route, running through a region once covered by more than 50 miles of native prairie grasslands; Belvidere/Caledonia Route, covering the county seat, Belvidere, and the Scottish settlements at Caledonia and Argyle; Piscasaw Route, which follows the Kishwaukee River and Piscasaw Creek to the Norwegian village of Capron; and the Blaine/State Line Route, beginning in the Kinnikinnick Creek Conservation Acre and traveling through historic Blaine village and across the rolling hills of the Illinois-Wisconsin border. Each route is about 30 miles long, approximating the length of one day's wagon trip in the early settlement days of the 1830s. The trail is designed to be covered by car, on foot by hikers, or on bicycles.

The first three routes begin in Belvidere's *Spencer Park,* on the western edge of the city on Lincoln Avenue. Before the arrival of white settlers, this was the permanent gathering place for the local Potawatomi Indians. At nearby Belvidere Park, the old *Baltic Mill* dates from 1845 and was in use up until 1918. The fall of water through the Kishwaukee River provided the energy to turn the heavy grinding wheel.

At 534 East Hurlbut Avenue, 61008, is the former home of one of its early Civil War heroes, Gen. Stephen A. Hurlbut. Hurlbut's forces at the Battle of Shiloh won an important victory for the Union, earning him national recognition. He served as a member of the Illinois Constitutional Convention, a state representative in the Illinois Legislature, a U.S. congressman, and a minister to Colombia and Peru. Hurlbut is buried in Belvidere Cemetery along with dozens of the city's pioneers.

Usually cemeteries are repositories of an area's history, and **Belvidere Cemetery,** at North Main and Harrison Streets, is no exception. Stop at the cemetery office, (815) 547–7642, for a copy of their historic walking tour. Established in 1847, the burial ground holds the graves of two Revolutionary War soldiers, Thomas Hart and Timothy Lewis; the first white woman in the county, Sara Loop; a black soldier in the Civil War and former slave, John Lawson; and blacksmith Samuel Longcor. Longcor was an early Illinois manufacturer of scouring plows, known as the S. Longcor's Iron Beam, a significant development in the cultivation of the state's prairie lands.

The **Pettit Memorial Chapel,** listed in the National Register of Historic Places, was designed by Frank Lloyd Wright in 1907 as a monument to a local physician, Dr. William H. Pettit. The chapel was restored by the Belvidere Junior Women's Club in 1977. It is a fine example of Wright's Prairie School style, with long, low lines. The stucco exterior is painted pale green with dark green wood trim and has a rough-sawn cedar shingle roof. Contact the cemetery office (number above) for viewing or a list of open dates.

Another historic home, the **Colonel Joel Walker Home,** stands at the corner of Lincoln Avenue and Main Street. The 1840 structure was the residence of a noted hero of the War of 1812.

Big Thunder Park honors the Potawatomi Indian Chief Big Thunder, who died before the first white settlers arrived on the scene in the 1830s. His method of burial, however, provided the town's very first tourist

If you're driving through northwestern Illinois, you'll note that the landscape is actually quite remarkable in some spots.

Far northwestern Illinois claims the state's most exciting topography up this way, especially if you head far west, from Stephenson County near Freeport into Jo Daviess County and onto the Mississippi River. Here the great glacier never leveled out the topography, and you'll note steep valleys and sharply sloping wooded hills. Of course, once you reach the river, you'll see magnificent bluffs lining both sides of it.

Much of the region south of here is undulating prairie, but it's still intriguing, especially when running through the Illinois and Rock River Valleys, where soaring cliffs and wooded bluffs jump out of the prairie flatness, only to disappear too quickly.

attraction. Following Indian custom, he was buried seated in his best attire, along with food, tobacco, and implements necessary in the afterlife, then surrounded by a 6-foot-tall log stockade and left to the elements. Early visitors, including travelers on the Chicago-Galena stagecoach who stopped here, were very curious and—like tourists today—took souvenirs. Soon, very little was left of Big Thunder. But undaunted, the local citizenry substituted bones of hogs and sheep, it is said, as relics for the eager and gullible tourists. A boulder with bronze plaque on the grounds of the Boone County courthouse serves as a memorial.

A greater exploration of local history can be undertaken at the *Boone County Historical Museum,* 311 Whitney Boulevard, 61008; (815) 544–8391. Featured are farm implements typical of those that shaped the county's character. Call for appointments.

The fall in Belvidere is the time for festivals. The third weekend in September brings *Oktoberfest* to town, with German bands, beer, and food, along with carnival rides and craft exhibits. The fourth weekend in September each year, the Boone County Conservation District sponsors the *Autumn Pioneer Festival* with pioneer ethnic gardens, produce, samples and crafts, volunteers in authentic period dress, and an Indian village. Call (815) 547–7935.

Northwest of Belvidere are remnants of the county's immigrant past when Scottish and Scandinavian settlers arrived to take up farming. *Caledonia* and *Argyle* (on the Winnebago County line) were, of course, Scottish settlements. In 1834 two Armour brothers and their cousin came to Ottawa, Illinois, from Kintyre, Scotland. Shortly thereafter they moved to this part of Boone County, which came to be known as Scotch Grove.

Capron, on Route 173 in the northeast part of the county, was home to Norwegian settlers. The first two Norwegian pioneers came to the area in 1842 and called their settlement Helgesaw, later known as Long Prairie.

The town of De Kalb can, quite legitimately, claim that it changed the future of the American West. Once known as the "World's Barbed Wire Capital," it was here in 1874 that inventor Joseph F. Glidden patented an improved method of producing barbed wire. An industry grew up around his invention, with other De Kalb pioneers involved in its manufacture— Jacob Haish and Isaac Ellwood. The *Glidden homestead* and barn at 921 West Lincoln Highway, 60115, is listed in the National Register of Historic Places. It's privately owned, however, and not open to the public.

The *Ellwood House Museum,* 509 North First Street, 60115, is an imposing Victorian mansion appointed with the finest furnishings of the period. Call (815) 756–4609 for hours. Also in Ellwood Park is the *Little House,* a 10-foot miniature mansion with carefully crafted interiors. The carriage house on the property has a fine collection of buggies and sleighs and samples of—what else?—barbed wire. Admission is $5.00 adults, children ages six through fourteen $1.00.

Northern Illinois University, founded in 1895, is located in De Kalb. The school, with 25,000 enrollment, is the second largest in the state. The architecture of some of the older buildings is worth exploring. Check with the Office of Admissions in Williston Hall for guided tours of the campus and self-guided walking tours; (815) 753–0446. NIU's O'Connell and Players' Theaters offer performances throughout the year; (815) 753–1600. Admission is free to the anthropology museum in the Stevens Building.

The *Egyptian Theater,* on North Second Street near Lincoln Highway, is a National Register of Historic Places building with a unique terracotta exterior and excellent acoustics. Built in the Egyptian Revival style, the theater is used for productions by traveling companies and local performing arts groups, as well as for movies; (815) 758–1215. Tours are scheduled by appointment.

The 1929 *Haish Memorial Library,* at Oak and North Third Streets, was a gift from another early barbed wire baron. Its art deco Indiana limestone structure, designed by White and Weber of Chicago, was also placed in the National Register.

And the *Gurler House,* 205 Pine Street, 60115, is home to a series of special events, such as the Summer's Eve Festival. The Greek Revival farmhouse, set in a parklike environment, is listed in the National Register. Historically speaking, De Kalb also claims the first county farm bureau—in 1912.

Festivals of all kinds are important in the county. Among the most popular is the annual *Sweet Corn Festival* each August in De Kalb, when thousands of pounds of fresh-roasted, hot, buttered sweet corn are given free to all "corny" visitors. Sycamore, the county seat, hosts a yearly *Pumpkin Festival* the last weekend in October with a variety of old-time activities including a parade and decorated pumpkins, some in fantastic shapes and others lampooning the politicians of the day, on the courthouse lawn; (815) 895–3456.

Shabbona Lake State Park, in the southwest part of De Kalb County, encompasses 1,550 acres and a 32-acre lake. Fishing is the thing here, and boats can be rented ($50/day for motorboats, $30/day for rowboats) at the marina. One hundred fifty campsites are available (all with

Sandwich Sampler

Sandwich might be the best place in Illinois to find a real deal on antiques and collectibles. The massive show, whose organizer holds to strict standards so that only authentic merchandise is sold, features more than 550 dealers, offering more than 330,000 items in a parklike setting of 160 acres.

Better yet, there's an unconditional ten-day, money-back guarantee on all purchases.

The popular antiques market prides itself on fine nineteenth and twentieth-century American and English furniture. Of course, primitives are still hot as collectibles, too.

But whatever kind of antique you're looking for, just figure that you'll find it here.

electrical hookups), and hiking trails, horseshoe pits, and a baseball diamond are in place. In the winter, cross-country skiing, ice fishing, and snowmobiling are enjoyed here. Write the Site Superintendent, RR 1, Box 120, Shabbona 60550; (815) 824–2106.

In the southeast corner of the county, Sandwich is home of the immensely popular **Sandwich Antiques Market,** held on Sundays May to October from 8:00 A.M. to 4:00 P.M. at the County Fairgrounds on U.S. Highway 34. Admission is $5.00; parking is free.

Indians and Soldiers

Ottawa is a town that remembers its soldiers well. **Washington Park,** in the center of town between Lafayette and La Salle Streets, has two war memorials, one dedicated to veterans of World Wars I and II, Vietnam, and Korea, and the other to the county soldiers in the Civil War. The Civil War monument was designed and erected by Edward McInhill, and it lists the names of the soldiers.

The park is a block square and is decorated with flowers and shrubbery. During the summer months an old-fashioned popcorn wagon does business, and piped music plays in the park. Many of the townspeople enjoy their lunch there.

The park also has a boulder for commemorating the first Lincoln-Douglas debate here on August 21, 1858. The memorial was erected by the Illinois Chapter of the Daughters of the American Revolution.

In 1856 Sheriff William Reddick built what is known as the **Reddick Mansion.** The building is at 100 West Lafayette Street, 61350, across the street from Washington Park and is listed as a national landmark. It serves as office space for the Ottawa Chamber of Commerce and as a tourist information center.

The **Third District Appellate Court of Illinois,** just east of the Reddick Mansion, was built in 1857 and served as the state's supreme court for a decade. The building is open to visitors during business hours.

Other attractions to see in Ottawa include the ***statue of W. D. Boyce,*** who founded the Boy Scouts of America in 1910. The statue is in the Ottawa Avenue Cemetery, 1 mile west of downtown Ottawa on Boyce Memorial Drive. Boyce is buried near the statue.

You must visit **Christ Episcopal Church,** the first Episcopal church to hold services in Ottawa in 1838. It is an example of English High Victorian Gothic architecture. The Wallace Window, patterned after a cathedral in Glasgow, Scotland, is a depiction of the Resurrection. It was designed by Professor Julius Herber of Dresden, Germany, one of Germany's finest artists. The church is located at 113 West Lafayette Street, 61350.

The **Ottawa Avenue Memorial Columns** are classic Roman architecture. The columns were built in 1918 as a memorial to Ottawa in honor of the centennial celebration of Illinois statehood. The columns are located next to the Ottawa Avenue Cemetery. Allen Park, along the Illinois River where it joins the Fox River, is a scenic park with tennis courts, public boat launches, picnic areas, and a beautiful view of the two rivers.

The Ottawa Chamber of Commerce publishes an auto tour of historic sites in the city. Contact the chamber for a copy of the tour at Ottawa Chamber of Commerce, 100 West Lafayette Street, P.O. Box 888, Ottawa 61350; (815) 433–0084, or call the Heritage Corridor Visitors Bureau at (815) 433–1355.

Two miles west of Ottawa in the Illinois Michigan Canal National Heritage Corridor is the **Effigy Tumuli.** These five massive earth sculptures have been shaped into a mile-and-a-half-long work, the largest outdoor sculpture in the world. Call (815) 942–0796 for information.

The **Starved Rock Land Tour,** also available at the Chamber of Commerce office, begins just outside the Ottawa Avenue Cemetery in the village of Naplate. The village was named for the former National Plate Glass Company and is now the home of the Libbey-Owens-Ford Glass Company.

The tour continues west through **Buffalo Rock State Park,** named for a rock that resembles a sleeping bison, to the Half-Way House, once the Sulphur Springs Hotel. The house is privately owned and not open to the public.

The **Grand Village of the Kaskaskia Indians** (1678 to 1700) is the site of three archaeological excavations near the Illinois River. Artifacts from the digs are on exhibit at the La Salle County Historical Museum in Utica.

The *Starved Rock Lock and Dam* and *Illinois Waterway Visitors Center* are next on the tour, followed by the *Father Marquette Memorial.*

The *La Salle County Historical Museum* in Utica, just outside Starved Rock State Park, was built during the term of President Zachary Taylor in 1848.

The tour ends at the Visitors Center in *Starved Rock State Park,* one of the finest state preserves in the Midwest. Starved Rock State Park is located 10 miles west of Ottawa on Route 71 or south of I–80 on Route 178.

The park's name was derived from an Indian legend, which originated during the 1760s when Pontiac, chief of the Ottawa tribe (which lived upriver from this area), was murdered by an Illinois Indian while attending a tribal council in southern Illinois. Many battles to avenge the death of Pontiac were fought, and the Potawatomi tribe, allies of the Ottawa, fought the Illinois Indians in the area now called Starved Rock. The Illinois Indians took refuge on top of a butte and were surrounded by the Ottawa and Potawatomi tribes. They eventually starved atop the rock.

There is evidence the Archaic Indians as well as the Hopewellian, Woodland, and Mississippian tribes lived in the area. Village sites and burial mounds have been mapped by archaeologists within the park boundaries.

The largest group of Indians to inhabit the area was the Illinois. They are believed to have lived here from the 1500s to the 1700s. The tribe's population was between 5,000 and 10,000 and was divided into subtribes. The Kaskaskias were a subtribe whose village extended along the north bank of the Illinois River, directly across from the park.

French explorers Louis Joliet and Father Jacques Marquette were the first known Europeans to visit the area. They canoed up the Illinois River from the Mississippi and stopped at the Kaskaskia village. Two years later, Father Marquette founded the Mission of Immaculate Conception, Illinois's first Christian mission, on the site of the Kaskaskia village.

Rene Robert Cavalier, Sieur de La Salle, came to the area to build a chain of forts to confine the English colonies in the East. Fort St. Louis was built on top of Starved Rock in the winter of 1682–83. It was a strategic post, towering above the rapids of the Illinois River and thereby controlling passage from Canada south. Many Indians settled near the fort for protection from the Iroquois tribe and to be near French trade goods.

NORTHWESTERN ILLINOIS

In the 1800s there was a movement to make Starved Rock the "Gibraltar of the West," but this plan was unsuccessful. The area was later developed into a vacation spot. In 1911 the State of Illinois purchased Starved Rock and the surrounding area. The park now consists of 2,630 acres and is bordered by a 582–acre nature preserve.

Many interesting rock formations are found in the park; they are primarily of St. Peter's sandstone, laid down by a huge, shallow inland sea more than 425 million years ago. It was brought to the surface by an enormous upfold known as the La Salle Anticline. Continual erosion has formed the existing flat surface.

Most of the flat land was glaciated during the past 700,000 years, resulting in a flat and gently rolling plain formed after the last glacier. Most of the prairie is now farmland, and the areas along the river are predominantly forest.

There are eighteen canyons in the park; they were formed by streams feeding into the Illinois River. The streams cut channels through the rock as they followed the cracks and crevices of the sedimentary layers. Waterfalls are found at the heads of all the canyons, especially after a hard summer rain. The most popular waterfalls are at the St. Louis, French, La Salle, and Ottawa canyons.

The park has a wide variety of plant and animal life. Red oak, basswood, and sugar maple trees grow in the moist, sandy soil along the northern slopes. Woodchucks feed on the lush undergrowth, and moles live on insects found in the soil. Vireos and catbirds fly above the ferns and shrubs. Trillium, Dutchmen's Breeches, and the large white flowers of the May Apple tree can be seen in spring.

Along the floodplain cottonwood, black willow, and ash trees grow. Skunk cabbage, marsh marigold, and wild iris live in the marshy areas. Wood ducks nest in hollow trees and can be seen paddling along the river's edge. Beaver and muskrat sometimes appear along the river.

The park has 20 miles of marked hiking trails, and hiking information is available at the visitors center and park office. The trails are open year-round, but hikers should be cautious near bluffs and stay on official park trails. Metal trail maps are located at all trail access points, trail intersections, and points of interest. Colored dots along the trails and on trees assist the hiker; they correspond to letter symbols on trail maps.

Picnicking is permitted, and picnic tables, drinking water, toilets, litter cans, and metal grills are provided at no charge.

Fishing is permitted but anglers must stay 600 feet from the dam. Channel catfish are caught between the lock and dam, bullheads from the seawall, white bass from both ends of Plum Island, sauger and walleye from below the dam in fast water, carp from both banks, and crappies from around the small Leopold Island.

Boats may be launched from the ramp at the west end of the park, and canoes are available for rent.

Ice skating is permitted at parking lot C, and cross-country skiing and snowshoeing are allowed in the picnic area and at **Mattiessen State Park** (just southeast of Starved Rock State Park off Route 178). Equipment can be rented on weekends, and tobogganing and sledding are permitted east of parking lot C. Heated washrooms are accessible from these areas. Snowmobiling is not allowed in the park.

The visitors center displays the park's cultural and natural history. A park interpreter posts a weekly schedule of activities. The center is usually open on weekend afternoons during peak visitor seasons. If the center is closed, contact the park office, which is open daily from 8:00 A.M. to 4:00 P.M.

Contact the visitors center or park interpreter at Starved Rock State Park, Box 116, Utica 61373; (815) 667–4906.

Camping is permitted except in the winter and during the spring thaw. There are 133 sites, and permits are obtained at the campground or park office.

There are horseback riding trails and a horseback riders' campground along Route 71 in the far western side of the park. Horse rentals are available on weekends on Route 71, half a mile west of Route 178.

The wonderful **Starved Rock Lodge,** inside the state park, is located on a high bluff overlooking the Illinois River. The Civilian Conservation Corps (CCC)–built lodge boasts seventy-two rooms and a rustic lounge with a large double fireplace. An indoor swimming pool, Jacuzzi, and sauna are also available. The Pow-Wow Room in the lodge basement offers refreshments. Eighteen cabins adjacent to the lodge are also for rent. Lodging is available year-round. For reservations and information call (815) 667–4211 or write Starved Rock Lodge, Schmidt Enterprises, Inc., P.O. Box 471, Utica 61373.

Norway, 12 miles northeast of Ottawa, is the site of the first permanent settlement of Norwegians in 1834. Inspired by their leader, Cleng Peerson, fourteen families purchased a tiny sailing vessel and set sail for America. They left Norway because of economic, political, and religious domination by the Swedes. Peerson became known as the Norwegian Daniel Boone because he helped settle the new land in America.

A historical marker on Route 71 commemorates the hundred-year anniversary of the settlement, and a plaque tells the Norsk story. The *Norsk Museum,* off Route 71 on County Road 2631, 60551, is open May through October, Saturday and Sunday from 1:00 to 5:00 P.M.

Great elm trees planted by the founding fathers line the streets of Princeton, a prosperous small town much as it was when it was part of the pioneer path to the west.

Princeton was the home of the abolitionist preacher Owen Lovejoy. Lovejoy, a close friend of Abraham Lincoln, was elected to the State Legislature in 1854 and then to the U.S. House of Representatives in 1856 where he served five terms. Lovejoy became nationally known for his work on behalf of the abolition of slavery. His house was one of the most important stations on the Underground Railway in Illinois. Runaway slaves were hidden here by the Lovejoy family until plans could be made for them to travel to the next station on their way to Canada.

The *Owen Lovejoy Homestead* is now a museum. Listed in the National Register of Historic Places, it has fifteen rooms and has been restored to reflect the typical furnishing of its era. The home is on U.S. Highway 6 in Princeton. Hours are 1:00 to 5:00 P.M. every day except Tuesday. For additional information write Tour Director, 451 South Main Street, Princeton 61356; (815) 875–2184.

More recent history can be found on the shelves of *Hoffman's Patterns of the Past,* a china and crystal replacement service at 513 South Main Street, 61356. More than 12,000 hard-to-find patterns are stocked. Hours are 9:00 A.M. to 5:00 P.M. Monday through Saturday; (815) 875–1944.

Other buildings to look for in Princeton are the *Cyrus Bryant House,* 1110 South Main Street, 61356, and the *John Bryant House* at 1518 South Main Street. Cyrus Bryant's house was built in 1844, and in the front yard is a boulder marking the site of the log cabin that he and his brother John built when they gained the right to buy public land by settling on it.

Covered Bridge in Princeton

Another attraction in Princeton is the red **covered bridge** built in 1863. The bridge is 2$^1/_2$ miles north of Princeton off Route 26.

The second weekend in September is the **Homestead Festival and Annual Pork Barbeque,** complete with an ice cream social, art show, beer garden, street dance, flea market, antique car show, pioneer crafts, horse-drawn wagons, and horse show. For information contact the Princeton Chamber of Commerce, 435 South Main Street, Princeton 61356; (815) 875–2616.

The **Hennepin Canal Parkway State Park,** 1 mile south of I–80 at Route 88, is a 104-mile waterway with canoeing, boating, hiking, and snowmobiling. It was here that engineers discovered how to make water run uphill. The park is open twenty-four hours a day. Call (815) 454–2328.

In 1846 a group of idealistic Swedish immigrants came to the Midwest looking for a place to build a communal society. Under the leadership of Erik Janson, a religious zealot, the group founded a commune in **Bishop Hill.** The group, industrious and optimistic, suffered through a harsh winter and epidemics. That year took many of its inhabitants with it. The survivors did establish their version of utopia, but dissension spread among the ranks, and in 1861 the commune dissolved. With the dissolution Bishop Hill faded into history.

Almost thirty years ago the descendents of the Jansonists decided to restore Bishop Hill. The town is now listed as a National Historic Landmark and as a historic district in the National Register of Historic Places. The preserved buildings, located mostly in the center of town, trace the history of the commune.

The **Steeple Building,** once the commune's church, is now a museum. In it craftspeople re-create colony life by demonstrating crafts and other skills practiced by the Jansonists. The museum also has an exhibit of world-famous primitive paintings by Olaf Krans. Donations accepted.

Where Does the Time Go?

The **Colony Church** has also been restored into a museum and has changing exhibits. It is open from 9:00 A.M. to 5:00 P.M., Wednesday through Sunday. The **Bjorklund Hotel,** now restored, is open for visitors but not overnight guests. Both the Steeple Building and the hotel are open daily from 9:00 A.M. to 5:00 P.M. except holidays.

Bishop Hill has twenty-two gift and craft shops that sell antiques, Swedish imports, and handicrafts. Local restaurants serve Swedish and American food. For information contact the Bishop Hill Heritage Association, P.O. Box 1853, Bishop Hill 61419; (309) 927–3899.

The **Henry County Historical Museum** is also located in Bishop Hill, a block south of the town park. Its thousands of artifacts tell of the county's history. Included in its collection are garments, tools, gadgets, and furnishings of the late nineteenth century. Five display areas are devoted to special interest subjects, and the exhibits are changed during the season. A nineteenth-century bedroom, a harness shop, and a parlor organ are on permanent display. Museum hours are daily from 10:00 A.M. to 4:00 P.M. May through October.

Perhaps the most unusual (and character-driven) feature of the Bishop Hill utopian village is found at the Steeple Building, completed in 1854, and constructed of handmade bricks and plaster.

But look up at that two-story wooden steeple with the clock. There are four faces to the clock—but only one hand!

The mystery might be explained by local folklore, which notes that this speaks directly to the Colony's work ethic: "If you take care of the hours, you don't have to worry about the minutes."

The last weekend in September is the **Jordbruksdagarna**—the harvest fest. Its Lucia Nights pre-Christmas celebration offers a chance to shop for gifts at the Colony's Craft Stores—all festooned for the holidays. And you will never forget its 6:00 A.M. Christmas Day nondenominational sunrise service once you've attended it. For specific dates and a list of activities, call the Bishop Hill Heritage Association at (309) 927–3899.

Two miles north of Woodhull on County Road 400 at 63E, 61490, is **Max Nordeen's Wheels Museum,** a personal collection of 2,300 items organized around automotive history. The museum is open July through August daily except Monday and on weekends only in May, September, and October. Hours are 9:00 A.M. to 4:00 P.M., or by appointment (call before leaving home); (309) 334–2589.

About 6 miles southeast of Bishop Hill on U.S. Route 34 is Galva, the sister city to Gävle, Sweden. Galva is the home of **Jacobsen's Home Bakery,** which specializes in rusks, a sweet raised bread toasted until brown and crisp. The rusks are sold in food stores in a 50-mile radius of Galva and can be mail-ordered around the country.

Jenny Lind, the famous Swedish opera singer, endowed a chapel in Andover, just northwest of Bishop Hill on Route 81. The chapel is open to the public.

The **Henry County Courthouse,** built in 1878–80, is located in Cambridge, the county seat. The main courtroom is worth a look. It is decorated with murals depicting the principal communities in the county.

Henry County has a number of lakes and recreational parks for camping, swimming, fishing, picnicking, hiking, boating, and waterskiing. **Johnson Sauk State Park,** off Route 78, 4 miles south of the Annawan exit of I–80, has 400 acres of campsites along the Old Sauk Trail. **Izaak Walton League Park,** Route 82, 1^1/$_2$ miles north of Genesco on Hennepin Canal Parkway, has eight acres of camping, fishing, hiking, and water sports. The **Circle S Campground** on Route 78 has eighty acres of wooded area and fifty campsites. Circle S is 4 miles north of the Annawan exit on I–80. The **Timber Campground,** 5 miles north of Bishop Hill, has twenty campsites with lake swimming, fishing, a pavilion, and planned activities. It is located on Route 81, 3 miles east of Cambridge and 1 mile north.

Rock Island, one of the Quad Cities, has the Mississippi River as its frontyard and the Rock River as its back. During the 1840s and 1850s, the height of the steamboat era, as many as 1,900 steamboats docked in Rock Island annually.

It was here in 1675 that explorers Marquette and Joliet came on their trip down the Mississippi River. Seven years later they were driven out by the Sauk and Fox tribes. In 1805 Zebulon Pike traveled up the Mississippi on a government inspection trip and found the land inhabited by more than 5,000 Indians.

In 1816 Rock Island was fortified by the government and Col. George Davenport became the first resident-settler. In 1828 other settlers started moving here in large numbers and began battling with the Indians. The Indians retaliated, and the settlers sent for help from the governor. They wrote that the Indians "threaten our lives if we attempt to plant corn, and say that we have stolen their land from them, and they are determined to exterminate us."

The result was the Black Hawk War in which the Sauk and Fox lost their fight, opening up all of northern Illinois for settlement.

The Rock Island Railway, the first to come to the area, completed its railroad bridge in 1855, the first bridge to span the entire Mississippi River.

In 1862 the *Rock Island Arsenal* was built. It originally served as a prison for Confederate soldiers, and more than 1,200 prisoners were confined here. When the Civil War ended, the arsenal was converted to its present use as the U.S. Army Armament, Munition, and Chemical Command.

The Rock Island Arsenal was built on what is now known as Arsenal Island, in the middle of the Mississippi River. The arsenal is one of the largest in the world.

The *Clock Tower,* the first permanent building of the Rock Island Arsenal, has a giant clock, over a hundred years old and still running. Visitors can tour the Clock Tower (on weekends and by appointment only) and other sights on the island—a replica of the *Fort Armstrong blockhouse,* the *Court of Patriots Memorial,* and a **Confederate Soldier cemetery.** For tour information contact the visitors center at Lock and Dam 15 on Arsenal Island.

Lock and Dam 15 Visitors Center stands above the Mississippi Waterway System, where you can get a great view of barges passing through the lock system. Admission is free. The center is open daily in the summer months 9:00 A.M. to 9:00 P.M.; spring and fall 9:00 A.M. to 5:00 P.M.; winter 9:00 A.M. to 5:00 P.M.; closed from December 15 to February 3.

The restored *home of Colonel Davenport* is open for viewing Saturday and Sunday from 1:00 to 3:00 P.M., from the first weekend in May through October. It is located on Davenport Drive on Arsenal Island (which was called Rock Island when he settled here, before the town of Rock Island grew in size).

For bikers an 8-mile bike trail around Arsenal Island begins at Terrace Drive at the corner of Gillespie Street.

To reach Arsenal Island take I–74 in Rock Island, exit at Seventh Avenue and go west to Fourteenth Street. Take Fourteenth Street north to the bridge to the island.

Rails to the River is a specially chartered, one-day rail tour from Chicago to the Quad Cities. The package includes rail connection, ground transportation, meals, and event admission to Bix Jazz Festival, Bishop Hill, Village of East Davenport, Civil War Muster, Mississippi Riverboat cruise, and rail attractions. Write 3716 Fourteenth Street, Rock Island 61201 (or call 309–786–7533) for information.

Rock Island is on the site of *Black Hawk State Park,* 1510 Forty-sixth Avenue (309) 788–0177. This is the site of the westernmost battle of the

Revolutionary War. On the grounds are the *Hauberg Indian Museum* and the *Watch Tower Lodge.* The museum contains a collection of Indian artifacts, paintings, and relics. A powwow is held every Labor Day. The museum has three rooms, one devoted to Black Hawk items including portraits of the chief, another devoted to the daily lives of the Sauk and Fox, and the third is a gallery of Indian chiefs and the soldiers who opposed them during the Black Hawk War.

The park is open daily from 8:00 A.M. to 10:00 P.M., and the museum and lodge are open 8:30 A.M. to 4:30 P.M.; closed for lunch from noon to 1:00 P.M. Admission is free.

The *Fryxell Geology Museum,* 639 Thirty-eighth Street, 61201, on the Augustana College campus, has a collection of fossils, which includes sauropod dinosaur eggs. Admission is free, and hours are Monday through Friday 8:00 A.M. to 5:00 P.M., Saturday and Sunday 1:00 to 4:00 P.M. Call (309) 794–1318.

The *Denkman Library,* also on campus, has the Augustana Historical Society collection of almost all the Swedish-American newspapers of North America.

Moline has a heritage of Belgian immigrants, and the *Center for Belgian Culture,* 712 Nineteenth Avenue, 61201, offers demonstrations of Belgian lace being made. Occasionally you can purchase samples. Call (309) 762–0167 for information.

A landmark in Moline is *Lagomarcino's Confectionery* at 1422 Fifth Avenue, 61201. The shop's specialty is golden sponge candy—dark chocolate coating around a crisp blond center. Everything is handmade and hand-dipped. Try the homemade ice cream and sinfully rich hot fudge sauce; (309) 764–1814.

Coal Valley is the home of the *Niabi Zoo.* Translated from the Indian, Niabi means "Spared of the Hunter's Arrow." The zoo is located on U.S. Route 6, 10 miles southeast of Moline. Besides a variety of animals, the zoo has a miniature railroad and a petting zoo designed for children. It is open daily 9:30 A.M. to 5:00 P.M.; (309) 799–5107. Admission is $4.25 for adults, $3.25 for seniors, and $3.00 for children three to eleven; children under three are free. Tuesday is free admission for everyone. Rides on the miniature railroad are $1.00.

Quad Cities Downs is one of the Midwest's finest harness-racing facilities. Located in East Moline at Morton Drive and Route 5, racing is nightly year-round. Post time is 7:30 P.M.; call (309) 792–0202 for specific times.

PLACES TO STAY IN NORTHWESTERN ILLINOIS

DE KALB
HoJo Motel by
Howard Johnson,
1321 West Lincoln
Highway, 60115
(815) 756–1451

University Inn,
1212 West Lincoln
Highway, 60115
(815) 758–8661

DIXON
Best Western
Brandywine Hotel,
443 Ill. Route 2, 61021
(815) 284–1890

EAST DUBUQUE
Timmerman's Lodge,
7777 Timmerman
Drive, 61025
(800) 336–3181

ELIZABETH
Elizabeth Guest House,
101 West Main, 61028
(815) 858–2533

FREEPORT
Country Inn & Suites
by Carlson,
1710 South Dick
Road, 61032
(815) 233–3300

Holiday Inn of Freeport,
1300 East South
Street, 61032
(815) 235–3121

GALENA
Aldrich Guest House,
900 Third Street, 61036
(815) 777–3323

Chestnut Mountain Resort,
8700 West Chestnut
Road, 61036
(800) 397–1320

DeSoto House Hotel,
230 South Main
Street, 61036
(800) 343–6562

Eagle Ridge Inn
and Resort,
Route 20 East, 61036
(800) 892–2269

Early American Settlement
Log Cabins,
9401 Hartjohn
Road, 61036
(800) 366–5647

Hellman Guest House,
318 Hill Street, 61036
(815) 777–3638

Pine Hollow Inn,
4700 North Council
Hill Road, 61036
(815) 777–1071

Queen Anne Guest House,
200 Park Avenue, 61036
(815) 777–3849

Stoney Creek Inn,
940 Galena Square
Drive, 61036
(800) 659–2220

LANARK
Standish House,
540 West Carroll
Street, 61046
(800) 468–2307

MORRIS
Comfort Inn,
70 West Gore Road, 60450
(815) 942–1433

Selected Visitors Bureaus and Chambers of Commerce

Illinois Bureau of Tourism/Travel Information,
(800) 2–CONNECT

Blackhawk Waterways Convention and Visitors Bureau,
201 North Franklin, Polo 61064
(800) 678–2108

Galena/Jo Daviess County Convention
and Visitors Bureau,
730 Park Avenue, Galena 61036
(800) 747–9377

Rockford Area Convention and Visitors Bureau,
211 North Main Street, Rockford 61101
(800) 521–0849

Stephenson County Convention and Visitors Bureau,
2047 Ayp Road, Freeport 61032
(800) 369–2955

Holiday Inn,
I–80 and Route 47, 60450
(815) 942–6600

MORRISON
Hillendale Bed
and Breakfast,
600 Lincolnway
West, 61270
(800) 349–7702

MOUNT CARROLL
Carrollton Inn,
1 Carrollton Drive, 61053
(815) 244–1000

MOUNT MORRIS
Kable House Country Inn,
Sunset Hill, 61054
(815) 734–7297

OREGON
Pinehill Bed and Breakfast,
400 Mix Street, 61061
(815) 732–2061

ROCKFORD
Best Western
Clock Tower Inn,
7801 East State
Street, 61108
(815) 398–6000

Fairfield Inn by Marriott,
7712 Potowatomi
Trail, 61107
(815) 397–8000

Hampton Inn Hotel,
615 Clark Drive, 61107
(815) 229–0404

Sweden House Lodge,
4605 East State
Street, 61108
(800) 886–4138

SYCAMORE
Stratford Inn,
355 West State
Street, 60178
(800) 937–8106

UTICA
Starved Rock State
Park Lodge,
Route 178 and
Highway 71, 61373
(815) 667–4211

**PLACES TO EAT IN
NORTHWESTERN ILLINOIS**

FREEPORT
Beltline Cafe,
325 West South
Street, 61032
(815) 232–5512

GALENA
Bubba's,
300 North Main, 61036
(815) 777–8030

Cafe Italia,
301 North Main, 61036
(815) 777–0033

Fried Green Tomatoes,
1301 Irish Hollow
Road, 61036
(815) 777–3938

Grant's Place,
5151 South Main, 61036
(815) 777–3331

Log Cabin,
201 North Main, 61036
(815) 777–039

Silver Annie's,
124 North Commerce
Street, 61036
(815) 777–3131

ROCKFORD
Great Wall Chinese
Restaurant,
4228 East State, 61108
(815) 226–0982

**OTHER ATTRACTIONS
WORTH SEEING IN
NORTHWESTERN ILLINOIS**

Fiorello's Pumpkin and
Christmas Patch,
Caledonia

Pecatonica Prairie Path,
Freeport

Silver Creek and Stephen-
son Railroad,
Freeport

Moo Cow Cafe,
Freeport

Vinegar Hill Historic Lead
Mine and Museum,
Galena

White Pines Ranch,
Oregon

Stockton,
Illinois's "highest" town

Warren Cheese Plant,
Warren

Eastern Illinois

The Heartland

Illinoisians tend to whiz through Vermilion County and its county seat, Danville, along I–74 en route to Indianapolis and other points east. Why, I haven't really figured out. Besides being the eastern-most big city in Illinois (apart from the really big one, Chicago), Danville has its charms. Among those are the area's many parks—more than 7,000 acres of parks, in fact, for only 39,000 residents, making this one of the most heavily "parked" cities in the state.

The largest is the 3,000-acre **Kennekuk Cove County Park,** where you will find the 170-acre **Lake Mingo,** which sounds like something from Flash Gordon. Actually, it's an inviting oasis where **Stephen's Beach** has all the charm of an old-fashioned swimming hole, replete with a noisy collection of boys and girls. There's fishing in the lake, too—for channel catfish, bass, and sunfish.

Follow **Lookout Point Trail** along a lush ravine system, through meadows and natural prairies. Stop to examine some of the 400 species of wild-flowers, plants, and trees that grow in the park. Watch for the population of white-tailed deer and dozens of species of birds that are occasional visitors. The park's solar-heated visitor center houses an interpretive display of area Indian history.

> ### Eastern Illinois Trivia
>
> *In Arcola's pharmacy, its Coffee Club displays more than 150 coffee cups, with customers' names affixed to them, behind the counter.*

Kennekuk Cove County Park is 8 miles northwest of Danville at Henning Road off U.S. Highway 150. Park hours are 6:00 A.M. to 11:00 P.M.

What once was an ugly strip mine is today **Kickapoo State Park,** 2,843 acres of woods and ponds popular for picnicking and camping. The Middle Fork of the Vermilion River flows through the park, offering the opportunity for fishing and boating. It's a nationally designated scenic river—the only one in Illinois. Half-, one-, and two-day canoe trips begin here, with overnight accommodations either at a park campsite or—for

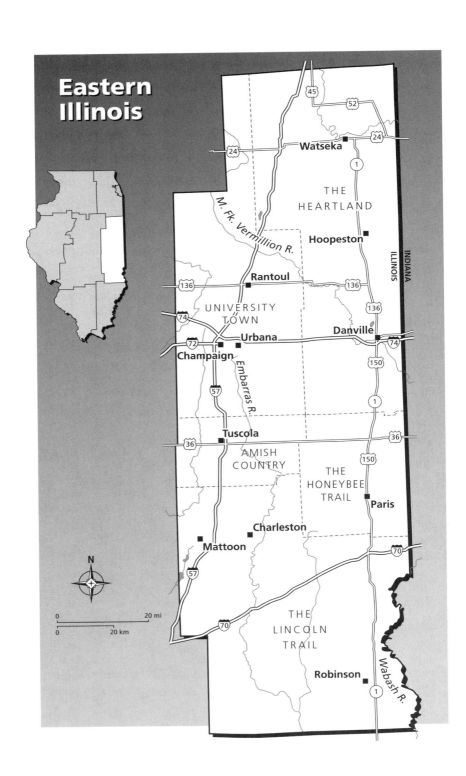

Eastern
Illinois

45

52

24

Watseka

1

THE
HEARTLAND

ILLINOIS   INDIANA

M. Fk. Vermillion R.

Hoopeston

136   **Rantoul**   136

136

UNIVERSITY
TOWN

74

72   **Urbana**   **Danville**   74

Champaign   150

Embarras R.

57   1

36   **Tuscola**   36

AMISH
COUNTRY   150

THE
HONEYBEE
TRAIL   **Paris**

Charleston

Mattoon   70

57

THE
LINCOLN
TRAIL

70

N

0   20 mi
0   20 km

Wabash R.

Robinson

1

the less adventuresome—at a hotel in Danville. Canoes, paddles, and life vests are provided.

State park employees conduct interpretive programs year-round. In the summer there is hiking and horseback riding. The park's winter activities include ice fishing, ice skating, cross-country skiing, and sledding. Kickapoo State Park is at exit 210 off I–74. Park hours are 8:00 A.M. to 10:00 P.M.; (217) 442–4915.

In the southern part of the county, near Georgetown, **Forest Glen Preserve** is unique because of its **Grove Handicapped Trail,** paved for access by wheelchairs and said to be the only nature trail for the handicapped in the Midwest. It boasts an unusual restored tall grass prairie. Among the park flora, surprisingly, are several varieties of orchids. Also, in mid-September each year, a one-day Revolutionary War reenactment is held here, complete with pioneer homestead and camp. On I–74, take the Main Street exit right onto Route 150. At the intersection of Main and Gilbert, turn right onto Route 1. Drive into the town of Westville, turn left (east) at the stoplight. The preserve's hours are 7:00 A.M. to 11:00 P.M.

But as a major city, Danville has much more to offer than its parks. Its **Civic Center,** built in 1980, is home to entertainment year-round, ranging from pop music concerts to exhibitions to hockey games played by the local team. The Civic Center is at 100 West Main Street, 61832; call (217) 431–2424 for information.

The **Vermilion County Museum** (116 North Gilbert, 61832, open Tuesday through Saturday 10:00 A.M. to 5:00 P.M. and Sunday 1:00 to 5:00 P.M.) is housed in an 1850-era house, once the home of Dr. William Fithian, a friend of Abraham Lincoln. Lincoln, in fact, spoke from the balcony while running for the U.S. Senate. The bed he spent the night in is still here. The local visitors bureau acknowledges the Lincoln connection with the slogan, "We knew Abe *before* they called him Mr. President." Of special note are the doll collection in the Child's Room and the summer herb garden on the southwest corner of the grounds. The building is listed on the National Register of Historic Places. Admission is $2.00 adults, 50 cents children. Call (217) 442–2922 for information.

The restored **Lamon House** at 1031 North Logan, 61832, in Lincoln Park is open to visitors on Sundays, May through October, or any time by appointment through the museum; (217) 442–2922. Built in 1850, it is possibly the oldest frame house extant in Danville. It is furnished with furniture of the period.

With a list of such celebrated native sons as Gene Hackman, Bobby Short, Donald O'Connor, and Dick Van Dyke, it's not surprising that the arts scene in Danville is an active one. Community theater, the Danville Light Opera, the Red Mask, and the Danville Symphony Orchestra—recently named Illinois Orchestra of the Year—provide cultural sustenance. Call the Danville Area Arts Council for information; (217) 431–6423.

For nourishment of a more basic order, country cooking is the key at **George's Buffet,** 1225 East Voorhees, 61832. From my travels in the state, we've derived the "pickup quotient" of rating places to eat; the more pickups in the parking lot, the better the food. George's gets a sixteen-pickup rating. It's all you can eat, and with hot baked rolls, grandmother-style chicken and noodles, and a dozen or more choices, that's a lot of food. Save room for dessert.

In the northern part of the county, Hoopeston and Rossville are good places to look for antiques. Hoopeston hosts the **National Sweetcorn Festival** each September. A beauty pageant, tractor pulls, and—of course—plenty of hot corn and butter are hallmarks of this event; (217) 283–7873.

What's Canoe With You?

*D*o you have your canoe handy? The Little Vermilion River State Natural Area and the Middle Fork River near Oakwood boast some of the state's top paddling possibilities.

About 2.2 miles of the Little Vermilion is listed as a statewide significant stream because its shoreline supports twelve state-endangered or threatened species and offers habitat for almost twenty-five additional forest interior species. The Middle Fork, the first Illinois stream included as part of the National Wild and Scenic River System, is contained in a narrow river valley, with 90-foot bluffs and few water ripples.

What all this means is some of the best scenery the state has to offer canoe lovers. Tulip trees 50 to 80 feet tall blossom here in springtime. Five natural prairies along the river are filled with 243 species of birds. You'll see Illinois's largest concentration of wild orchids. There are Indian mounds and burial sites with archeological digs everywhere. There's even an active 50-foot beaver dam.

Yes, these rivers are something special. For more information, call (217) 442–4915.

Top Annual Events

From Sheep to Clothing, Lincoln Log Cabin State Historic Site, *Lerna, early May, (217) 345–1845*

Raggedy Ann and Andy Festival, Arcola, mid-May, *(800) 336–5456*

The Market at the Square, Urbana, *Saturdays, June–October, (217) 384–6304*

Taste of Champaign-Urbana, Champaign, late June, *(217) 398–2550*

Moultrie-Douglas County Fair, Arthur, late July, *(800) 722–6474*

Sweetcorn Festival/ National Sweetheart Pageant, Hoopeston, early September, *(217) 283–7873*

Broom Corn Festival, Arthur, mid-September, *(800) 336–5456*

Boo! at the Zoo!, Scovill Zoo, *Decatur, mid- to late October, (217) 421–7435*

University of Illinois Football Games, Champaign, September–October, *(217) 333–5000*

Prairie Christmas, Lincoln Log Cabin State Historic Site, *Lerna, early December, (217) 345–1845*

Rossville, on the other hand, calls itself "the village of unusual shops," a very apt description. Along Main Street shops selling antique furniture, glass, china, primitives, and country crafts provide ample fodder for the most ambitious shopping spree. Perhaps the most unusual of these unusual shops is **Aunt Jody's Christmas Bank,** a remarkable display of nativity scenes, angels, nutcrackers, and ornaments. Open March through December; most shops closed on Monday.

Serendipity is opening an oyster and discovering a pearl. Serendipity, too, is driving through miles of central Illinois farmland and coming upon **The Heartland.** Here in Gilman this comfortable spa is remarkably unexpected, a Thoreauvian vision of a peaceful retreat some 28 miles from Kankakee down country back roads.

The facility was once the bucolic country estate of Dr. Karl A. Meyer, former medical director of Cook County Hospital. Meyer transformed the farmland, planting thirty-one acres of woods and creating Kam Lake. When Chicagoans Gerald S. Kaufman and Charlotte Newberger bought the property in 1983, they decided to preserve much of Dr. Meyer's healthful environment and to expand upon it.

At the edge of the spring-fed lake sits the main house—Meyer's mansion—with accommodations for only twenty-seven guests and a pretty little dining room overlooking the lawn and lake. Here, too, are the Wood Room, where Heartland Institute lectures are held, and the cozy White Room for reading and conversation. An underground passageway leads to the old barn, magically transformed into a three-story fitness center with an aerobics loft, a Cam II gym, sauna, whirlpool, and massage and facial rooms. Behind it is an enclosed swimming pool.

Guests begin their stay on Friday or Sunday for either a two-day weekend or a five- or seven-day program. The all-inclusive holiday begins with a tour of the facilities and an orientation, where one of the friendly staff members explains The Heartland fitness and nutrition philosophy.

That's Flat!

If it's flat, open prairie you're aiming to see, you're in the right part of Illinois. The eastern portion of the state, and to an even greater extent, the central breadbasket of Illinois, is the heart of the heartland, where you car will roll past neat rows of croplands planted with everything from sweet corn to soybeans.

It's where Amish buggies clip-clop past black earth that has nurtured a nation for more than 200 years. And where for miles and miles you'll see nothing but miles and miles.

So you've made it to the prairie flatlands, where the spirit of the sodbuster lives proudly among the fields of harvest. Enjoy the heartland hospitality. Feel the sun on the back of your neck. Relax and look around.

Guests exchange tired big-city clothes for furnished workout togs, the uniform for all occasions throughout the stay. It's all part of the comfortable, casual attitude here.

After an optional body fat evaluation, guests move on to dinner; like all meals, it's a fish or vegetarian affair, beautifully presented and served. Meals are kosher-supervised, as well. Calories are limited to 1,200 for women and 1,500 for men. Cholesterol, sodium, and fats are also limited. But no one goes hungry here. Seconds are okay, if you're not trying to lose weight. In addition to breakfast, lunch, and dinner, snacks are available at midmorning and in the afternoon. A fruit basket is always standing ready on the sideboard for those who just can't make it through. One of Chef Robert McGarrigle's menus might look like this: minestrone soup, eggplant Parmesan, steamed zucchini, fruit garnish, and carob coconut cookie. Or for lunch: Waldorf salad, frittata, green beans, and almonds.

A day's activities begin early. Wake-up comes at 7:00 A.M. (optional) followed by a morning stretch and a walk before breakfast. After the morning meal is a ninety-minute aerobics class in the fitness center where inhibitions are shed along with pounds and friendships are formed as guests struggle together through exercise class. By the end of a visit, the spirit of camaraderie is strong, along with the commitment to take home this awareness of healthy living.

Activities, it should be noted—like dance classes or horseback riding (extra fee)—are optional. So at any time you can wander away for a swim or a hike around the lake, or just take a lazy siesta in the sun with a good book. If it sounds like work, it isn't. As Director of Nutrition Susan Witz explains, rest and relaxation are among the important benefits of The Heartland, and her presentations, plus those of outside experts, address the issues of dieting and stress.

The Heartland advocates a three-part approach to stress management. The first phase, exercise, focuses on increasing body awareness. Guests explore a variety of exercise techniques. Yoga, guided relaxation, and stretching classes increase the participants' awareness of their bodies, using progressive muscle relaxation and controlled breathing.

Education is the second component of the program. Instruction here will help guests become more aware of how tensions accumulate and will introduce various attitudinal approaches, from positive thinking and calming mental imagery to improved communication strategies for defusing harmful stress.

Step three is nutrition, and the spa's balanced vegetarian menus serve that role.

For reservations call (800) 545–4853. To reach the spa from Chicago, take the Dan Ryan Expressway south to I–57. Go 52 miles to Kankakee exit 308. Turn right at the top of the cloverleaf onto U.S. Highway 52/45 (which becomes Route 49) to U.S. Highway 24 (at the flashing red light). Turn right onto U.S. Route 24 for 2 miles to The Heartland sign and Camp Wahanaha sign (County Road 1220E). Turn left and continue for 2 miles to The Heartland sign. Turn left. The driveway to The Heartland is on the immediate right. The Heartland is 80 miles south of Chicago.

University Town

The 56,000-student *University of Illinois,* the state's largest, shapes the landscape of the twin cities of Champaign/Urbana like nothing else. Lying at the dividing point of the two towns, the university, founded in 1867, is internationally known for its physics and engineering departments. It houses the National Center of Supercomputing Applications and is one of only five universities in this country to have a supercomputer on campus (two, in fact). It's a mecca for computer buffs.

> ### Eastern Illinois Trivia
>
> *Mammoths and mastodons once lived in east-central Illinois, and were driven out of the state during the Ice Age.*

Wander around campus and enjoy the architecture, or stop at the *Krannert Art Museum,* 500 Peabody Drive, 61820, for its collection of sculpture, old masters, and the Ewing collection of Malayan art (open daily except Monday); call (217) 333–1860. Also on campus is the *World Heritage Museum,* 702 South Wright, 61820, which exhibits the story of humankind from earliest times to modern day. Open daily except Saturday during the academic year.

Another treasure house, the *Museum of Natural History,* 1301 West Green, 61821, is one of the finest in the Midwest, with thousands of specimens on display. It's the perfect place to take children. The Discover

Room has hands-on exhibits—shells, teeth, and other artifacts—that kids can touch and examine closely. Open daily except Sunday. For the lively arts the *Krannert Center for the Performing Arts,* 500 South Goodwin Avenue, 61801, offers a full program of dance, theater, and music throughout the year. For schedule information call (217) 333–6280. Lively sports are represented each season when the "Fighting Illini" play in the Big Ten at *Memorial Stadium,* (217) 333–3470. For maps, walking tours, or directions, check in at the information desk at the Illini Union building at Wright and Green Streets; (217) 333–4666.

Other sites associated with the University of Illinois are worth a visit, too. The *Morrow Plots* at Gregory near Mathews Street in Urbana are the oldest permanent soil experiment fields in the country, in continuous use since 1876, in keeping with the original agricultural mission of the land grant school. Similarly, *three round dairy barns* built between 1902 and 1910 are part of the university's agricultural program (St. Mary's Road, Urbana). Renowned sculptor Lorado Taft studied here, graduating in 1879. *Taft's student residence,* built in 1871, is located at the Illini Grove on Pennsylvania Avenue in Urbana. One of his works, a *Lincoln statue,* sits opposite Urbana High School on Race Street.

A number of historic buildings are scattered throughout the area. The *Wilbur Mansion,* 709 West University, 61820, in Champaign, is a 1907 structure that now houses the *Champaign County Historical Museum.* Also in Champaign, the *Cattle Bank Building,* 102 North First, 61820, is the oldest remaining business building in the city, incorporated

Old West Family Fest

The first time I walked into the Colorado Steak House with my family, we thought we'd stepped back into the Wild West. It wasn't that the ambience was unexpected; after all, the restaurant's outside facade resembles a rustic log cabin.

Inside it's more of the same, with cowboy boots, saddles, and all other kinds of cowboy-iana decorating the walls. The food was a throwback to the West, if not the Wild West. Entrees included

Rocky Mountain rainbow trout (which was breaded, sautéed and wonderful), and plenty of hamburger choices for the kids.

However, I went as crazy as a wild mustang over the aged sirloin steak, which is marinated and charbroiled to your liking. All in all, I'd say mosey on down to this here bunkhouse, pardner, for some really good chow. Located at 1805 South Neil Street, Champaign, 61820; (217) 359–6776.

as a branch of the Grand Prairie Bank of Urbana in 1856.

In Mahomet, on Route 47, 10 miles west of Champaign/ Urbana, *Lake of the Woods County Park* is a pleasant diversion in the Illinois farm country. Here, a twenty-six-acre lake with a sandy beach, canoes, rowboats, fishing, and paddleboat rentals attracts families from miles around.

They come, too, for the unique *Early American Museum and Botanical Garden,* located within the park. The museum, opened in 1968, began with the collection of local history buff William Redhead and has grown over the years. Volunteers present a fascinating series of pioneer life programs year-round—from a colonial muster in September, to an exhibition of farm life a century ago. You might encounter a costumed interpreter making soap or stitching a quilt, dipping candles or spinning a tall folk tale. The demonstration of Christmas past is especially nice during the holidays. For children 5 to 9 years of age, Wednesday mornings in June and July mean a chance to put on a pioneer costume and spend time just as a youngster of the 1800s might have, learning antique crafts, games, and music.

One of my favorite off-the-beaten-path museums in this hearty college town is one that'll bring music to your ears. It's the John Philip Sousa Library and Museum, located on campus on the second floor of the Harding Band Building.

Maybe it's because I remember my mom playing Sousa marching songs on her old Victrola in the living room of our old house that I have a soft spot for Sousa's rousing flourishes. Here in the library and museum, you can see his personal music sheets, period band uniforms, musical instruments, and more.

In the garden special plantings include the Heritage Garden, the Roses of Yesteryear, the Dye-Plant Garden, and a Prairie Sampler of native prairie plants. An eighteen-hole golf course, hiking trails, plus a covered bridge round out the park's attractions. Call (217) 586–3360 for information. The park is open daily year-round. Admission is free.

Two other parks in the Champaign County Forest District are worth mentioning. *Middlefork River Forest Preserve* near Penfield has year-round camping in addition to three fishing lakes, swimming, and an activity center. The preserve is on County Road 22, about 7 miles north of Penfield; (217) 595–5432. *Salt Fork River Forest Preserve* near Homer encompasses the eighty-acre Homer Lake, popular with area fishing enthusiasts. The Trailside Visitors Center features nature displays, live animals, and educational exhibits. In early June stop by for the Salt Fork Summerfest, with nature walks, fishing demonstrations, and canoe and kayak races; (217) 896–2455. From I–74, exit at Ogden and proceed south on Route 49 for 3 miles. Turn right at the sign for the preserve onto County Road 19. The entrance to the preserve will be in 1 mile.

Amish Country

Douglas and its neighboring county, Moultrie, are the center of Amish culture in Illinois. The first Amish in Illinois, however, came to the area around Peoria along the Illinois River in the 1830s. These early settlers immigrated from Europe—Alsace and Lorraine, Bavaria, and Hesse-Darmstadt. In the succeeding decades, though, Amish from Ohio and Pennsylvania joined those pioneers in Illinois, settling around Arcola and Arthur in the years immediately following the Civil War.

Today things haven't changed that much. You can still see a plainly dressed family riding to town in a black horse-drawn buggy. Indeed, they are called the "Plain People," for their belief in life's simple things. They eschew modern conveniences, electricity, and stylish clothes. Men dress in black or dark blue suits with "front-fall" pants (sometimes called "barn-door britches"), held up by suspenders. Shirts are of plain color and style. A flat-crowned, broad-brimmed black felt hat is worn in winter, exchanged in summer for one of straw. Amish women dress alike in almost every detail, with dresses of solid color in a pattern handed down over generations. On their heads they wear a white prayer cap covered by a black bonnet. As you drive down country back roads, you'll find horsepower of the original sort on display—Amish farmers hitched to teams of plow horses. Tractors are not used. Visiting this part of the state is a bit like stepping into a time machine, going back to an era when things were simpler.

Hitchin' a Ride

It's always interesting to visit Illinois's Amish Country because you seem to discover something new every trip.

Like the time a few years ago when my family and I were driving through Arcola, the largest of the twin towns that claim most of the state's Amish population. As we passed along one of the "downtown" streets, my daughter, Dayne, yelled out, "Pa! Look at that!"

What did she discover? Only that the local Hardee's fast-food restaurant had a hitching post right out front of its building to accommodate those Amish families with horse and buggy who might want to stop in and grab a bite to eat.

I guess you would call that the original drive-thru.

You can begin a trip here with a stop at *Rockome Gardens,* a park 5 miles west of Arcola on Route 133. Here, on fourteen landscaped acres, nearly everything—from fences to arches to garden walls—is constructed of rocks inlaid in cement. The Gardens's *Old Bagdad Town* is a re-created frontier village with a general store, bakery, calico workshop, quilt shop, working candy shop, and a gift shop with locally made items from the Rockome Gardens Craft Guild. At the shops you can find good reproductions of Amish furniture as well. A popular feature with children is the petting zoo populated with goats, peacocks, chickens, and other farm animals. They'll also enjoy the doll shop, the tree house, and the Old Hickory Railroad. Other attractions include a "haunted" cave, a replica of an Amish home, and an antiques museum. You can get in the spirit of things by taking a buggy ride around the grounds (additional fee).

A schedule of weekend festivals and special events runs all season long—from Horse Farming Days to the Quilt Show. Every September, weekends bring the Harvest Days with threshing, corn shucking, plowing demonstration (you can join in), cider pressing, and apple butter making. *Rockome Family Style Restaurant* serves up Amish-style cooking, including a wonderful shoofly pie. Admission to Rockome Gardens is $8.50 for adults, $6.50 for children four to twelve. The park is open daily from Memorial Day to Labor Day; call for the schedule during the rest of the year. The gate opens at 9:00 A.M. and closes at 5:00 P.M.; (217) 268–4216.

For shopping the *Arcola Emporium,* at 201 East Main Street in downtown Arcola, offers the conveniences of a mall with a collection of charming shops selling antiques, art, women's fashions, toys, cookware,

Baguettes & Bowling

*T*here may be only one place in the world where you can enjoy fancy French gourmet cuisine and then work off the heavy sauces by bowling a few frames. So spare some time to strike out and visit the French Embassy Bowling Restaurant in Arcola—inexplicably located in the heart of Amish country.

Chef Jean-Louis Ledent serves up all kinds of Gallic delicacies, like quail

with onions, sautéed lamb with white Bordeaux sauce, and bouillabaisse. And his wine selections, heavy on choices from the Alsace region, are great, too.

But when you're finished, just walk over to the bowling lanes inside the restaurant and try your luck knocking down those pins. I'm told it's what the French do after almost every meal.

Amish Country

gourmet foods, and handcrafted solid wood furniture. A number of antiques shops are also in the region.

The weekend after Labor Day, Arcola hosts the annual **Broom Corn Festival,** recalling the days when it was Broom Corn Capital of the world. A parade, a 10,000-meter road race, a flea market and street fair, plus demonstrations of broom-making, and other old-fashioned crafts, highlight the celebrations. Or course, most people visit Illinois's Amish country to see the "Plain People." Keep in mind, however, that this is a lifestyle—not actors from Central Casting in Hollywood. So please take steps to be respectful: Don't intrude, try to engage in conversation, or point. And note that the Amish do not like to have photographs of themselves taken. So if they turn away when you point and shoot, they're not being unfriendly. It's just part of their cultural milieu. For more information contact the Arcola Chamber of Commerce, Arcola 61910; (217) 268–4530.

The Lincoln Trail

The *Lincoln Log Cabin State Historic Site* near Charleston was the last home of Thomas and Sarah Bush Lincoln, Abraham Lincoln's parents. The cabin was built in 1837 and is now reconstructed on an eighty-six-acre lot that includes a pavilion, picnic area, and historical farm museum. The cabin is furnished with period pieces, and a kitchen building, log barn, and smokehouse from the

Lincoln Log Cabin

1840s have been added to the site. They are being restored to represent New England or "Yankee" culture in Illinois, in contrast to the Lincolns' southern upland culture.

The cabin is open 9:00 A.M. to 5:00 P.M. daily in June, July, and August, weekends 9:00 A.M. to 5:00 P.M. in May and September; (217) 345–6489. Costumed guides conduct tours during the summer, and admission is free. Special events at the cabin include the July Fourth 1845 Independence Day and Militia Muster, the Bluegrass Festival in August, the Harvest Frolic and Trades Fair in October, and the 1884 Prairie Christmas in December. You'll see signs for the site on Fourth Street Road, 8 miles south of Charleston.

Fox Ridge State Park is 8 miles south of Charleston on Route 130. A wooded tract with rolling hills running along the Embarras River, the park has fishing, boating, hiking, picnicking, and camping. For information contact the Park Manager, R.R. 1, Box 234, Charleston 62910; (217) 345–6416.

The *Shiloh Cemetery* is located about 1¹/₂ miles southwest of Campbell, along the Lincoln Heritage Trail. Previously called Gordon's Cemetery, it is the resting place of Thomas and Sarah Bush Lincoln. When historians discovered Thomas Lincoln's cabin and began to restore it, the citizens of Coles County dedicated themselves to perpetuating the gravesite. It is also a major cemetery for Civil War veterans.

A few miles north of the Lincoln Cabin on the Lincoln Heritage Trail is the *Moore House* in Campbell. It was the home of Rueben and Matilda Moore. Matilda was the daughter of Sarah Bush Lincoln and was Abraham Lincoln's stepsister. In January 1861 Lincoln paid his last visit to Coles County and his stepsister at this home. The grounds of the home are open to the public.

The **Stephen Sargent Farm** is located 10 miles south of the Lincoln Cabin. It is open to the public when staffing permits. It is a fine example of progressive farming of the 1840s. This is in contrast to the Lincoln Farm, which exemplifies subsistence farming. For more information contact the Lincoln Log Cabin State Historic Site, R.R. 1, Box 172A, Herma 62440 or call (217) 345–6489.

The **Indian Church** is 3½ miles west of the Lincoln Heritage Trail between County Roads 1150E and 250N. Built in 1832, this was the first church on the Little Indian Creek.

The **5-Miles House** at the corner of Route 130 and the Westfield Road (about 5 miles southeast of Coles County Courthouse in Charleston) was built in 1836. It was originally a wayside tavern and a place to water and care for horses. In 1849 it was an outfitting shop for travelers to the gold fields. It now contains a display of contemporary implements in front of the house (now a private residence).

Eastern Illinois University is the cultural center of Coles County. The battlements of Old Main, an example of German Gothic architecture, tower over the campus. The museum and greenhouses of the Life Science Building are open to the public. Various artworks are on display in the lobby of the Fine Arts Building, and the **Paul Sargent Art Gallery** is in the Booth Library. The **Tarble Arts Center** displays fine art and has changing exhibits. Check with the university for hours; (217) 581–5000. Admission is free.

The university sponsors a **Celebration in Arts Festival** the last weekend in April. Call (217) 581–5000 for information.

Riot!

*E*ver hear about the "Charleston Riot"? In March 1864, six Union soldiers and three civilians were killed here when a riot broke out right before a local Democratic Congressman was about to give a speech about reuniting the country. It is said to be "the largest battle fought between soldiers and civilians in the North over an issue other than the draft."

Eventually fifteen people were arrested and imprisoned at Fort Delaware, Delaware. Eight months later, President Abraham Lincoln, himself, stepped in and ordered all fifteen to be returned to their homes in Coles County, Illinois.

The authorities here in Charleston released thirteen of the rioters on their arrival, while two stood trial and were eventually acquitted of inciting a riot. A marker on the Coles County Courthouse lawn (Monroe and 7th Street), marks the site of the tragic incident.

EASTERN ILLINOIS

A *replica of the Liberty Bell* became part of Charleston's heritage during the Bicentennial celebration of 1976. The bell hangs in Morton Park on Lincoln Street (Route 16).

The *Coles County Courthouse,* built in 1898, was remodeled in 1951. Located in Charleston's town square, it is where Lincoln practiced law, and it is the scene of the Charleston Riot, which involved 300 men in an armed conflict during the Civil War.

The *Will Rogers Movie Theater,* 705 Monroe Street, 61920, named after the comedian and philosopher, is an example of art deco architecture and is listed on the National Register of Historic Places.

The fourth Lincoln-Douglas debate was held in Charleston on September 8, 1858. The site of the debate is now the *Coles County Fairgrounds* on Route 316 on the west end of Charleston. A display of the debate and six other historic debates, replicas of historic documents relating to the debates, and a stone marker commemorate the site.

East of the debate site are the *Old Cemetery* and *Chambers Cemetery.* Here are the graves of Col. and Mrs. Augustus C. Chapman and Mr. and Mrs. Dennis Friend Hanks, relatives of Lincoln. Hanks supposedly taught Lincoln to read and write. There are also graves of many of the early settlers, including Charles Morton, founder of Charleston.

Charleston and Coles County celebrate a variety of festivals. In July Charleston has its nineteenth-century trade fair. More than a dozen tradespeople, dressed in period clothing, demonstrate such trades as tinsmithing, blacksmithing, woodworking, tailoring, and shoemaking. The weekend of activities is held at the Lincoln Log Cabin State Historical Site from 10:00 A.M. to 5:00 P.M.

In July the 1845 Militia Muster presents a reenactment of early Illinois militia training with weekend drills, shooting competitions, and military inspections. A mock battle is the highlight of Sunday. This is also at the Lincoln Log Cabin site.

For information on the festivals, contact the Charleston Chamber of Commerce, 501 Jackson Street, P.O. Box 99, Charleston 61920; (217) 345–7041.

Although primarily an agricultural county, Clark County has two literary associations worth noting. James Jones, author of *From Here to Eternity,* made his home in Marshall, the county seat. Indiana writer Booth Tarkington visited Marshall often as a boy and then recounted those experiences in his nostalgic novel, *Penrod.*

The Lewis Home

The town of about 4,000 has a wealth of charm that could easily serve as writerly inspiration—quiet streets with leafy canopies of oak and maple, solid turn-of-the-century brick homes. One of the best examples is the 1908 **Lewis Home,** 503 Chestnut, 62441, with its dramatic two-story columned veranda (listed in the National Register of Historic Places, but not open to public inspection). The old-fashioned bandstand at the county courthouse is home to the oldest continuing city band in the state. The band, with a century-long history, performs every Friday night on the courthouse lawn from the end of May through August.

The original inhabitants of the county were the Kickapoo Indians, who ceded the land to the United States government in 1819. By 1832 they had been moved from the area. A year later the site on which Marshall was built was purchased by Col. William Archer and Joseph Duncan, later the sixth governor of Illinois. The town was named after the fourth chief justice of the United States, John Marshall.

Like the eastern states, which are dotted with spots that claim "George Washington slept (or ate or visited or whatever) here," we in Illinois have the Lincoln legend at every turn. The **Lincoln Heritage Trail,** created in 1963, marks the route the family traveled from their original home in Kentucky, through Indiana, to Macon County, Illinois. Here in Clark County, the **Lincoln Trail State Recreation Area** marks the area through which the Lincolns passed in 1830 on their way to a new home in Decatur. The 146-acre Lincoln Trail Lake is its focal point. The park offers camping (electricity, showers, and toilets available), fishing (bass, bluegill, crappie, channel catfish), picnicking, and hiking on trails up to 2 miles long. Boats are available for rental. In the winter enjoy ice fishing, ice skating, and cross-country skiing. For information contact the Site Superintendent's office, (217) 826–2222. The recreation area is 2

Eastern Illinois Trivia

miles south of Marshall on Route 1; then drive 1 mile west.

Mill Creek Park, 7 miles northwest of Marshall, is operated by the Clark County Park District, the first county park district to be formed in Illinois (1967). The 2,600-acre park encloses Mill Creek Lake, an 811-acre flood control reservoir. The park opened in 1982. The campground has 192 sites (electric hookups available). For reservations write Clark County Park District, R.R. 2, Marshall 62441, or phone (217) 889–3601. Besides fishing for bass, walleye, catfish, crappie, and bluegill, sample the equestrian or RV trails and the picnicking and swimming areas in the park. Mill Creek Park is on the Lincoln Heritage Trail 1 mile west of Clarksville.

In Arcola's "Dutch Kitchen" restaurant, Amish German sayings are translated on the walls; a couple of the more colorful ones are: "Don't eat yourself full. There's more back yet"; and "Eat your mouth empty before you say."

In Marshall visit the **Clark County Historical Museum,** 502 South Front Street, 62441, built in 1833 as the home of early postmaster Uri Manly. The museum is open free of charge on Sunday 1:00 to 4:00 P.M. during the summer. At the First Methodist Church, the **Hinners Track Action Pipe Organ** dates from 1909. Find these sights on the walking tour sponsored by the Marshall Area Chamber of Commerce. Write for a brochure: 708 Archer Avenue, P.O. Box 263, Marshall 62441; phone (217) 826–2034.

Casey, on U.S. Highway 40 at Clark County's western border, is famous for **Richard's Farm Restaurant,** which is situated in an old barn. The specialty of the house is a "one-pound pork chop." Enjoy the decor and a seat in the hayloft and perhaps a chat with owners Diane and Gary Richards. Open daily for lunch and dinner; (217) 932–5300. Dinners range from $10 to $18. The restaurant is 1 block east of the intersection of Route 49 and U.S. Highway 40.

Plan a visit for Saturday night and take in Casey's famous **Saturday Night Auction,** held weekly at 5:30 P.M., with collectibles from area shops and individuals. It's held at the auction house in downtown Casey on Route 49; (217) 932–6186. Or stop by the auction house's salesroom any day from 8:00 A.M. to 4:00 P.M.

The Honeybee Trail

his may be Illinois's most international county, with a Paris, Scotland, Palermo, and even a Kansas within its borders. The county seat, Paris, lies in the heart of a rich farming area. Both Paris and the county date from 1823 when pioneer Samuel Vance donated twenty-six acres. Today's wonderfully ornate *county courthouse* (listed in the National Register of Historic Places) sits at the center of that land. Vance laid out many of the county's earliest roads, some still traveled today. The county seat gets its name from settlers arriving from Paris, Kentucky, it is believed. Forty years later those southern settlers sympathized with the Confederacy during the Civil War and came to be known as Copperheads. When first established, Edgar County extended north all the way to Lake Michigan. Paris was incorporated as a village in 1849.

A number of historic homes grace this lovely little town. The **Milton K. Alexander Home,** at 130 South Central Avenue, 61944, was the residence of a brigadier general in the Illinois Mounted Volunteers during the Black Hawk War of 1832. The house was built in 1826, with additions in 1840. It is now home to the **Bicentennial Art Center,** open noon to 4:00 P.M. Tuesday through Friday and 1:00 to 3:00 P.M. Saturday and Sunday; (217) 466–8130.

The **Daniel Arthur Home,** 414 North Main Street, 61944, was built in 1872 and now houses the **Edgar County Historical Museum.** Open Wednesday through Friday 9:00 A.M. to 4:00 P.M., other times by appointment. For more information call (217) 463–5305.

Each year at the end of September, the town is abuzz with the excitement of the annual **Paris Homecoming and Honeybee Festival.** Known as the honeybee capital of the nation, the community features the best-known product as well as arts and crafts, an antique car show, and a parade. Concurrently, the museum sponsors **Prairie Settler Day,** with exhibits and demonstrations of pioneer life. Call the Paris Chamber of Commerce for further information, (217) 465–4179.

Twin Lakes Park, the largest of ten in the city, offers camping (tent or RV, toilets, showers, electric hookups), boating, fishing, picnic areas, and cooking grills. The star attraction of West Lake is a small amusement park. The park is on the northern edge of the city on Route 1 and U.S. Highway 50; (217) 465–7601.

Palermo, in the northwest corner of the county, is the site of a historic meeting and peace council between Ottawa Indian Chief Pontiac and George Croghan, the British deputy superintendent of Indian Affairs. The 1765 parley settled the uprising known as Pontiac's Conspiracy, which occurred shortly after the French and Indian War.

PLACES TO STAY IN EASTERN ILLINOIS

ARCOLA
Amish Country Inn,
640 East Springfield
Road, 61910
(217) 268-3031

Best Western Regency Inn,
I-57 and
Route 133, 61910
(217) 268-4000

ARTHUR
Arthur's Country Inn,
Route 133, 61911
(217) 543-3321

CHAMPAIGN
The Chancellor Hotel,
1501 South Neil
Street, 61820
(800) 257-6667

Comfort Inn,
305 Marketview
Drive, 61822
(217) 352-4055

Radisson Suite Hotel,
101 Trade Center
Drive, 61820
(217) 398-3400

University Inn,
302 East John Street, 61820
(800) 322-8282

DANVILLE
Budget Suites and Inn,
411 Lynch Road, 61834
(800) 369-1339

Days Inn,
77 North Gilbert
Street, 61832
(217) 443-6600

Ramada Inn,
388 Eastgate Drive, 61834
(217) 446-2400

URBANA
The Lincoln Lodge,
403 West University
Avenue, 61802
(217) 367-1111

Europe Inn,
520 North
Cunningham, 61802
(217) 367-8377

Holiday Inn Hotel,
1001 Killarney
Street, 61801
(217) 328-7900

Illini Union Guest Rooms,
1401 West Green
Street, 61801
(217) 333-1241

Jumer's Castle Lodge,
209 South Broadway
Avenue, 61801
(800) 285-8637

PLACES TO EAT IN EASTERN ILLINOIS

ARCOLA
Dutch Kitchen,
127 East Main, 61910
(217) 268-3518

French Embassy,
112 West Springfield
Road, 61910
(217) 268-4949

Rockome Family Style,
125 North County
Road 425E, 61910
(217) 268-4106

CHAMPAIGN-URBANA
House of Hunan,
403 North Mattis Street,
Champaign, 61821
(217) 398-3388

Ned Kelly's,
1601 North Cunningham
Avenue, 61802
Urbana, (217) 344-8201

Selected Visitors Bureaus and Chambers of Commerce

Illinois Bureau of Tourism-Travel Information,
(800) 2-CONNECT

Arthur Visitor Center,
106 East Progress, Arthur 61911,
(800) 72-AMISH

Champaign-Urbana Convention and Visitors Bureau,
40 East University Avenue, Champaign 61820,
(800) 369-6151

Danville Area Convention and Visitors Bureau,
100 West Main Street, 61832
(800) 383-4386

CHARLESTON
Tapestries,
920 West Lincoln
Highway, 61920
(217) 348–8165

OTHER ATTRACTIONS WORTH
SEEING IN EASTERN ILLINOIS

Rockome Gardens, Arcola,
(217) 268–4106

William M. Staerkel
Planetarium, Champaign,
(217) 351–2446

Danville Stadium,
Exit 215 off I–74,
Danville,
(217) 431–2261

Middle Fork National
Scenic River,
Oakwood,
(800) 383–4386

Central Illinois

History, Lakes, and Rivers

Illinois may be known for its cornfields, but beginning in the central part of the state, history, lakes, and rivers abound.

Vandalia was the second capital of Illinois, but it was the first capital in the state to build a statehouse from scratch.

The first Illinois statehouse was a rented building in Kaskaskia. It was the seat of state government from 1818 to 1820. When the capital was moved to Vandalia, a two-story frame building was rented and the first session of the Second General Assembly met here on December 4, 1820. On December 9, 1823, fire destroyed the building.

The State Bank Building was remodeled and repaired and became the new statehouse. In spite of the repairs, the building was still in poor condition. It was so unsound that by 1836, no one dared hold a meeting there for fear of the building collapsing.

Lincoln's Statehouse Days

Historians tell us that Abraham Lincoln saw Illinois's first capital for the first time as his stagecoach driver "dramatically blew a horn to signal the end of the 75-mile, thirty-six-hour journey" from his home in New Salem. Lincoln roomed with the Whig floor leader during the 1834 legislative session, taking his place when the House of Representatives convened in Vandalia's old bank building, first-floor chambers.

When his first session as a state House member was completed in February 1835, Lincoln was paid $258 for his services and traveling expenses, and returned to New Salem by stagecoach in subzero temperatures.

But the taste of real politics had whetted his appetite for more. When he returned to his little log cabin village, he undertook the study of law with new zeal.

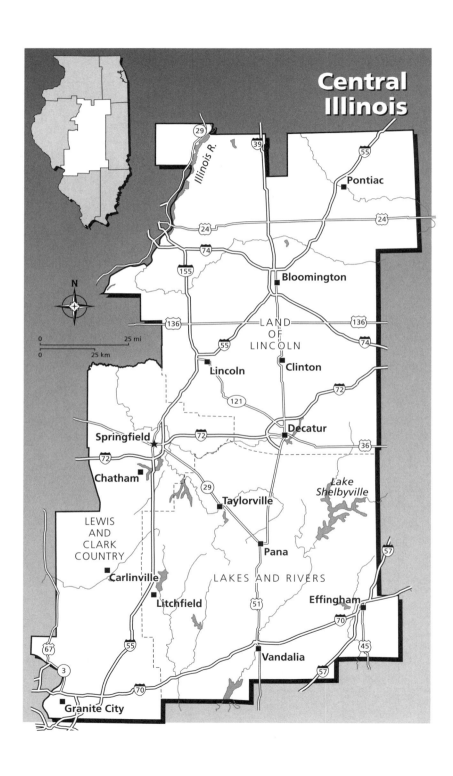

Central Illinois

Illinois R.

Pontiac

Bloomington

LAND
OF
LINCOLN

Lincoln   Clinton

Springfield

Decatur

Chatham

Lake
Shelbyville

Taylorville

LEWIS
AND
CLARK
COUNTRY

Pana

Carlinville

LAKES AND RIVERS

Litchfield

Effingham

Vandalia

Granite City

N

0   25 mi
0   25 km

29
39
55
24
74
155
136
136
74
55
121
72
72
36
29
51
57
67
3
55
70
45
57
70

In August 1836 Gov. Joseph Duncan authorized Auditor Levi Davis to either have the building repaired, rent an assembly hall, or build a new statehouse. It was decided to forget the old plans and build a new statehouse in the style of vernacular Federal architecture.

A bill of $16,378.22 was presented to the legislature for the building. The legislature appropriated $10,378.22 and Duncan drew $5,500 more from the contingency fund. The balance was contributed by individuals. The total cost of the building was $23,241.45.

Some of the important issues discussed at the **Vandalia Statehouse** were slavery and the establishment of Illinois as a free state. The first school laws of Illinois were enacted here and the controversial State Bank was debated here. The city of Chicago was also incorporated by the 1836–37 legislature, which included Stephen A. Douglas and Abraham Lincoln.

As the population shifted proposals were made to move the capital. On February 18, 1837, the General Assembly voted to move the capital to Springfield.

In 1933 the Illinois Department of Conservation began restoration of the old statehouse. At 315 West Gallatin, Vandalia 62471, it is open daily to visitors from 9:00 A.M. to 5:00 P.M. year-round except Thanksgiving, Christmas, and New Year's Day. Admission is free, and guided tours are available. For information call (618) 283–1161.

The area around **Ramsey Lake State Fish and Wildlife Area** was originally called Old Fox Chase Grounds and was popular with fox and raccoon hunters. It was first considered as a public recreation area in the late 1920s during the administration of Gov. Len Small. In 1947 the state of Illinois purchased 815 acres for a lake site, and additional land acquisition increased the area to 1,880 acres.

Ramsey Lake is 1 mile northwest of Ramsey off U.S. Highway 51 in a rolling, wooded terrain. The lake was constructed in a valley with an elevated timbered shoreline of almost 4 miles.

AUTHOR'S TOP TEN PICKS

1. *Springfield,*
   (800) 545–5781

2. *Cahokia Mounds,*
   Collinsville,
   (618) 346–5160

3. *Vandalia Statehouse*
   State Historic Site,
   Vandalia,
   (618) 283–1161

4. *Lake Shelbyville,*
   Findlay,
   (217) 774–2244

5. *Horseshoe Lake State*
   Park, Edwardsville,
   (618) 931–0270

6. *Lincoln,*
   (217) 732–8687

7. *Fort Creve Coeur State*
   Park, Creve Coeur,
   (309) 694–3193

8. *Scovill Children's Zoo,*
   Decatur,
   (217) 421–7435

9. *Mari-Mann Herb Farm,*
   Decatur,
   (217) 429–1404

10. *Central Illinois Jazz*
    Festival, Decatur,
    (217) 422–8800

Ramsey Lake has fishing, hunting, camping, picnicking, hiking, horseback riding, and snowmobiling facilities. *White Oak Campground* has 100 sites with a sanitary disposal station, electric hookups, flush toilets, and shower building. Two other campgrounds have more rugged facilities. Reservations are available from the site staff.

There are several picnic shelters, which have water, tables, and stoves. Fox Knoll, Coon Ridge, and Blackberry Fork picnic areas are small, shady, secluded knolls that overlook the lake.

Hikers will find a 1-mile designated trail and several miles of unmarked land.

The lake is stocked with largemouth bass, bluegill, red-ear sunfish, channel catfish, and black crappie. Boats can be rented, but only electric trolling motors are allowed. Fishing is also allowed in the small ponds. Check with the park office for catch and size limits on fish.

The horse trail, at the north end, is 13 miles long. A small equestrian campground is 1 mile north of the park entrance.

Dove, squirrel, quail, pheasant, and deer hunting are permitted in season, deer hunting only with a bow. Shotguns only are permitted, and no hunting is allowed inside of Lake Circle Drive.

Ice fishing, snowmobiling, cross-country skiing, sledding, and ice skating are permitted in winter.

For information and reservations contact the Site Superintendent, Ramsey Lake State Fish and Wildlife Area, P.O. Box 97, Ramsey 62080; (618) 423–2215.

Shelby County is blessed with natural resources set aside for public recreation. Within its boundaries lie Hidden Springs, Wolf Creek, and Eagle Creek state parks; Lake Mattoon; Lake Pana; and—most importantly—*Lake Shelbyville.* This giant lake is one of the state's largest, covering 11,100 acres with 172 miles of wooded shoreline protected from development by the U.S. Army Corps of Engineers. It reaches 20 miles from Shelbyville, the county seat in the south, to Sullivan in Moultrie County in the north.

Begun in 1963 and completed in 1970 as a flood control project, the lake contains the Kaskaskia and Okaw Rivers. Today the recreational benefits are primary on the minds of most visitors, with camping, boating, fishing, picnicking, hiking, and swimming all available to weekend adventurers. Call (217) 774–2020 for recorded lake fishing conditions. Your

TOP ANNUAL FESTIVALS

Mari-Mann Herb Festival,
Decatur, mid-May,
(217) 429–1404

*Springfield Scottish
Highland Games,*
Springfield, mid-May,
(217) 241–3000

*Illinois Shakespeare
Festival,* Bloomington, late
June, (309) 438–2535

*Annual Battle of the
Bands,* Normal, mid-June,
(217) 774–3951

*Bloomington Gold
Corvettes USA Show,*
Bloomington, late June,
(309) 829–3976

*Springfield Air
Rendezvous,* mid-July,
(217) 789–4400

Logan County Fair,
Lincoln, late July,
(217) 732–3311

Illinois State Fair,
Springfield, early August,
(217) 782–6661

Apple 'n' Pork Festival,
Clinton, late September,
(217) 935–6066

*Lake Shelbyville Festival
of Lights,* Findlay, late
November–mid-January,
(800) 874–3529

Christmas on the Square,
Mt. Pulaski, early December,
(217) 732–8930

First Night Springfield,
Springfield, late December,
(217) 753–3519

catch might be white or largemouth bass, walleye, crappie, channel catfish, northern pike, or any of two dozen or so varieties of fish found in the lake.

There are only three marinas on the lake—Fox Harbor in Moultrie County and **Lithia Springs** and Findlay in Shelby County. Lithia Springs is closest to Shelbyville and boasts a modest motel, the Lithia Resort, only a short walk away. An alternative accommodation choice, however, is offered in the houseboat rental. Lithia rents spacious houseboats by the week for prices ranging from about $1,000 to $2,000; (217) 774–4121. For that you can bring six or eight people and make it a party. To reach Lithia Springs Marina, drive 3 miles east of Shelbyville on Route 16; then turn north and follow the signs.

Sailboats and fishing boats, water-skiers, and naturalists happily coexist on the lake where deep forested coves seem far away from the flat farmland not too distant. On shore, campers will find more than 500 campsites with electrical hookups. During the summer season Corps of Engineer personnel present a schedule of interpretive programs on a range of spiffy topics: "Family Water Safety," "Through an Insect's Eye," "Wild Edible Plants," and others. Be sure to stop at the visitors center at the **Dam East Recreation Area,** 1 mile east of Shelbyville on Route 16 (open Memorial Day through Labor Day), which offers audiovisual programs, exhibits, and an unmatched view of the dam.

Apart from the lake there's plenty to see ashore. In Shelbyville, named for Revolutionary War Gen. Isaac Shelby, drive up Washington Street to view the handsome Civil War–era homes. Downtown the French Second Empire–style **county courthouse** is a local point of interest. The old, multisided **Chautauqua Auditorium** in Forest Park dates from the period around 1903 when evangelist Jasper L. Douthit held his celebrated religious meetings here.

Although farming may be the primary enterprise in Moultrie County, fishing is probably the primary pastime. Sullivan, the county seat, advertises itself as the "northern gateway to beautiful Lake Shelbyville." It shares the 11,000-acre lake with Shelby County to the south. So at the same time that the county claims first place in statewide corn-per-acre production, its production of walleye, crappie, and largemouth bass isn't bad either.

If you're camping, try *Sullivan's Marina and Campground,* south of town on Lake Shelbyville; (217) 728–7338. There are boat rentals and plenty of wooded terrain just across from the *Sullivan Recreation Area,* which has a well-maintained swimming beach.

Sullivan is situated on the Lincoln Heritage Trail. It claims to be the only town with a National Guard unit once commanded by Abraham Lincoln. Less honorably, it was also the scene of a near-riot on the day that both Lincoln and Douglas were in town to give speeches.

The *Little Theatre on the Square* is the town's pride and joy and Sullivan's claim to summer culture fame. Founded in 1957, it bills itself as the only professional Equity theater between Chicago and St. Louis. And each year from the end of May through mid-August, a program of musicals and plays is presented by the Little Theatre's own company; (217) 728–7375.

On the north side of town, *Wyman Park* and *Wyman Lake* make up

Holidazzle

Many people come to giant Lake Shelbyville in Findlay during the summer months, when camping, fishing, and boating are the main activities.

My family likes to come here during the winter, in the heart of the Christmas season, for the Lake Shelbyville Festival of Lights. From early November through mid-January, this award-winning holiday bash boasts a winter wonderland of more than two-and-a-half-million twinkling electric lights, creating America's second-largest Yuletide light show.

With most action taking place in Eagle Creek State Park, you can drive through more than 200 holiday displays that wind around the lake and through the woods. Better yet, drive through the 3-mile-long "holiday tunnel" with Christmas scenes adorned with more twinkling lights.

Of course, you won't be alone here. During its almost three-month run, the Christmas fest draws more than 200,000 Yuletide revelers. Why not be one of them?

Illinois's Witchhunt

*A*ccording to my map for Illinois, a bit of the state's Mississippi River coastline is included in the section of the book I call Central Illinois. Well, just ignore this quirky geography classification, and listen to this.

In the late 1600s the French settled in what is called the Illinois French Colonial district in Cahokia, just south of St. Louis (on the Missouri side) on the Mississippi. The French also brought the first West Indian slaves into the area in the 1730s, primarily to work in the region's lead mines.

By 1732, the village of Cahokia listed 182 slaves as part of their cache; there were 106 listed as "Negro" and 76 as "Indian."

These Caribbean slaves brought their own culture with them and, in return for inhumane treatment at the hands of their French owners, poisoned some of their masters "using secret rituals of sorcery." Then, resembling a "mini-Salem" atmosphere, local authorities put several of these slaves on trial, not for murder but for "witchcraft."

Located behind Cahokia's Church of the Holy Family is a large white cross. This spot designates where some of the "poisoned" French victims were buried. Slavery was practiced in this area until the nineteenth century.

forty acres of recreational area offering tennis, a playground, and room for picnicking. Nearby, the ***Civic Center*** has an Olympic-size indoor heated pool with diving area, racquetball courts, and a gymnasium.

Also in town is ***The Depot,*** an antiques shop with a split personality—one store a chock-full antique mall, and across the tracks, a gallery. Hours are Monday through Saturday, 10:00 A.M. to 5:00 P.M.

Just outside of town, east on Route 121, is the ***Illinois Masonic Home.*** Land for the home was given before the century by Mason Robert A. Miller upon which to build a residence for Masons and their widows. The first building was dedicated in 1904. Today more than 300 retired persons reside here. Its beautiful grounds include a deer park, a landscaped lake, and a greenhouse that furnishes fresh flowers daily for the home. A small collection called ***Ward's Museum*** is housed in the main building. Open to the public, it includes 10,000 specimens of seashells, plus primitive furniture and other antiques. In a separate building is an old-fashioned ice cream parlor complete with a marvelous player piano. Visitors are welcome at the home year-round; (217) 728–4394. Hours are 8:00 A.M. to 4:30 P.M. Monday through Friday, 8:00 A.M. to 4:00 P.M. Saturday and Sunday. No admission charge.

Lewis and Clark Country

Commemorating the starting point of the famous expedition to the Pacific Coast is *Lewis and Clark State Park* in Madison County. South of Wood River on Route 3, 2 miles north of I–270, the monument to the expedition consists of eleven concrete pylons that form the rotunda and represent the eleven Trail States traversed by the expedition. Individual plaques briefly review the party's activities as it traveled cross-country.

Cahokia Mounds in Collinsville are recognized as a World Heritage site by the United Nations Educational, Scientific, and Cultural Organization (UNESCO). The organization offers educational programs and publications here. (There is also a gift and book shop.) Take I–55/70 to exit 11 at Route 157, then south to U.S. Highway 40, then west to Cahokia Mounds World Heritage Site.

The most spectacular features are the sixty-five intact mounds. Originally there were approximately 120 mounds and most were ceremonial. *Monk's Mound* is the largest prehistoric mound north of Mexico. You can walk up countless wood-and-earthen steps to reach the top of the mound for panoramic vistas of the surrounding prehistoric mounds— or for great sunrises and sunsets. The museum is open daily from 9:00 A.M. to 5:00 P.M. except on major holidays.

Edwardsville, at the center of the county, boasts two areas listed on the

Without A Trace

Here's a mystery worthy of X- Filers Mulder and Scully.

What happened to the people who built Cahokia Mounds, the largest prehistoric Indian city north of Mexico?

They just disappeared!

That's what archaeologists can't figure out. This stretch of floodplain just 6 miles east of the Mississippi River was home to the ancient "City of the Sun," a town that was crammed with

20,000 people by A.D. 1100. Homes were arranged in rows around open plazas. More than 100 earthen-man-made mounds dotted the city. And a wooden wall about 15 feet high surrounded about 300 sacred acres of the central city.

It was an advanced civilization, scientists say. But by A.D. 1500, less than 300 years after its heyday, Cahokia was abandoned, leaving no clues about what happened to her people or where they went.

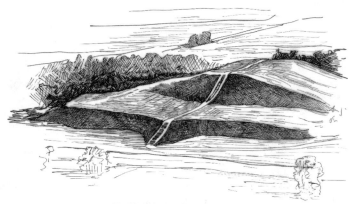

Monk's Mound at Cahokia Mounds

National Historic Register—the *St. Louis Street Historic District* and the *LeClaire Historic District,* as well as the handsome campus of *Southern Illinois University* at Edwardsville.

Horseshoe Lake State Park on 2,600 acres on Route 111, west of Edwardsville, offers a wide variety of family fun: picnicking, boating, fishing, hunting, camping, bird-watching, and cross-country skiing. The area was inhabited by Indian groups, with the earliest evidence dating from 8000 B.C. during the Archaic Period. Artifacts have been found that fall into the Woodland Period, 1000 B.C. to A.D. 1000. The park is open year-round except for holidays. Contact the Site Superintendent, Horseshoe Lake State Park, P.O. Box 1307, Granite City 62040; (618) 931–0270.

Turf enthusiasts will savor the excitement at the *Fairmount Park Race Track* on Route 140 in Collinsville. Both harness and thoroughbred racing are on the bill from January through November.

For an unusual event Collinsville sponsors an annual *Horseradish Festival.* These homemade concoctions can set your intestines on fire, though. Contact the Collinsville Chamber of Commerce, 221 West Main Street, Collinsville 62234, (618) 344–2884, for more information.

Alton was the site of *Alton Prison,* the state's first penitentiary. The remnants of a cell block wall have been restored as a monument to this primitive penitentiary, which housed Confederate prisoners during the Civil War. The *penitentiary monument* is at the corner of Broadway and Williams Streets near downtown Alton.

The town's colorful history includes Rev. Elijah P. Lovejoy, a newspaperman who crusaded against slavery and was shot down by a hostile mob.

Central Illinois Trivia

One of the funniest Illinois newspaper headlines ever in print occurred when a downstate publication described the wedding of a couple from different small towns; it read "Oblong Girl Weds Normal Boy."

He was shot on November 8, 1837, and sixty years later, a 90-foot *stone memorial to Lovejoy*—the tallest memorial in the state—was erected near his grave. In 1915 the frame of his printing press went on display in the lobby of the Alton Telegraph Building.

Carlinville is home to the *Million Dollar Courthouse,* more affectionately termed the "White Elephant." The courthouse was far beyond the needs of the county and cost much more than anticipated when construction began in 1867. Within a few months the building commissioners and the county court knew that the building would be more than double the $150,000 estimated cost.

It was 2 1/2 years before the building was finished and forty years before it was paid for. When it was finally completed, the move from the old courthouse to the new was quietly made. The eventual cost was $1,300,000.

The building is made of limestone and consists of two rectangles that cross at the center and are surmounted with a dome. The dome rises 191 feet above the street, and 40-foot columns support the roof. Every door is made of iron, and each outer door weighs more than a ton. All interior trim is of iron or stone. The judge's chair, costing $1,500, is mounted on a track behind the varicolored marble bench.

Macoupin County Historical Museum has a collection of county historical items; a music room with an old grand piano; exhibits of furniture, pottery, china, and glass; stained glass windows from a German exhibitor at the 1893 World's Fair in Chicago; an 1890 bathroom; and memorabilia of early Macoupin County doctors. The museum celebrates three special events: a Strawberry Festival the last weekend in May, a Fall Festival the third weekend in September, and special holiday decorations for the Christmas season.

A gift shop on the premises carries postcards, county history reprints, and craft items. Hours are April through November, Wednesday 10:00 A.M. to 2:00 P.M., June through August, Sunday 1:00 to 5:00 P.M. Admission is $2.00 for adults, $1.00 for children 6 to 16, no charge for children under six. The museum is on Breckenridge Road in Carlinville; (217) 854–2850.

Land of Lincoln

ocal residents say, "Lincoln never lived here, but he left a lot of tracks." Abraham Lincoln gave Logan County its name, owned property here, practiced law at the Eighth Judicial Circuit Court at Mount Pulaski, and his funeral train stopped here.

Logan County was a result of Abraham Lincoln's efforts to divide Sangamon County into four smaller counties in 1839. At his suggestion one of the counties was named after Dr. John Logan, a friend of Lincoln's who was instrumental in helping persuade the legislature to move the state capital to Springfield.

The town of Lincoln is the only one named after him with his knowledge and consent. The honor evolved from three partners in Postville, who engaged Lincoln as a lawyer to establish joint ownership of the tract of land near Postville. The partners decided to name the town Lincoln, against the advice of Lincoln himself. He said, "Never knew anything named Lincoln that amounted to much."

Customized tours of Lincoln are available from the Abraham Lincoln Tourism Bureau of Logan County at no charge and by appointment only. Phone (217) 732–8687 (TOUR).

Other historical events involving Abraham Lincoln include his and Stephen A. Douglas's visit to the area during their senatorial campaign in the summer of 1858. On November 21, 1859, Lincoln gave a farewell address to the citizens here, and on May 3, 1865, his funeral train was greeted with mourners singing hymns and paying their last respects.

The **Lincoln Gallery,** 111 North Sangamon, 62656, has a statue of Lincoln christening the town. Lloyd Ostendorf's oil paintings depict Lincoln's life in Logan County, Washington, D.C., and Gettysburg. They are inside the Olympia Savings and Loan Association building. Hours are Monday through Wednesday 8:30 A.M. to 3:00 P.M., Thursday 8:30 A.M. to noon, Friday 8:30 A.M. to 5:00 P.M., and Saturday 8:30 A.M. to noon.

Central Illinois Trivia

It's said that Abe Lincoln started studying law books by candlelight in a room at the Onstot Cooper Shop in Lincoln's New Salem Historic Site in Petersburg, where he rented a room.

Lincoln College was established in 1865 with the donation of ten acres of land by John D. Gillett and Robert B. Latham, two of the college's founding fathers. The cornerstone of the **University Hall** was laid on February 12, 1865, Lincoln's last living birthday. The hall is listed in the National Register of Historic Places.

The McKinstry Library, on campus, houses the **Museum of the Presidents,** an outstanding collection of more than 2,500 Lincoln artifacts. The **Merrill Gage Statue** showing Lincoln as a student is also on campus.

Lincoln Rustic, 412 Pulaski Street, 62656, is the site where a conspiracy developed to steal Lincoln's body from Oak Ridge Cemetery in Springfield.

The **Postville Courthouse,** 914 Fifth Street, 62656, is open Friday and Saturday from 9:00 A.M. to 5:00 P.M. (217–732–8930), and it was here that Lincoln received his nickname "Honest Abe." The building was completed in 1840, and Lincoln served here as a member of the bar for a quarter of a century. The building was reconstructed in 1953; the original stands in Greenfield Village, Michigan.

Another site of interest in Logan County is the **Atlanta Public Library and Museum,** Race Street, Atlanta (217–648–2112). The museum contains artifacts from the area, and the building is actually Logan County's first bank. The library is listed in the National Register of Historic Places and is one of only a few octagonal-plan libraries in Illinois. Closed Sunday and Monday.

The **Middletown Stage Coach Inn** in Middletown was established in 1832 and still stands. Middletown is believed to be the oldest town in Logan County and served as a midpoint and stagecoach stop on the Peoria-Springfield Road. The **bank building** in Middletown is thought to be the oldest building in Logan County.

Elkhart Cemetery in Elkhart has the **John Dean Gillett Memorial Chapel,** a charming country chapel that is privately owned and self-supporting. It was built in 1890 and erected in memory of John Dean Gillett, the "Cattle King of America."

Richard S. Oglesby, three-time governor of Illinois, is also buried in this cemetery. Oglesby was the person who nominated Lincoln for the presidency and was the first to call him the "Railsplitter." The **Logan Railsplitting Festival,** held the second weekend after Labor Day, is a nineteenth-century-style festival featuring a railsplitting contest, flea market, food, and entertainment. Contact the Logan Railsplitting Festival and Association, P.O. Box 352, Lincoln 62656; (217) 732–4795.

Mount Pulaski was named for Count Casimir Pulaski, a Polish-born soldier who joined the Continental army of George Washington in 1777. The **Mount Pulaski Courthouse** is Greek Revival architecture and one of the two surviving courthouses from Lincoln's days in the Eighth Judicial Circuit Court. It is located in the town's square and is open daily from 9:00 A.M. to 5:00 P.M.

CENTRAL ILLINOIS

Pekin, once a major port on the Illinois River during the steamboat era, is one of the oldest settlements in Tazewell County. Like many other towns in western Illinois, it was visited by Abraham Lincoln and was used as a fort during the Black Hawk War.

Pekin is also the home of the **Everett McKinley Dirksen Congressional Leadership Center,** the nation's only educational institution devoted to the study of congressional leadership. The center is located at Broadway and Fourth Streets. It contains the late senator's office files, speeches, audio-and videotapes, records, photographs, books, and memorabilia. The major exhibit is "Congress: The Voice of the People." This exhibit shows examples of how the citizenry participates in the legislative process.

In addition to the Exhibition Hall, the center has a growing collection of memorabilia relating to Congress. Senator Dirksen began the collection with contributions of his own artwork, sculpture, photographs, flags, letters, and political mementos. These objects are used in special exhibits.

You may have read that Illinois is one of the flattest states on all the prairie. It's true. And travelers here will discover that the last great glacier, which swept through central Illinois about 10,000 years ago, leveled much of the local topography.

So, indeed, Illinois's central heartland is truly an outpost for flatlanders.

Of course, this makes it easier to get around, for all you have to do is follow roads that cut a swath through seemingly endless cornfields. Negatively speaking, it can make for some spectacularly boring driving. On the positive side, the landscape is a kind of throwback to the wide open prairie that greeted the pioneers.

Visitors can tour the Exhibition Hall and also view special programs offered in the Assembly Room. These programs must be arranged by advance request. Admission is free, and the museum is open to the public Monday through Friday 8:00 A.M. to 4:00 P.M.

The Pekin area lies at the boundary between the Bloomington Ridge Plain that was formed by Wisconsin glaciers nearly 22,000 years ago and the Springfield Plain formed by the Illinoisan glaciers about 200,000 years ago. The geological history of the Mississippi and Illinios Rivers can be studied through field trips sponsored by the Illinois Department of Energy and Natural Resources, State Geological Survey Division, Natural Resources Building, 615 East Peabody Drive, Champaign 61820. Call (217) 344–1481 for information.

In mid-September Pekin holds its **Annual Marigold Festival** to celebrate the flower that blooms throughout the city. A parade and art fair are part of the celebration. Contact the Pekin Chamber of Commerce, 116 South Capitol, P.O. Box 636, Pekin 61554, (309) 346–2106, for a list of activities.

The *Spring Lake State Conservation Area*—1 mile south of Pekin on Route 29, 9 miles southwest on Manito Blacktop, and 3 miles west on Spring Lake Blacktop—is a 1,996-acre park with a fish hatchery and fishing, boating, hiking, cross-country skiing, and picnicking facilities. Contact the Park Manager, R.R. 1, Box 248, Manito 61546, (309) 968–7135, for information.

East Peoria, at the base of the bluffs on the floodplain of the Illinois River, is the home of *McGlothlin Farm Park.* Located on Neumann Drive off Meadows Avenue at U.S. Highway 150, the park is a timeless picture of farm life. It has duck ponds, a schoolhouse, barn, brooder, blacksmith shop, and hen house. Animals on the farm are typical of those on many area farms and are free to roam the grounds. Visitors are allowed to pet and feed them. For information call (309) 694–2195.

The *General Store,* on the grounds of the park, offers a variety of toys, country items, and candy. The *Country Kitchen* is open to view antiques, and when a special event is scheduled, baked goods are baked in an old woodstove on the premises. Concessions as well as picnic tables are available. Summer hours are 10:00 A.M. to 4:00 P.M. Tuesday through Saturday and 1:00 to 6:00 P.M. Sunday. Closed mid-October to May 1. Admission is $2.00 for adults, $1.50 for children.

Fond du Lac Park at Springfield and Steward Avenues in East Peoria has an extensive view of Peoria and the Illinois River Valley. Its more than 2,000 acres on the east bank of the Illinois River offer picnic areas, hiking, golf, tennis, camping, and swimming facilities. Call (309) 699–3923.

Central Illinois Trivia

The last Illinois buffalo roamed these parts as late as 1808—when it was promptly killed by hunters.

The Oliver Parks Telephone Museum in Springfield doesn't have its own telephone.

But a "must visit" in these parts is *Fort Creve Coeur State Park* in Creve Coeur, once the site of the explorer La Salle's outpost. The fort, established in 1680, was ill-fated. It was a proposed base for exploration and colonization of the Mississippi Valley, but when La Salle went to Quebec and left another man in charge, the dissatisfied troops destroyed the fort and went into the wilderness with all the powder and provisions. The fort was never rebuilt. A granite marker commemorates the founding of the fort and tells the story of its desertion.

The *Fort Creve Coeur Rendezvous* is an annual event held the fourth weekend in September. The festivities feature voyageurs with canoes, buckskin-garbed troops, flintlocks, and crafts. Contact Fort Creve Coeur State Park at (309) 694–3193 for dates and information.

At the heart of the Illinois prairie sit the sister cities of Bloomington and Normal. The earliest records show the first white people were here around 1800—traders and trappers who made a living roaming the region bordering the Mississippi River. A local legend says that one such group hid a keg of whiskey here in a thick grove of trees, only to have it discovered by an Indian party that finished it off handily. Thus, when the first settlers arrived in 1822, the place was called Keg Grove. Seven years later, when the first post office was established, the settlement called itself Blooming Grove for the area's profusion of flowers.

McLean County was organized in 1830; a year later, Bloomington, laid out on 22 1/2 acres donated by James Allin just north of Blooming Grove, was designated the county seat. Normal, once North Bloomington, takes it name from what was the State Normal University, now Illinois State University (founded in 1857). Bloomington's university, Illinois Wesleyan, was chartered in 1853. Apart from being university towns and a center of county government, the communities have a rich business and industrial base. For example, the home office of State Farm Insurance Company is based here.

History and politics have long been intertwined here, as well. Some say Bloomington's David Davis was the man who "made Lincoln president." A noted lawyer and member of the state legislature, Davis was elected judge of the Eighth Judicial Circuit in 1848, a position that put him in frequent contact with the lawyer Abraham Lincoln. At the 1860 Republican Convention, Davis worked behind the scenes to organize support for Illinois's favorite son. In 1862 Lincoln rewarded him with an appointment to the Supreme Court. Davis was elected to the U.S. Senate in 1877.

His mansion, *Clover Lawn,* is one of the top attractions for visitors. A state historic site, the twenty-room Italian villa includes much of the original furnishings from the 1872 period. The house is built of yellow-faced brick with stone quoins in the corners. Its tower rises 50 feet above the ground. Inside, eight marble fireplaces decorate rooms done in high Victorian style, a fine example of upper-class life of the period. The home is open from 9:00 A.M. to 4:00 P.M. Monday through Thursday. Admission is free. Call for further details; (309) 828–1084.

Another mansion cum museum is the *Ewing Manor Cultural Center,* the former home of Hazel Buck Ewing, whose father was associated with William Wrigley, Jr., in the foundation of the Wrigley Company of Chicago. Also known as the Ewing Castle, the 1929 estate is done in the style of a Norman castle. Upon the death of the wealthy philanthropist, the property became part of the Illinois State University Foundation. It's not open to the public, but drive by and enjoy the architecture. Emerson Street at Towanda Avenue.

In July and early August, the *Illinois Shakespeare Festival* presents three Shakespearean plays here in repertory nightly Tuesday through Sunday. Picnicking on the lawn of the Ewing Manor is especially popular with festival-goers; (309) 438–2535.

The *McLean County Historical Society Museum* catalogues the county's past with exhibits of Indian artifacts, decorative arts, military souvenirs, and crafts. Upstairs there's a neat gift shop and genealogy collection. One of the star attractions is the *"Tilbury Flash,"* a 1930s racing plane built in Bloomington, among the smallest in the world. Special shows are mounted throughout the year. The museum is open daily at various hours; call for details. Tuesday admission is free; the remainder of the week it's $2.00 for adults and $1.00 for children 12 and under. The museum is housed in the old McLean County Courthouse at 200 North Main Street, 61701; (309) 827–0428.

At the McLean County Fairground in Bloomington, the *Third Sunday Market* is like an attic full of collectibles and antiques. Show admission is $3.00; parking is free. For information phone (309) 452–7926. The monthly event is managed by Don and Carol Raycraft, authorities and authors on country antiques.

Central Illinois Trivia

Abe Lincoln's bronze bust, which stands at the entrance to his tomb in Springfield's Oak Ridge Cemetery, has a golden nose thanks to millions of tourists rubbing it for good luck.

Illinois State University provides plenty to keep a visitor busy. Stop at the university art galleries, the Funk Gem and Mineral Museum, the planetarium, the Hudelson Museum of Agriculture, or the school's historical museum. The Adlai E. Stevenson Memorial Room honors one of Bloomington's most famous citizens. And there really is an academic ivory tower here—Watterson Towers, at twenty-eight stories the world's largest college residence hall. Most campus attractions are free, and tours can be arranged. Call (309) 438–2111 for ISU information. Regular performing arts events are scheduled at Braden Auditorium; call (309) 438–5444.

Illinois Wesleyan, too, boasts a number of treasures including Evelyn Chapel, a focal point of the private school. The chapel is an example of Moravian-style architecture in Flemish patterned brick. The interior woodwork and acoustics are superb. Sheean Library holds the Indian pottery collection of Maj. John Wesley Powell, a former faculty member

CENTRAL ILLINOIS

and first explorer of the Colorado River and Grand Canyon. Call (309) 556–3034 for campus information. McPherson Theater has a busy schedule of productions throughout the year; (309) 556–3232.

Bloomington's **Miller Park Zoo,** 1020 South Morris Avenue, is one of Illinois's best. The **Tropical Rain Forest,** 80 feet in diameter, has overhead skylights, a profusion of tropical plants, and colorful exotic birds flying free through the exhibit. Outside, the antics of the California sea lions or the American river otters captivate crowds. The **James E. Gardner Memorial Children's Zoo** features farmyard animals for kids to pet. The zoo is open every day of the year, 10:00 A.M. to 5:00 P.M. Admission: $3.00 adults, $2.00 children three to fifteen, and seniors 60+. Call (309) 434–2250.

A major seasonal event is Bloomington's **American Passion Play**. Since 1924 community players have enacted the life of Christ, from his Baptism to the Resurrection, in an annual spring tradition with a cast of more than 300, with nearly fifty scene changes. Sundays, mid-March to early May at the Scottish Rite Temple, 110 East Mulberry Street, 61701; (309) 829–3903.

At 901 North McLean in Bloomington, 61701, is the site of the **Adlai E. Stevenson I** home. Stevenson was vice president of the United States from 1893 to 1897. Both he and his grandson Adlai Stevenson II, former governor of Illinois, are buried at Evergreen Cemetery here. Another Illinois governor—this one a Republican—also lived in Bloomington. Joseph W. Fifer, governor of Illinois from 1889 to 1893, lived at 909 North McLean, near the Stevensons. Both homes are privately owned and not open for tours.

Southwest of the county's two major cities is historic **Funks Grove.** One of the county's first settlements, several of the original buildings still remain—the Funk Prairie Home, the 1865 Funk's Grove Church, and the syrup factory. Here, 1,200 gallons per year of maple syrup are produced by the same family that first settled here in 1824. Nearby, stop at the **Lafayette Funk Rock Museum.** To reach Funks Grove take I–55 south to the Shirley exit; the town is about 10 miles southwest of

Faith-filled Moment

For me, the most electrifying moment of the American Passion Play comes during the scene that shows Jesus calming the storm on the sea while his Apostles cower in their boat; then, like the Scripture verse, He walks on the water.

Lightning bolts flash, thunder rumbles, and rain pelts the water (on stage only). What a compelling moment in the depiction of the life of Christ.

More than 15,000 people come to see the show during its run, some from as far away as the East Coast, just to glimpse a bit of its Easter message of hope.

Bloomington. Call (309) 874–3360 for information on the early spring maple tapping, or you can just take home a souvenir bottle or two.

Five miles west of Bloomington on County Road 1650 North, *The Apple Barn* sells tasty bakery products, jams, cider, and fruit from McLean County's oldest commercial orchard. Open daily July through early December; (309) 963–5557.

In Lexington, northeast of the major cities, stands the *Patton Cabin,* built in 1829 by John Patton, one of the county's first white settlers.

For campers *Moraine View State Park,* near rural LeRoy, offers 1,700 acres of rolling terrain plus the 160-acre Dawson Lake. Boating, fishing, camping (142 sites, most with electrical hookup), and hiking are popular activities. Call (309) 724–8032.

The center of this county, situated at the center of the state, is *Lake Clinton,* a 5,000-acre cooling lake for the Illinois Power Company's nuclear power plant. (Insert your own presidential joke here.) With 130 miles of wooded shoreline, the lake development is managed by the Illinois Department of Conservation, which has thoughtfully stocked it with largemouth and smallmouth bass, walleye, crappie, and catfish. Sailboats share the lake with fishing boats, which stop for supplies at Dockside Marina, off Route 10, about 8 miles east of Clinton. In season, hunting is allowed on the land surrounding the lake.

Three miles southeast of Clinton is *Weldon Springs State Recreation Area,* just east of U.S. Highway 51. Prior to 1936 the park was privately owned and the site of a well-known chautauqua each summer. From 1901 to 1920 programs of educational, cultural, or religious interest were presented. By 1904 the yearly event drew so many people that it was necessary to build an auditorium accommodating 4,500 people. They came to hear the stars of the day—William Jennings Bryan, President William Howard Taft, Helen Keller, evangelist Billy Sunday, and temperance leader Carry Nation, among others. The park is open year-round and offers campsites (electric hookups, toilets), picnicking area, hiking trails, fishing, and boating. Weldon Springs has a special handicapped-accessible fishing dock, as well.

The *DeWitt County Museum* is located in the *Homestead* in Clinton, a restored Victorian mansion listed in the National Register of Historic Places. The 1867 Italianate residence was home to Clinton H. Moore, a former law partner of Abraham Lincoln. The architectural highlight here is a two-story library with a vaulted ceiling and an iron railing around the open upper gallery. Children will love the antique doll collection and the child's room with its child-sized four-poster bed. Period rooms, a carriage collection, and the farm and railroad museum are among the exhibits. On the last weekend in September the museum sponsors an *Apple 'n' Pork Festival,* featuring stick-to-the-ribs home cooking with plenty of smoked ham and apple cider. During the Christmas season the house is beautifully decorated in the style of the late 1800s. Candlelight tours are also available in December. The museum is open April through December Tuesday through Saturday 10:00 A.M. to 5:00 P.M. and Sunday 1:00 to 5:00 P.M., $2.00 admission. At 219 East Woodlawn, 61727; (217) 935–6066.

A *statue of Lincoln* at the square commemorates the speech delivered in Clinton in 1848 in which Lincoln remarked, "You can fool some of the people all of the time, and all of the people some of the time, but you can't fool all the people all of the time."

Decatur has a cornucopia of architectural styles popular from the Civil War to the Great Depression. Eighty acres of its buildings are listed in the National Register of Historic Places. In addition, the Historic and Architectural Sites Commission has published five walking tours, which take you past examples of Italianate, Second Empire, Queen Anne, Romanesque Revival, Shingle, Stick, Georgian Revival, Tudor, Art Deco, and neoclassical styles. The walking tours are free and can be obtained from the Decatur Area Convention and Visitors Bureau, 202 East North Street, Decatur 62523; (217) 423–7000.

Highlights of the tours include the *Milliken Homestead* at 125 North Pine, 62522, a Victorian mansion with fine woodwork, leaded glass, and elegant fireplaces. The *Oglesby Mansion,* 421 West Williams, 62522, is an Italianate-style building with diamond-shaped glass in its bay windows. It was the home of the former United States senator and three-time governor of Illinois, Richard J. Oglesby.

> ### Central Illinois Trivia
>
> *Illinois has three nicknames: Inland Empire, Land of Lincoln, and Prairie State. Carl Sandburg's "Hog Butcher to the World" never stuck.*

Abraham Lincoln was no stranger to Decatur. It was here at the 1860 Republican Party Convention that he was unanimously nominated for president and also dubbed the "Railsplitter." A *statue of the barefoot Lincoln* stands in Lincoln Square in the center of downtown.

The *Scovill Children's Zoo* is a special treat because it is designed to look as if the animals and visitors are in the same environment. The zoo encompasses ten acres and lies above the east shore of Lake Decatur. It is open 10:00 A.M. to 8:00 P.M. in the summer and on weekends, May

The Milliken Homestead

through Labor Day, and 10:00 A.M. to 4:00 P.M. when school is in session. The zoo features rides on the ZO&O Express; admission is $2.75 for adults, $1.00 for children, and $1.50 for seniors. Tours are available by advance arrangement.

To get to Scovill Zoo, take U.S. Highway 36 east and cross Lake Decatur to 71 South Country Club Road. For information call (217) 421–7435.

The *Macon County Museum Complex,* 5580 North Fork Road, 62521, prides itself on preserving and presenting the heritage of Macon County. The museum has a collection of historic artifacts as well as examples of 1890s houses, a prairie village, and an 1860s schoolhouse. A "hands-on" approach is used in the displays so you can see, smell, and touch the past as well as the present. Museum hours are Tuesday through Sunday 1:00 to 4:00 P.M.; (217) 422–4919.

The *Mari-Mann Herb Farm and Gingerbread House* is at the north end of St. Louis Bridge Road. Visitors can walk among the herb beds, wildflower fields, deer trails, and formal gardens. The Gingerbread House offers herb products, Special Spoon Herbal Sauce, herbal jellies, and other herbal condiments. Teas, herbs, gourmet spices, fragrances with potpourri, and essential and fragrant oils are also sold.

The herb greenhouse carries a selection of year-round herbal plants.

The farm is open 9:00 A.M. to 5:00 P.M. Monday through Saturday and noon to 5:00 P.M. Sunday. Demonstrations, luncheons, teas, tours, and classes are available by appointment. Contact Mari-Mann Herb Company, Inc., R.R. 4, P.O. Box 7, Decatur 62521; (217) 429–1404.

Decatur is also the home of the *Central Illinois Jazz Festival,* which attracts thousands of jazz musicians and enthusiasts from across the nation. For information call the Holiday Inn, (217) 422–8800.

BLOOMINGTON-NORMAL
Best Inns of America,
1905 West Market Street,
Bloomington, 61701
(800) 237–8466

Best Western University Inn,
6 Traders Circle,
Normal, 61761
(309) 454–4070

Comfort Suites,
310B Greenbriar Drive,
Normal, 61761
(309) 862–1166

Holiday Inn,
8 Traders Circle,
Normal, 61761
(309) 452–8300

Jumer's Chateau,
1601 Jumer Drive,
Bloomington, 61704
(309) 662–2020

Ramada Inn Fundome,
1219 Holiday Lane,
Bloomington, 61704
(309) 662–5311

Signature Inn,
101 South Veterans
Parkway, Normal, 61761
(309) 454–4044

CLINTON
Days Inn,
Route 51,
Bypass and Kleeman
Drive, 61727
(217) 935–4140

DECATUR
Shelton Inn,
450 East Pershing
Road, 62526
(217) 877–7255

Country Inn
and Suites Hotel,
5150 Hickory Point
Frontage Road, 62526
(217) 872–2402

Fairfield Inn,
1417 Hickory Point
Drive, 62526
(217) 875–3337

Holiday Inn
Conference Hotel,
Route 36 and Wyckles
Road, 62526
(217) 422–8800

Ramada Limited,
355 Hickory Point
Road, 62526
(800) 272–6232

FINDLAY
Inn at Eagle Creek Resort,
Eagle Creek State
Park, 62534
(217) 756–3456

SHELBYVILLE
Shelbyville Historic
House and Inn,
816 West Main
Street, 62565
(800) 342–9978

SPRINGFIELD
Best Inns of America,
500 North First
Street, 62702
(800) 237–8466

Selected Visitors Bureaus and Chambers of Commerce

Illinois Bureau of Tourism/Travel Information,
(800) 2–CONNECT

Bloomington–Normal Area
Convention and Visitors Bureau,
210 South East Street, Bloomington, 61701
(800) 433–8226

Collinsville Convention and Visitors Bureau,
1 Gateway Drive, Collinsville, 62234
(800) 289–2388

Decatur Area Convention and Visitors Bureau,
202 East North Street, Decatur, 62523
(800) 331–4479

Springfield Convention and Visitors Bureau,
109 North Seventh Street, Springfield, 62701
(800) 545–7300

Best Western Lincoln
Plaza Hotel,
101 East Adams
Street, 62701
(217) 523–5661

Capital Plaza Hotel,
418 East Jefferson
Street, 62701
(800) 448–3635

Comfort Suites,
2620 South Dirksen
Parkway, 62703
(217) 753–4000

Crowne Plaza Springfield,
3100 South Dirksen
Parkway, 62703
(800) 2–CROWNE

Holiday Inn East,
3100 South Dirksen
Parkway, 62703
(217) 529–7171

Mansion View Inn
and Suites,
529 South 4th
Street, 62701
(800) 252–1083

Pear Tree Inn,
3190 South Dirksen
Parkway, 62703
(800) 282–8733

Renaissance Springfield,
701 East Adams
Street, 62701
(217) 544–8800

Springfield Hilton Hotel,
700 East Adams
Street, 62701
(217) 789–1530

**PLACES TO EAT IN
CENTRAL ILLINOIS**

BLOOMINGTON
Central Station Cafe,
220 East Front
Street, 61701
(309) 828–2323

Jim's Steak House,
2307 East Washington
Street, 61704
(309) 663–4142

COLLINSVILLE
Maggie's,
2102 North Keebler
Road, 62234
(618) 344–8283

LINCOLN
Tropics,
1007 Hickox Drive, 62656
(217) 732–6710

SPRINGFIELD
Baur's,
620 South First
Street, 62704
(217) 789–4311

Heritage House,
3851 South 6th
Street, 62704
(217) 529–5571

Maldaner's,
222 South 6th
Street, 62701
(217) 522–4313

**OTHER ATTRACTIONS
WORTH SEEING IN
CENTRAL ILLINOIS**

Beer Nuts Products,
Bloomington

Miller Park Zoo,
Bloomington

Prairie Aviation Museum,
Bloomington

Children's Museum
of Illinois, Decatur

Scovill Zoo,
Decatur

Andersen Prairie, Pana

Daughters of Union
Veterans of the
Civil War Museum,
Springfield

Dana-Thomas State
Historic Site, Springfield

Illinois State Capitol,
Springfield

Illinois State Museum,
Springfield

Lincoln National Home
State Historic Site,
Springfield

Lincoln Memorial Garden,
Springfield

Old State Capitol
State Historic Site,
Springfield

Oliver Parks
Telephone Museum,
Springfield

Washington Park
Botanical Gardens,
Springfield

Western Illinois

River Towns

The most impressive feature of Quincy, a river town on the east bank of the Mississippi River, is its architecture. Stately mansions and fine old commercial buildings of Italianate, Greek Revival, Romanesque, Queen Anne, Prairie, and Moorish designs fill the town.

The **John Wood Mansion,** 425 South Twelfth Street, 62301, is an example of Greek Revival architecture. The home was built in 1835 by John Wood, founder of Quincy and a former governor of Illinois. Take an escorted tour of the restored home and see the audiovisual presentation. The **Osage Orangerie Gift Shop** is on the premises and offers handcrafted items reminiscent of the early nineteenth century.

The fourteen-room mansion is listed in the National Register of Historic Places. It was originally located across Twelfth Street, but Wood had the house moved to its present site in 1864.

On display are furnishings and many personal items of the Wood family as well as objects recalling Adams County's history. Included are a Victorian dollhouse, the first piano in Quincy, Quincy-made stoves, a table used by Abraham Lincoln, a chandelier from a Mississippi River steamboat, and a sunstone from the Mormon Temple in Nauvoo.

> **Western Illinois Trivia**
>
> *Abe Lincoln's "lost love," Ann Rutledge, is buried in a cemetery just outside Petersburg.*

Museum hours are 1:00 to 4:00 P.M. daily. Other times by appointment. Admission is $2.00 for adults, $1.00 for students; (217) 222–1835.

The **Quincy Museum** is housed in the Newcomb Stillwell Mansion. Built in 1891, it is listed in the National Register of Historic Places. The exterior has leafy carved ornamentation and window transom bars of solid stone. Building materials of contrasting colors and textures enhance its bold facade and forceful design. It is an example

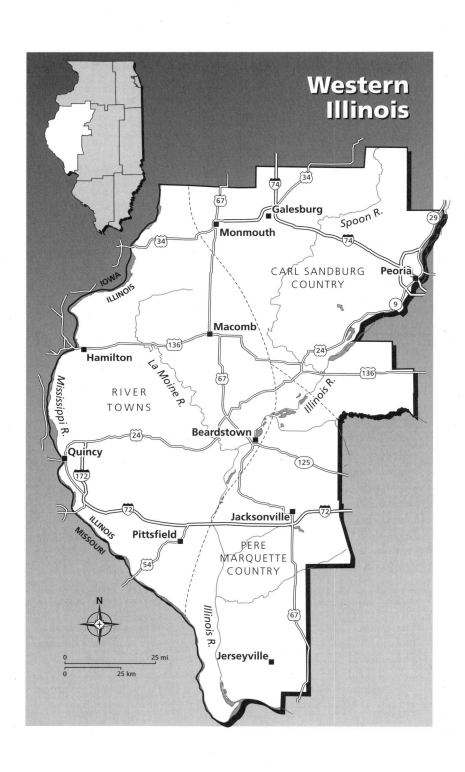

AUTHOR'S TOP TEN PICKS

1. *New Salem State Historic Site,* Petersburg, *(217) 632–7363*
2. *Wildlife Prairie Park,* Peoria, *(309) 676–0998*
3. *Village of Elsah,* *(800) 266–3228*
4. *Père Marquette State Park,* Grafton, *(618) 786–2331*
5. *St. Francis Monastery,* Peoria, *(309) 688–0094*
6. *Hobson's Bluffdale,* Eldred, *(217) 983–2854*
7. *Nauvoo,* *(217) 453–2237*
8. *Carl Sandburg Birthplace State Historic Site,* Galesburg, *(309) 342–2361*
9. *Villa Katherine,* Quincy, *(217) 224–3688*
10. *Wyatt Earp Birthplace Historic House Museum,* Monmouth, *(309) 734–6419*

typical of American architectural style of the late 1800s.

The museum exhibits a collection of Indian relics, clothing, weapons, and accessories. There are also African safari trophies and a large collection of fossils, seashells, and butterflies.

In the special discovery area, children can touch museum objects and learn through observation and creative activities. A miniature circus for children, the work of the late Milton Kalmer of Quincy, contains virtually every element of an old-fashioned circus—tiny circus animals, clowns, acrobats, a train, a band with musical instruments, and circus-goers in the stands.

The museum is located at 1601 Maine Street, Quincy 62301; (217) 224–7669. Hours are Tuesday through Sunday 1:00 to 5:00 P.M. Guided tours are available. Admission is $2.00 for adults, $1.00 for students, and free for children under five.

The *Villa Katherine,* 532 Gardner Expressway, 62301; (217) 223–1000, is a Moorish-style castle. It is located on a bluff overlooking the Mississippi River and is listed in the National Register of Historic Places. The visitors center is open daily 10:00 A.M. to 4:00 P.M. Admission is $2.00 for adults, $1.00 for children.

And the *Quincy Art Center* is located on the grounds of the *Lorenzo Bull Home,* 1515 Jersey Street, 62301. The Carriage House was designed by Joseph Lyman Silsbee, a prominent Chicago architect and mentor of Frank Lloyd Wright. The center contains a permanent collection of paintings, sculpture, and graphics, and a library of art books and periodicals. It also has temporary and traveling exhibits. Hours are 1:00 to 4:00 P.M. Tuesday through Sunday. No admission fee, but donations gratefully accepted. Call (217) 223–5900.

Quincy has a number of other museums that are worth visiting. The *Quinsippi Island Antique Auto Museum* is located in Quincy's All-American Park on the banks of the Mississippi River. Sixty-five antique cars and related displays make up the exhibit. The museum's collection includes a 1917 Chevrolet Royal Mail Roadster, a 1911 Little, a St.

FF THE BEATEN PATH

Louis–built Diana, a 1901 Columbia Electric, a Ford Roadster pickup featured in television's *Hee Haw,* and a horse-drawn hearse.

The museum is located at Front and Cedar Streets; (217) 223–4846. Hours are 11:00 A.M. to 5:00 P.M. Sunday and by appointment. Admission is $1.00 for adults, twelve and under 50 cents. The group rate is 75 cents per person.

The **Gardner Museum of Architecture and Design** is in the Old Public Library Building built in 1888. At Fourth and Maine Streets, it is open from 1:00 to 5:00 P.M. Tuesday through Sunday. The museum contains stained-glass windows from Quincy churches, photographs, and examples of terra-cotta, metal, fine woodwork, and other ornamentation from early Quincy homes. Admission is $2.00 for adults, $1.00 for seniors, and 50 cents for students; (217) 224–6873.

All Wars Museum, 1701 North Twelfth Street, 62301, (217) 222–8641, displays military memorabilia with a military library and films. It is on the grounds of the Illinois Veterans Home, one of the nation's largest. Tours are by appointment only; admission is free.

The **Lincoln-Douglas Valentine Museum,** 101 North Fourth Street, 62301; (217) 224–3355, has a unique collection of old and unusual valentines on exhibit. It is open 10:00 A.M. to 2:00 P.M. Monday through Friday. Admission is free.

Quincy's public square at the center of the uptown historical district was originally called John's Square, honoring the United States president for

Eagle Eyes

*O*ne of my favorite times to visit the Quad Cities area is mid-January during Rock Island's Bald Eagle Days. I put on some warm winter clothing, insulated boots, hat and gloves, and bring along a pair of binoculars, then head to the fields along the Mississippi River to look for traces of America's national symbol.

According to the U.S. Army Corps of Engineers, which operates a series of dams on the river (keeping open winter waters in which eagles can feed), as many as 1,500 bald eagles winter between Minneapolis and St. Louis.

A lot of these magnificent birds can be found here. Watch as they swoop over the Mississippi in search of prey, then dive down with talons exposed to snatch an unsuspecting fish right out of the water, only to carry their catch to aeries located high in trees hugging the river.

There may be no more exciting sight in the Midwest's natural winter world.

whom both Adams County and Quincy were named. The square became *Washington Square* in 1857. One year later it was the site of the sixth senatorial debate between Lincoln and Douglas. The spot is marked by a commemorative plaque sculpted by Lorado Taft in 1935.

The *Clat Adams General Store* at 200 Front Street, 62301, was once a favorite haunt of river men, and it is still open to the public. The *Quincy Levee* has steamboats for moonlight excursions and runs daily trips to Hannibal, Missouri, in the summer. Several warehouses and buildings along the levee are from the steamboat era.

Riverview Park on the northeast corner of Quincy, overlooking the Mississippi River, has a statue of George Rogers Clark. This was the site of the Black Hawk War skirmish in Quincy. In *Woodland Cemetery,* South Fifth Street, is a Soldier's Monument dedicated to Adams County men killed in the Civil War, along with the grave of John Wood.

Quincy celebrates its *Annual Dogwood Festival* the first week in May. Festivities include a parade, crafts fair, and military band concert along with the sight of all the dogwood trees in bloom. For a list of events and times, contact the Quincy Chamber of Commerce at (217) 222–7980.

Pittsfield, the county seat of Pike County, was a genuine transplant of New England culture when it was founded in 1833. The settlers came from Pittsfield, Massachusetts, and purchased the site from the federal government for $200.

Pork packing became the chief local industry, and Pittsfield now has the distinction of being the "Pork Capital of the World," with 400,000 to 500,000 hogs marketed there annually. Pittsfield and Pike County residents celebrate *Pig Days* with a day of activities and pork sandwiches and a pork chop dinner. The festival is held during the summer, and the Chamber of Commerce is happy to supply information. Write the chamber at P.O. Box 283, Pittsfield 62363, or call (217) 285–2971.

Pittsfield also has a *Fall Festival* in September that signals the beginning of the harvest season. Again, the Chamber of Commerce has information.

One of the sights to see in Pittsfield is the *home of John Nicolay,* Abraham Lincoln's private secretary. The home is now owned by a private citizen but can be viewed from the street. Nicolay collaborated with John Hay, a personal friend of Lincoln's, in writing a biography of the president. The house is at 500 West Washington Street, 62301.

The home of town philanthropist William Ross no longer stands, but a marker designates the site near the city limits. Ross's mansion was destroyed by fire in 1896. Abraham Lincoln was an overnight guest here when he debated with Stephen A. Douglas in Pittsfield in 1858.

The *Lewis M. Grigsby, Sr., Home,* 830 East Washington Street, 62301, was built by Colonel Ross's daughter, Mrs. Earl Grigsby, and her friend

Fountain of Youth

*T*here was a time in Illinois history when people came from all parts of the Midwest to take advantage of waters known for their alleged wonderful curative powers. The legendary medicinal value of the region's springwater was thought to cure everything from skin conditions to ulcers.

Today you can see for yourself when visiting Siloam Springs State Park, boasting 3,300 acres of pristine natural beauty, to say nothing of its "sparkling water" lake, surrounded by dense forests dotted with wildflowers in the spring.

Can these waters still cure what's ailing you? Depends. If you're looking for a natural way to reduce stress and tension, then I guess a stay at this state park and a splash in these "curative waters" will do the trick just fine. Call (217) 894–6205.

Mrs. F. M. Lewis, Sr., in 1930. Six generations of the Ross family have resided in Pittsfield, and four generations have lived in this house.

The historic **East School** has recently been restored and is listed in the National Register of Historic Places. The building, built in 1966, is now a museum and a John Wood Community College Learning Center. The building was designed by architect John M. Van Osdel, the "grandfather of Illinois architecture," and includes a renovated clock tower. This building is one of two remaining examples of Osdel's work.

The local community theater group, the **Pittsfield Theatre Guild,** presents five productions a year and is based in the school building. The Chamber of Commerce has information.

There is no record of Abraham Lincoln having served in the **Pike County Courthouse,** but nearly 500 documents of cases associated with Lincoln were found in the courthouse. The courthouse is open Monday through Friday 8:00 A.M. to 4:00 P.M.

Griggsville is the "Purple Martin Capital of the World." These purple birds are the largest of the swallows, which feed only on flying insects, thus cleaning the air of millions of insects every day.

Purple Martin Junction is a ten-acre complex on Route 107 at the south end of Griggsville. A factory that makes aluminum martin houses and an experimental martin colony are on the grounds as is Nature House. The best time to view the martins at Purple Martin Junction is from May to July. Hours are 8:00 A.M. to noon, and 1:00 to 5:00 P.M. Monday through Friday. For information call (217) 833–2393.

Griggsville may seem an unusual spot for a spice factory, but owner Wayne Riley got his start raising cattle and hogs and found that a tasty mix of seasonings did wonders for a roast. He bottles about six tons of his secret recipe when he isn't preparing hog roasts throughout the Midwest. Contact Riley's Seasoning and Spices, R.R. 2, Box 17, Griggsville 62340; (217) 833–2207.

Anybody who travels in western Illinois soon discovers that the geography of the region is dominated by the Mississippi River. Especially in far western Illinois, the winding channels of the Mississippi and the high, tree-studded bluffs that line its shores provide great vistas for off-the-beaten-path wanderers, especially along the Great River Road, a National Scenic Byway that is marked by large green signs.

And once you head to the southern reaches of the western portion of Illinois, you start to arrive at the beginnings of the Ozark Plateau, covered with dense forests, hills that stack up to more than 1,000 feet high, and deep limestone and sandstone canyons.

But you'll learn more about this magnificent and undiscovered part of Illinois in later chapters.

Western Illinois Trivia

Pine Lakes Camping and Fishing Resort, 1½ miles north of U.S. Highway 36 near Pittsfield, has camping facilities that include water and electric hookups, laundromat, camp store, recreation room, paddleboat rental, rowboats, bathhouse, and snack bar. Enjoy swimming with attendants on duty, fishing in a forty-five-acre lake, horseshoe pits, hayrides, and a playground.

Besides campgrounds, six two-bedroom cottages are available for rent. Contact Pine Lakes Resort, R.R. 3, Box 130A, Pittsfield 62363; (217) 285–6719.

Pike County has its share of natural beauty. Bound by the Mississippi River on the west and the Illinois River on the east, it has rolling countryside and majestic bluffs. Streams, ponds, and small lakes abound for fishing, boating, and swimming. Hunting and camping are also plentiful.

The town of Barry's business district is a turn-of-the-century architectural delight due to a fire in 1894 that caused the town to be rebuilt. The **Barry Museum,** established in 1984, is housed in the local library and is open year-round by appointment only; (217) 335–2149.

Now a trading center for coal mining and a grain- and fruit-growing region, Rushville began as a tiny wilderness village of twelve families in 1825. It was named for a famous Philadelphia surgeon, Dr. Benjamin Rush. It has stayed a small town with only 3,348 residents.

The community is rich in nineteenth-century history. During the Black Hawk War, Abraham Lincoln and his troops camped near Rushville. It is believed that in 1844 Governor Ford left Springfield with a company of militia and camped overnight in the town square. A tablet in the center of the town square reads, ABRAHAM LINCOLN ADDRESSED THE PEOPLE OF RUSHVILLE ON OCTOBER 20TH, 1858. Lincoln also practiced law in the county courthouse that once stood on this spot.

When Stephen A. Douglas came to Rushville to speak in the senatorial campaign of 1858, his followers arranged a welcome that would be remembered in the town's history. They borrowed a cannon from the nearby community of Beardston, brought it over to the town square, and loaded it with a heavy charge of powder and wet scraps of leather. When the salute to Douglas was fired, the cannon was blown into pieces; miraculously, no one was hurt.

The **Schuyler County Courthouse** dates back to 1881. It is a two-story building of faded brick and topped with a square clock tower. The cornerstone is dated according to the Masonic calendar and reads June 24 A.L. 5881. The first county building was a log cabin on the north side of the square. In 1829 it was replaced by a plain unornamented brick building, which served until the present courthouse was built on the corner of Lafayette and Congress Streets.

The *Schuyler-Brown County Historical Society* at 200 South Congress, 62681 (on U.S. Highway 24, just a block from the courthouse corner) displays genealogical materials and the history of Schuyler and Brown Counties. The center of the building is an old jailhouse. A collection of undertakers' sticks, used to measure the deceased for custom-built coffins, is on display. The society's museum is open daily 1:00 to 5:00 P.M. March through November, and on Sunday the rest of the year.

At the same location is the *Jail Museum,* open daily 1:00 to 5:00 P.M. April 1 to November 1. Winter hours are Saturday and Sunday 1:00 to 5:00 P.M. Admission is free. The museum is open at other times by appointment only. Special exhibits change monthly. Call (217) 322–6975 for more information about these museums.

Tasty souvenirs are to be found at *Bartlow Brothers Meats,* (217) 322–3365. The retail store next to the plant sells heavenly honey-cured hams, bacon, sausages, and a local specialty, Korn Top Wieners.

Scripps Park was formerly the eighty-acre farm of Edward Wyllis Scripps, founder of the Scripps-Howard newspaper chain. The park was given to the town in 1922 by Scripps and his two sisters, Virginia and Ellen Browning Scripps. The latter contributed the $100,000 to build the *Community House* that marks the site of the Scripps homestead, the birthplace of Edward Wyllis Scripps. The park is located outside of Rushville, southwest of the junction of U.S. Highway 67 and U.S. Highway 24; (217) 322–3028.

Founded in 1899, *Western Illinois University,* 900 West Adams, 61455, is an important landmark in Macomb and throughout the western part of the state; (309) 295–1414. Over 13,000 students attend the institution.

On campus is the *Western Museum,* on the third floor of Sherman Hall. Its collections feature Civil War memorabilia, American Indian costumes, antique farm implements, and historical materials from the region. Open by appointment only; (309) 298–1727. Free.

If you've got a green thumb, or need to develop one, you'll enjoy the *WIU Greenhouse* at 316 Wagner Hall on campus; (309) 298–1004. The 4,500-square-foot space houses an international collection of plants used in classroom analysis.

The *university library* is known for its unusual pinwheel floor design and a six-story atrium with exhibits and displays throughout. Housing more than 60,000 volumes, it ranks among the top ten largest libraries in the country for nondoctoral degree-granting universities.

On the square in downtown Macomb, the stately *old brick courthouse* is worth a visit, too. Built in the summer of 1872 at a cost of $155,370, the recently renovated building still serves as the center of government. For that matter, there's plenty of history in Macomb. To begin with, the city, founded in 1830, is itself named after Gen. Alexander Macomb, a hero of the War of 1812.

The *Clarence Watson/Wiley Schoolhouse Museum,* 301 West Calhoun, 61455, is a restored 1877 one-room schoolhouse, evocative of the days of pigtails and inkwells. Open 8:30 A.M. to 4:30 P.M. Monday through Friday. It's on the grounds of the United Way. Call (309) 837–9180.

Western Illinois Trivia
G. W. Gale Ferris, who built the world's largest entertainment ride (which still bears his name) for the 1893 World's Columbian Exposition in Chicago, lived in Galesburg.

Home of the McDonough County Preservation Society is the *Old Bailey House,* an 1887 Eastlake-style residence at 100 South Campbell, 61455, built by the founder of Macomb's Union National Bank.

Theatergoers have various options. The *Pat Crane Memorial Playhouse* is a popular community theater, with productions running from September through May. Call (309) 837–1828 for ticket information. The playhouse is on St. Francis Road, 2 miles south of Macomb. Western Illinois University has its own *Summer Music Theater* at Brown Hall; (309) 298–1543.

Argyle Lake State Park, 7 miles west of Macomb and 2 miles north of Colchester off U.S. Highway 136, has 1,148 acres of recreational land within its boundaries, including the ninety-five-acre Argyle Lake. Interestingly, the State Department of Conservation in 1970 showed a remarkable sense of doing a job right when, after twenty years of poor fishing, the department simply drained the whole lake to remove undesirable species, and restocked it with the fish the department wanted. The park takes its name from a group of early settlers of Scottish descent, who called the area Argyle Hollow. The old Galena-to-Beardstown stagecoach passed through here in the early 1800s. Today the park offers visitors picnicking, boating, fishing (for bluegill, largemouth bass, crappie, and channel catfish), camping (electrical outlets available), hiking, and a summer interpretive program. Boats and canoes can be rented. The park is open year-round, and winter brings cross-country skiing, snowmobiling trails, ice skating, and sledding. For more information contact the Site Superintendent, R.R. 2, Colchester 62326; (309) 776–3422.

Hancock County, at the western edge of the state where the Mississippi turns and bends its way around Illinois's bulging middle, has a rich and colorful history inextricably linked with the Mormon religion. It was here, at Nauvoo and Carthage, that some of the most significant—and tragic—chapters of Mormon history were written.

What was once the site of Sauk and Fox Indian villages, had come by the 1830s to be a sleepy river village known as Commerce. After being driven out of Missouri in the spring of 1839, church founder Joseph Smith brought his followers here, to the place he called Nauvoo, to create a homeland for his people. By special negotiation with the Illinois Legislature, the group obtained a charter that allowed its members extraordinary powers—their own courts, militia, university—and any other authority not prohibited by the United States or Illinois constitutions. Nauvoo became virtually an autonomous state. With Mormon converts arriving from across the country and from overseas, the town grew to be Illinois's largest, with 8,000 homes and a population of 15,000 by 1842.

Discontent with the leaders' power grew within and outside of the church. When a group of dissidents published an anti-establishment newspaper with views critical of the leadership, the paper was shut down. For that, Joseph Smith and his brother, Hyrum, were jailed at the county seat, Carthage. An anti-Mormon mob stormed the jail and murdered the two churchmen. Brigham Young took control of the group and led it west to Utah in 1846.

Nauvoo was abandoned until 1849, when a group of French communalists, the Icarians, arrived from Texas to practice their own brand of philosophy under their leader, Etienne Cabet. Their experiment lasted until 1856. During their tenancy, however, they began the production of wine and cheese.

Today groups associated with branches of the Mormon church have extensively restored Nauvoo and the old Carthage jail. The ***Nauvoo Restoration Visitor Center*** at Young and Main Streets includes a historical exhibit and a short film on the early days of the community. Admission is free. Call for hours (217) 453–2237. Just outside the center is a sculpture garden, the ***Monument to Women.***

Some of the historic homes and shops open to visit in Nauvoo are the **Brigham Young Home**; the Mormon newspaper office of the *Times and Seasons;* the Joseph Smith Mansion; Jonathan Browning's gunsmith shop; and the Clark store. Many have guides and period craft demonstrations. The historic homes are open from 9:00 A.M. to 6:00 P.M. in the summer and from 9:00 A.M. to 5:00 P.M. in the winter. Visit around mid-August and enjoy the annual **City of Joseph Smith Pageant**—an outdoor musical event, handsomely costumed and well performed.

Also in Nauvoo be sure to visit the **Joseph Smith Historic Center,** on Water Street off Route 96. Here there is a film, a history of the town, and a walking tour to the log cabin homestead where Smith first lived and the family cemetery.

On the hill overlooking the river plain where the temple community grew are the ruins of Smith's **Great Temple.** The Nauvoo Chamber of Commerce Tourist Reception Center, on Route 96 in the center of town, has a self-guided cassette tape tour and maps of the area available. Open daily 9:00 A.M. to 5:00 P.M. April through October; (217) 453–6648.

Illinois's Mormon Legacies

The name, Nauvoo, given to the settlement by Prophet Joseph Smith, who led his Mormon followers here in 1839, means beautiful place in Old Hebrew. But many of the historical memories here are anything but beautiful.

You can almost feel the ghosts in historic Nauvoo. More than 15,000 people lived here by 1842. But when a schism developed within the ranks of the religious leaders, discontent grew. And when the community's special city charter was repealed, armed clashes broke out.

In nearby Carthage, leader Joseph Smith and his brother, Hyrum, were killed by a mob of anti-Mormons, a sentiment that was growing steadily on the Illinois prairie. So Brigham Young assumed control, and led the

population to its final westward destination in Utah.

The people left by wagon, handcart— and some walked. Houses were left abandoned. Even the great temple, on which construction had begun in 1841 and which was almost completed, was abandoned. (Eventually it was burned by an arsonist.)

Nauvoo became a ghost city of 8,000 houses and no people.

In 1849, a group of French communalists called Icarians came to the deserted Nauvoo from Texas to make their attempt at communal living. That experiment lasted until 1856.

Yes, there are lots of ghosts in Nauvoo. Sometimes you can hear them whispering in the prairie wind.

Nearby, the **Nauvoo State Park** features a museum operated by the Nauvoo Historical Society. Camping, a playground, a picnic area, and a stocked fishing lake are also available at the park. For more information contact the Site Superintendent, Nauvoo State Park, P.O. Box 337, Nauvoo 62354; (217) 453–2512.

Labor Day weekend marks the annual **Nauvoo Grape Festival**, (217) 453–6600, with tastings of the local blue cheese and wine, some of the area's best souvenirs. Stop by **Baxter's Winery** on East Parley Street, (217) 453–2528, for tours and tastings. It's recently been reopened by members of the family who've owned the historic winery since the 1800s. Throughout the year, some delightful tastes come from the kitchen of the **Hotel Nauvoo**. The hotel, once a private home, dates from the Mormon period around 1840. In addition to the restaurant, where dinner prices range from $7.00 to $14.00, there are a limited number of overnight accommodations; a double costs $49.50 and up. At 1290 Mulholland, 62354; (217) 453–2211.

In Carthage the old jail, which once held Joseph and Hyrum Smith, is at 307 Walnut Street, 62354.

Also of interest is the **Hancock County Courthouse**, a Greek Revival structure that's one of the prettiest in the state. It was here, on October 2, 1858, that Abraham Lincoln addressed a crowd of 6,000 in his senatorial campaign against Stephen A. Douglas. A stone marker commemorates the event.

The **Kibbe-Hancock Museum**, across from the old jail on Walnut Street, is the personal collection of a former biology professor at the now-closed Carthage College. In addition, area residents have contributed their treasures. The collection includes Civil War relics, World War II memorabilia, Indian artifacts, fossils and rocks, and a natural history exhibit. Free. Call (217) 357–3119 for hours.

Along the western edge of the county, the **Great River Road** runs next to the Mississippi, providing dramatic views and scenic photographic opportunities. In the winter months, from early November through early March, scores of bald eagles roost in the vicinity. January is the best time for observation around the open waters below Lock and Dam No. 19 near Hamilton. From sunrise to around 10:00 A.M. is the best time to catch the eagles feeding. The **Alice Kibbe Life Science Field Station** of Western Illinois University on the Hamilton-Warsaw Road is open for nature observation and hiking at most times of the year. Hank Courtois, resident manager of the station, is available by appointment from 8:00 A.M. to 5:00 P.M. to explain the eagle's natural environment. Call (217) 256–4519.

Carl Sandburg Country

alesburg is a city that retains the flavor of the nineteenth century through its architecture. The city is so proud of its treasures that it has published six walking tours, thirty to forty-five minutes each, that take you through the historic districts, pointing out buildings and telling tales of Galesburg's history. Walking tours are available through the Illinois Department of Tourism or from the Galesburg Area Convention and Visitors Bureau, 154 East Simmons Street, 61401; (309) 343–1194.

In the mid-1830s George Washington Gale, Galesburg's founding father, came to the area to create a labor collective similar to the Oneida Institute of Science and Industry, a collective he founded in New York. Galesburg began as a religious colony under Gale's leadership, and in June 1836, 560 acres were allocated for the town and 104 acres for a college. By the end of the first year, forty families were established in Galesburg.

Railroads were the mainstay of the town. In 1854 the first train, called Reindeer, came to Galesburg. The railroads allowed for area produce to be shipped to other markets and employed a major portion of the town's workforce. By 1880 the town had quadrupled in size and had grown in prosperity as evidenced by the many large Victorian homes here.

Galesburg's public square was the starting point for commerce in the town. The first general store was established at the northwest corner of Broad and Main Streets. The square was traversed by trolley tracks and was proposed as the site of the courthouse or post office. But, after 140 years the square still remains an open, grassy area.

Galeburg's most prominent citizen was Carl Sandburg, noted poet, socialist, biographer, historian, minstrel, and lover of humanity. He lived in Galesburg until he was twenty-four years old. ***Sandburg's birthplace,*** 331 East Third Street, 61401, the second house east of the Chicago, Burlington, and Quincy Railroad tracks, is now a museum. The house is a three-room cottage bought by August Sandburg, Carl's father, in the fall of 1873. A neighboring house is open as a visitors center housing Sandburg exhibits and memorabilia. The museum is open June 1 through Labor Day, 10:00 A.M. to 4:00 P.M. Tuesday through Sunday. Call to arrange a tour during the rest of the year; (309) 342–9400.

Carl Sandburg Park is located behind the birthplace. Legend says that Sandburg was so taken with the spot's beauty that he requested it be his final resting place.

In 1966 a memorial named ***Remembrance Rock,*** after Sandburg's only novel, was erected here. The memorial is a large, red granite boulder unearthed during highway construction northeast of Galesburg. It is a glacial remnant and product of the prairie.

Sandburg's ashes were placed beneath Remembrance Rock in 1967. Ten years later his wife, Lilian Paula Sandburg, was buried beside him.

The house is located in the southwest section of Galesburg. Enter Galesburg via the Main Street off I–74 and follow directional signs through the town. For more information or group appointments, call (309) 342–2361. Museum hours are 9:00 A.M. to 5:00 P.M. daily; closed New Year's, Thanksgiving, and Christmas days.

Another worthwhile sidetrip is the ***Galesburg Railroad Museum*** at South Seminary and Mulberry Streets. The museum houses a Pullman parlor car, locomotive #3006, and caboose #13501 among other railroad memorabilia. The museum was once the Burlington Northern Depot. Tours of the trains are available during Railroad Days.

Galesburg holds an annual national ***Stearman Fly-In*** every September. Stearmans are the biplane trainers that gave wings to more military pilots than any other aircraft series in the world. The celebration lasts five days with commercial exhibits, mini-air shows, Stearman contests, aerobatic competition, short-field takeoff, flour-bombing, spot landing, and formation flying contests. For information call the Galesburg Area Convention and Visitors Bureau, (309) 343–1194.

Carl Sandburg Birthplace

Railroad Days is another yearly event in Galesburg. Railroad memorabilia, a street fair, and a carnival are part of the festivities. There are also tours of Galesburg's historic sites. Railroad Days is always the fourth weekend in June. For more information contact the Galesburg Area Convention and Visitors Bureau, 154 East Simmons Street, Galesburg 61401; (309) 343–1194.

The Seminary Street Historic Commercial District on Seminary Street in downtown Galesburg is 2 blocks of restored, turn-of-the-century buildings that house specialty shops and restaurants. For information call the Seminary Street Ltd. office at (309) 342–7061.

And yet another Galesburg annual event is the *Heritage Festival* in August. A tram tour through the historic district features shops with "ghosts" from the past. Also featured are old-time craft demonstrations, entertainment, and a Civil War battle reenactment. For information call (309) 344–2839.

The Orpheum Theater, 57 South Kellogg Street, 61401, first opened in 1916 as William J. Olson's vision to raise the public's perception of the meaning of the word "theater" to a level never imagined by local builders and audiences of the time. Employing the Chicago architectural firm of C. W. & George L. Rapp, whose philosophy was that a theater should be "a shrine to democracy where the wealthy rub elbows with the poor," Olson created a perfect microcosm of nineteenth-century eclectic architecture. The Orpheum was billed as a vaudeville house and hosted such stars as Jack Benny, George Burns, Houdini, and Fanny Brice. Converted to a movie theater by the late 1970s, the Orpheum was forced to close down in 1982 due to high operating costs. The theater is now renovated and is a not-for-profit community performing arts center. For a schedule of events, call (309) 342–2299.

Knox College, Cherry and South Streets, (309) 343–0112, was built in 1857 and has been described as "a monument to the vision of the founding fathers of both the college and city." *Old Main,* the administration building, was restored and stabilized during the 1930s. It is registered as a national landmark and is an example of American Gothic Revival architecture. Old Main is the only building left standing where Lincoln and Douglas debated in 1858. Hours are 8:00 A.M. to 4:00 P.M.

Knox County Scenic Drive through the Spoon River Valley is a self-guided driving tour when the surrounding countryside is transformed by Mother Nature's autumn palette into a kaleidoscope of colors. The first two weekends in October are a festival with music, flea markets, arts and crafts, exhibits, and good country cooking. For information call the Galesburg Area Convention and Visitors Bureau.

For fans of old TV westerns, the most important sightseeing stop in the county is surely the house in Monmouth in which Wyatt Earp was born on March 19, 1848; 406 South Third Street, 61462. Earp's birthplace is now a small museum with period furniture. Open 1:00 to 4:00 P.M. Sunday, Memorial Day through Labor Day or by appointment; (309) 734–6419. A memorial to Earp stands in **Monmouth Park.** Although he found a final resting place in California, many of his relatives are buried in Monmouth's **Pioneer Cemetery** on East Archer near Fifth Street. In fact a walk around the old cemetery gives you some historical perspective on the town, which was founded in 1831.

A county landmark is **Monmouth College,** established in 1853 by a group of Scottish Presbyterians who pioneered the settlement of this part of the state. The campus has many attractive brick buildings in the Greek Revival style. The white-framed **Holt House,** at 402 East First Avenue, 61462, is the birthplace of Pi Beta Phi Sorority. Architecture buffs will also enjoy a drive down **East Broadway,** where the homes bring memories of a more gracious period. Historic district status for the area is being pursued.

A-OK at the O.K. Corral

*O*n October 26, 1881, Wyatt Earp marched down the streets of Tombstone, Arizona, with his brothers Virgil, Morgan, and notorious gunman Doc Holliday to have it out with so-called cattle rustlers.

All hell broke loose at a livery stable on the outskirts of town. But that fifteen-second shootout, immediately labeled the Gunfight at the O.K. Corral, may be the most celebrated shoot-em-up of the Wild West era.

Every year in early June, visitors to this tiny western Illinois town get to see a reenactment of the famed gunfight

that sealed Wyatt Earp's name in the logs of western lore; it's called Wyatt Earp's Birthday Celebration. And be careful what you say about Earp around these parts, pardner. Several Earp relatives still live in the town where Wyatt was born.

Of course, if you miss the June bash, you'll get to see the O.K. Corral gunfight again in October, when the Earp Birthplace Historic House Museum commemorates the celebrated shootout. There'll even be an Earp look-alike contest. Start growing those mustaches now.

In front of the castlelike 1895 "Richardsonian Romanesque" county courthouse in Monmouth stands a *statue of Gen. Abner C. Harding,* a hero at the second battle of Fort Donaldson during the Civil War.

And though Dixon claims the title as Ronald Reagan's boyhood home, Monmouth, too, shares the honor, for the family lived here briefly during the former president's early years, at 218 South Seventh Street (now a private residence).

Western Stoneware Company, 521 Sixth Avenue, 61462; (309) 734–2161, is the oldest maker of pottery and stoneware in the Midwest. The maple-leaf emblem that appeared on Western Stoneware's jugs and crocks produced here came from Monmouth's epithet as Maple City (especially well-earned in the fall when the city's thousands of maple trees are ablaze with color). Though no factory tours are available, the retail outlet, *The Pottery Barn,* located at U.S. Highway 34 and U.S. Highway 67, is open daily. Hours are 9:30 A.M. to 4:30 P.M. except Sunday, noon to 4:30 P.M.

Each year right after Labor Day, the *Warren County Prime Beef Festival* is held in Monmouth. There are livestock shows, parades, a demolition derby, and a carnival. Call (309) 734–3181 for more information.

For recreation during the warmer months, the eighteen holes of *Gibson Woods Golf Course* are open to the public. The course is adjacent to Monmouth Park on U.S. Highway 34 immediately northeast of Monmouth, (309) 734–9968.

Monmouth Airport, northeast of town on U.S. Highway 34, is the oldest continually operating airport in the state.

Out in the rural part of the county, visit the *County Historical Museum* in Roseville.

If old bones, skulls, and Indian burial grounds grab your interest, Fulton County is the place you should visit. It is one of the richest archaeological areas in the Midwest. There are 800 mounds in Fulton centered at the junction of the Spoon and Illinois Rivers. The most famous is the *Dickson Mound* near Lewiston.

The Dickson Mound is on a high bluff overlooking the two rivers. It was originally crescent-shaped with the points facing east. It measures 550 feet along its outer curve and is 35 feet high. A reproduction of one of the burials is exhibited at the Field Museum of Natural History in Chicago.

The mound is located off Route 97 and Route 78 near Havana, 5 miles south of Lewiston. Grounds are open to dusk from May 1 to November 1. Admission is free; (309) 547–3721.

For the literary-minded, Edgar Lee Masters immortalized the Spoon River Country and particularly Lewiston in his *Spoon River Anthology*. Masters's home was in Lewiston, and **Oak Hill Cemetery** on North Main Street shows many names identical to characters in the anthology. The area is also filled with interesting buildings, historic markers, and antiques shops.

The **Ross Mansion,** 409 East Milton Avenue, 61542, was the inspiration for the McNeely Mansion in the anthology. The mansion was modeled after a home on the Hudson River that Col. Lewis W. Ross admired. The New England–style home has seventeen rooms and is made of stone from the Spoon River Valley.

Maj. Newton Walker's house had the honor of having Abraham Lincoln as a guest. The home was built in 1833 and is located at 1127 North Main Street, 61542. Unfortunately, it is not open to the public.

Other places of interest in Lewiston are the **Phelps Store,** Main and Washington Streets (originally an Indian trading post), and the **Church of St. James** at Broadway and Illinois Streets, an example of Victorian Gothic architecture.

In the nearby town of Ellisville is an **opera house** from the nineteenth century, and in London Mills is the **Ross Hotel,** an authentically restored hotel.

The **Spoon River Scenic Drive,** especially dramatic in the color-filled fall, takes you through 60 miles of woodland and towns. To obtain a map from the Spoon River Scenic Drive Associates, write to them at Box 59, Ellisville 61431, or call (309) 293–2143. Special signs mark the drive.

The first two weekends in October are the **Annual Spoon River Festival.** Spoon River Country also has a **Spoon River Country Christmas Festival** the first Saturday in December. The festival offers crafts, music, dancing, and food. Contact the Spoon River Scenic Drive Associates for information.

Some of the greatest concentrations of wild ducks and geese in the nation are to be found in the **Illinois River Wildlife and Fish Refuge** in Mason County. These feathered creatures contribute to the area's reputation as a hunting and fishing paradise.

The refuge is a vital link in the chain of resting, feeding, and wintering areas for migratory birds along the Mississippi Flyway. During the annual migration ducks and geese are often so numerous their masses darken the sky.

The refuge has 4,500 acres of land and water where wild ducks and geese can be observed each fall and winter. The average peak concentration during early winter exceeds 100,000 ducks and up to 40,000 Canada, blue, and snow geese. Mallards make up most of the duck population, with smaller numbers of wood ducks, pintail, widgeon, black duck, blue-winged teal, scaup, shoveler, gadwall, goldeneye, and mergansers.

The wood duck is the most common nester in the refuge. Wood ducks normally rest in natural cavities in hardwood timber, but they have adapted to nesting boxes erected in the refuge.

Bald eagles winter in several concentrated groups here. More than 240 eagles have been counted along the river. Eagles usually arrive in October and stay until the ice disappears in the spring.

More than 275 species of birds reside in the refuge. Great blue herons, green herons, great egrets, and black-crowned night herons are generally summer residents. Marsh, water, and shorebirds are common during the spring and fall, and their migration is spectacular during August and early September.

The refuge is open to the public, and an interpretive foot trail is located in the headquarters. Roads next to portions of the refuge offer opportunities for viewing wildlife without disturbing them.

Fishing, mushroom and berry picking, and hiking are permitted. *Lake Chautauqua* is known for its bluegill, crappie, and catfish fishing, especially during April, May, and early June.

Waterfowl hunting is permitted in the Liverpool section, located outside Lake Chautauqua.

For additional information contact the Refuge Manager, Illinois River Wildlife and Fish Refuge, R.R. 2, Havana 62644; (309) 535–2290. The refuge is 8 miles northeast of Havana on the Manito blacktop. A sign marks the entrance.

The *Jack Wolf Memorial Fish Hatchery,* 4 miles west of Manito on Oil Well Road, has 160 acres within the Sand Ridge State Forest. The hatchery is named after the late Jacob John "Jake" Wolf, who was once deputy director of the Department of Conservation for the State of Illinois. Wolf is remembered as a friend of the outdoor sportsman and sportswoman. During Wolf's career as a state legislator and a member of the Department of Conservation, numerous conservation bills were passed that benefited hunting and fishing enthusiasts statewide.

The complex includes a 36,000-square-foot hatchery building, fifty-six indoor rearing tanks, spawning and egg incubation facilities, modern fish harvest, and distribution and feeding systems. Outside are twenty-two acres of solar ponds that use energy from the sun to heat water for fish production, twenty-eight rearing raceways, and seven brood raceways.

Specialties of the hatchery are chinook, coho salmon, rainbow and brown trout, walleye, muskellunge, northern pike, striped bass, bluegill, channel catfish, and large- and smallmouth bass. The fish produced at the hatchery are used to stock Lake Michigan, private farm ponds, state-owned lakes, reservoirs, streams, and rivers. Anticipated production at the hatchery is forty-two million fish a year.

Tours are on a self-guided basis, although employee-guided tours can be scheduled for large groups. Visiting hours are 8:30 A.M. to 3:30 P.M. daily; (309) 968–7531.

New Salem State Historic Site, located 2 miles south of the county seat, Petersburg, on Route 97, is a reconstruction of the village in which Lincoln lived from 1831 to 1837. Admission to the park is free.

Here homes, shops, and taverns take you back to the time when Lincoln was just beginning his political career. He served here as postmaster and deputy surveyor and was defeated for election to the Illinois General Assembly in 1832, then elected two years later.

Western Illinois Trivia

In Nauvoo, the historic first settlement in western Illinois, , you'll find millers still grinding wheat and corn for baking; there is a 140-year-old vineyard still producing wine; and the area remains famous for its homemade blue cheese.

The 1835 ***Onstot Cooper Shop*** is the only original building on the site, and it was here that Lincoln studied law books late in the night. The ***Lincoln-Berry store*** is an authentic re-creation of the general store in which Lincoln was a partner. At the ***Rutledge Tavern*** lived his first love, Ann Rutledge (who is buried in Oakland Cemetery in Petersburg).

Costumed interpreters run the shops and exhibits, so you may encounter a blacksmith at a forge, a baker taking freshly baked bread from the oven, or a candlemaker working with tallow. Oxen and other farm animals are part of the scene. Inside the park flowers and plants have been planted for historic authenticity. Vegetable gardens and herb

OFF THE BEATEN PATH

gardens are tucked behind the cabins and wild plum, blackberry, goose-berry, and other trees and shrubs add to the look of the 1830s village.

And the park's outdoor amphitheater, surrounded by tall trees, features a special Lincoln production every summer.

The park has camping facilities available on the grounds (178 camp-sites, with showers and electric hookups available). For more informa-tion contact Site Superintendent, R.R. 1, Box 244A, Petersburg 62675; (217) 632–4000.

In Petersburg at Jackson and Eighth Streets, is the **Edgar Lee Masters Memorial Home.** The poet and author of *Spoon River Anthology* lived here as a boy. Much of his work reflects the feeling of this part of Illinois. Restored to its 1875 period, the home holds memorabilia of the family and his work. Open Memorial Day through Labor Day daily afternoons only. Admission is free; (217) 632–7363. Masters is buried in the town's **Oakland Cemetery.**

Petersburg is home to a wonderful bed-and-breakfast: **Bit of Country,** 122 West Sheridan, 62659; (217) 632–3771. Bit of Country is in a restored 1868 home with a guest house.

They used to ask, "Will it play in Peoria?" These days it decidedly does. Named one of the country's "All-American" cities, and called an "in" place to live by *Business Week* magazine, Peoria's a hit.

The **George L. Luthy Botanical Gardens,** 2218 North Prospect Road, 61603; (309) 686–3362, has a rose garden with more than 800 all-American award-winning selections. The All-Seasons Garden has plants selected for their unique characteristics that provide beauty all year-round. The herb garden has plants that are pleasant to smell and add zest to culinary arts.

The conservatory is the permanent home of a collection of tropical plants and fragile specimens and the bio-center has education pro-grams, workshops, films, and seminars.

Admission to the gardens is free, and they are open from dawn to dusk. The conservatory and gift and plant shop are open Monday through Thursday 10:00 A.M. to 5:00 P.M., Friday and Saturday 10:00 A.M. to 8:00 P.M., Sunday noon to 5:00 P.M.; call for special winter hours.

The **Lakeview Museum of Arts and Sciences,** 1125 West Lake, 61614; (309) 686–7000, has antiques, archaeology, astronomy, geology, folk art, music, wildlife, and movie exhibitions. The main exhibit is "Man and Nature: The Changing Relationship." It is a multimedia program telling the story of humankind's ties with nature from prehistoric to present times.

The Decorative Art Gallery has English, French, and American furniture from the eighteenth to the twentieth centuries. Other collections include fine arts, anthropology, history, and natural sciences.

The Planetarium gives laser light concerts and has a museum shop, sales/rental gallery, and bookstore. For a listing of planetarium shows, call (309) 686–6682.

Museum hours are Tuesday through Saturday 10:00 A.M. to 5:00 P.M., Wednesday evening 7:00 to 9:00 P.M., and Sunday noon to 5:00 P.M. The museum is closed on Monday and major holidays. Admission to the museum is free; the Planetarium show is $4.00 for adults, and $2.50 for seniors and students four and up.

But Peoria's Showplace might be **Wildlife Prairie Park,** which began as a project of the Forest Park Foundation. The theme was native North American animals living in natural habitat enclosures, with other areas of the park portraying Illinois's natural history. You can watch wolf

Honest Abe's "Turkey Harvest"

*W*hy not spend Thanksgiving with Honest Abe?

Of course, back in the mid-1800s, there was no such thing as "Thanksgiving Day." In fact, Illinois's first official statewide Thanksgiving Day was held on December 29, 1842.

But Abe Lincoln, who lived in the log cabin village of New Salem from 1831–37, did celebrate a "Thanksgiving Day" of sorts.

That's because the village usually celebrated a harvest feast sometime in mid-November, which featured all kinds of goings-on, like games, music, hearty meals, dancing, and maybe even a wrestling match outside the local tavern.

And that's the kind of festival you'll enjoy during New Salem's annual Harvest Feast, held in mid-November. There'll be costumed village residents performing period crafts; period music and eat treats; kids games; even a grand military parade, which pays homage to the New Salem Militia of the 1830s, an organization whose membership was compulsory for all male residents of the villages between the ages of eighteen and forty-five.

The irony about celebrating "Thanksgiving Day" in New Salem is that Lincoln, himself, declared in 1864 that the last Thursday in November be set aside for an annual national day of thanksgiving.

You can see an 1872 wind-powered grinding mill with the original grist stones and wooden gears still intact in Golden.

packs roam the park; see herds of buffalo thunder across the prairie; watch antelope gracefully run through the grasses. Better yet, rent the Cabin in the Woods for a night's stay at the preserve and listen to the wolf pack howl at the moon.

The park offers special events that include the Illinois Art League show, tree-planting parties, and Pops on the Prairie Concerts with the Peoria Symphony Orchestra.

From May through October, hours are 9:00 A.M. to 6:30 P.M. From November to April, weekday hours are 11:00 A.M. to 4:00 P.M.; weekends, 9:00 A.M. to 4:30 P.M. A 24-inch-gauge railroad system travels through the park. A gift shop and country store are on the grounds.

The park is located 10 miles west of downtown Peoria, off I–74 via exit 82 on Taylor Road. Admission is $5.00 for adults, $3.00 for children ages four through twelve and free for children under four. Call (309) 676–0998.

The **Peoria Historical Society,** 942 N.E. Glen Oak, 61603; (309) 674–1921, offers scenic and historic bus tours of Peoria. The tour starts downtown and travels through the Fort Clark site on the Illinois riverbank, the historic courthouse plaza, and city hall. Narrated group tours are available for half a day or a full day and include lunch. For information contact the society.

Two houses that are of interest and available for viewing are the **Flanagan House,** 942 N.E. Glen Oak Avenue, 61603, and the **Pettengill-Morton House,** 1212 West Moss Avenue, 61603. Both houses were constructed in the 1800s and are furnished in period style. Call (309) 674–1921 for tours. Admission is $2.00 for adults, 50 cents for children under twelve. The houses are open Sunday 2:00 to 4:30 P.M. March through December or by appointment.

Père Marquette Country

ather Jacques Marquette, a French Jesuit missionary, and explorer Louis Joliet, were the first Europeans to come to this area in 1673. The history of the area, however, is traceable back some 200 million years when movements of the earth resulted in dislocation of rocks, producing the Lincoln Fold in Père Marquette State Park.

Père Marquette State Park lies 5 miles west of Grafton on Route 100 in

Jersey County. The 8,000-acre park, lying on bluffs that overlook the confluence of the Mississippi and Illinois Rivers, is the largest state park in Illinois.

Another trace of prehistoric times is **McAdams Peak,** where twin springs flow from Ordovician-Silurian rocks that were deposited in the sea more than 350 million years ago. All the ridges have loess (pronounced *less*) on them. Loess is windblown dust laid down a million years ago during the Great Ice Age. The river's banks of yellow clay are composed of loess and capped with black topsoil that supports the forest.

Prehistoric people also left their mark here. There are eighteen sites indicating their presence, and a village once stood where the park lodge now stands. Nomadic hunters and fishers lived in the Illinois valley about the beginning of the Christian era, and Stone Age people left remnants of arrowheads and coarse, heavy pottery.

When the French came to this region, the tribes of Illinois, Potawatomi, and Kickapoo Indians remained near their ancestral cemeteries and burial mounds. Their houses and village sites dotted the Illinois Valley and are still visible throughout the park.

The **Père Marquette Lodge,** located in the park, (618) 786–2331, has been wonderfully remodeled. It boasts fifty rooms and twenty-two cabins, plus an indoor swimming pool. There is a dining room and a 700-ton stone fireplace in the lobby. The park also has what is believed to be the world's largest chess set. The board is 12 feet square and has figures bigger than the average six-year-old.

Within the grounds is an amphitheater with a movie screen. The theater seats about 200 people. There are also facilities for boating, camping, fishing, and picnicking, and more than 15 miles of hiking trails and horseback riding. Watch for American bald eagles in the bluffs throughout the area.

The visitors center displays the history of the park, and a park interpreter is available for assisting bus tours, hikes, demonstrations, and talks to large groups. The visitors center is open 8:30 A.M. to 4:00 P.M. year-round. For reservations with the interpreter, call (618) 786–3323 or write Park Interpreter, Père Marquette State Park, Box 325, Grafton 62037.

Just downriver away from Grafton is the quaint **Village of Elsah,** the first entire community to be listed on the National Register of Historic Places. On the Great River Road, this Mississippi River town seems more like a New England village. Plan a stay at the charming **Corner Nest Bed**

and Breakfast, 3 Elm Street. The 1883 French-American mansion overlooks the river with an inviting screened porch. Each of the four rooms is decorated with antiques. Phone (618) 374–1892 or write P.O. Box 220, Elsah 62028.

Greene County lies in the west-central part of the state on the Illinois River, about 20 miles from its mouth. Primarily an agricultural region, the terrain is marked by broken, hilly land as its western edge along the river bluffs. Here fruit cultivation is an important industry.

A number of historic sites are found throughout the county: In Carrollton, the county seat, the **Hodges Building** on the northwest corner of the town square houses the Greene County Historical Society. The **County Courthouse,** along with the entire square, is listed in the National Register of Historic Places. On the west side of the town square is the former **home of Maj. Marcus Reno,** who fought with Custer in the Battle of Little Big Horn.

The **Henry T. Rainey Home** is one-half mile east of Carrollton on Route 108. The three-story brick house faced with columns holds a wealth of historical artifacts. Rainey was the Speaker of the House in the Seventy-third Congress. In **Rainey Memorial Park,** on the north edge of town, a bronze statue honors the legislator who served in every session except one from 1903 until his death in 1934.

One of the few working farm vacations in the state can be had at **Hobson's Bluffdale Farm,** 4 miles north of Eldred on the Bluff blacktop road. It's good old-fashioned fun with plenty of outdoor activity. The farm holiday includes lodging, truly memorable meals, horseback riding, boating, hayrides, and swimming—as well as a chance to lend a hand with farm chores, like collecting eggs, feeding animals, baling hay, and more. The historic 1828 **John Russell House** is situated on the property as well. For reservations, call (217) 983–2854.

Other recreational opportunities are available at **Greenfield Lake,** 1 1/2 miles east of Greenfield, and **Roodhouse Reservoir,** 2 miles east of Roodhouse. Both offer camping, fishing, and boating. But, of course, the **Illi-**

Farm Follies

*H*obson's Bluffdale, a 320-acre farm run by the same family since 1828, is one of the best country-time getaways for city folks—or any other kind of folks.

I mean, where else can you help feed the chickens and pigs, gather eggs, move geese, bottle-feed calves, pick fresh blackberries, and harvest vegetables from a two-acre garden—and have loads of fun doing it?

Or enjoy horseback riding up in the nearby bluffs, take daylong canoe trips, go arrowhead hunting, take a hayride, stomp your feet during square dancing, or just hang out at the outdoor heated pool?

Everybody loves Bluffdale—even Charles Dickens, who visited the farm in the 1840s. So if you want a farm vacation that's filled with history and loaded with all kinds of great activities, point the nose of your car to Eldred right now, and put the pedal to the metal.

nois River is the major body of water in these parts. Try waterskiing downstream or take a free ferry from the terminus of Route 108, west of Eldred, across to Calhoun County.

For golfers there is the **Lone Oak Golf Course,** 3 miles east of Carrollton on Route 108, then right 1 ¼ miles on the country road. The nine-hole course is situated in a beautiful rural setting; (217) 942–6166.

In Whitehall, which is in the northern part of the county, the **Annie Louise Keller Memorial** is a sculpture by the famous artist, Lorado Taft, dedicated to a schoolteacher who lost her life rescuing her pupils during a tornado in 1927. Here, too, is the **grave of the Little Drummer Boy of Shiloh.**

Plan a drive along the river bluffs from Eldred to Hillview. It's especially pretty in the fall.

PLACES TO STAY IN WESTERN ILLINOIS

ELSAH
Corner Nest Bed
and Breakfast,
3 Elm Street, 62028
(800) 884–3832

Green Tree Inn,
15 Mill Street, 62028
(618) 374–2821

Maple Leaf Cottage Inn,
12 Selma Street, 62028
(618) 374–1684

GALESBURG
Comfort Inn,
907 West Carl Sandburg
Drive, 61401
(309) 344–5445

Holiday Inn Express,
I–74 at East Main
Street, 61401
(309) 343–7100

Jumer's Continental Inn,
East Main Street
at I–74, 61401
(309) 343–7151

Ramada Inn,
29 Public Square, 61401
(309) 343–0157

Regency Hotel,
3282 North Henderson
Street, 61401
(390) 344–1111

GRAFTON
Père Marquette Lodge,
Route 100, 62037
(618) 786–2331

LEWISTON
Cottonwood Motel,
805 South Main
Street, 61542
(309) 547–3733

MACOMB
Amerihost Inn,
1646 North
Lafayette, 61455
(309) 837–2220

Days Inn,
1400 North
Lafayette, 61455
(309) 833–5511

Olson Conference Center,
Western Illinois
University Campus, 61455
(309) 298–3500

Rams Inn,
1414 West Jackson, 61455
(309) 833–4521

MOLINE
Exel Inn,
2501 52nd Avenue, 61265
(309) 797–5580

Hampton Inn,
6920 27th Street, 61265
(309) 762–1711

Holiday Inn Express,
6910 27th Street, 61265
(309) 762–8300

Radisson on John Deere
Common,
1415 River Drive, 61265
(309) 764–1000

Ramada Inn,
Airport Road, 61265
(309) 797–1211

NAUVOO
Hotel Nauvoo,
1290 Mullholland, 62354
(217) 453–2771

Mississippi Memories,
1 Riverview Terrace, 62354
(217) 453–2771

Nauvoo Family Motel,
150 North Warsaw
Street, 62354
(217) 453–6527

NEW SALEM
Thomas Benton
Gray House,
R.R. 1, Box 30, 62357
(217) 285–2230

PEORIA
Best Western Eastlight Inn,
401 North Main
Street, 61611
(309) 699–7231

Comfort Suites,
4021 North War
Memorial Drive, 61614
(309) 688–3800

Fairfield Inn,
4203 North War
Memorial Drive, 61614
(309) 686–7600

Holiday Inn City Center,
500 Hamilton
Boulevard, 61602
(309) 674–2500

Jumer's Castle Lodge,
117 North Western
Avenue, 61604
(309) 673–9782

Mark Twain Hotel,
255 N.E. Adams
Street, 61602
(800) 325–6351

Père Marquette,
501 North Main
Street, 61610
(309) 637–6500

Red Roof Inn,
4031 North War Memorial
Drive, 61614
(309) 685–3911

Signature Inn,
4112 North
Brandywine, 61614
(309) 685–2556

PETERSBURG
The Oaks,
510 West Sheridan, 62659
(217) 632–5444

PITTSFIELD
Green Acres Hotel,
625 West Washington
Street, 62363
(217) 285–2166

Motel Pike Highway,
106 West, 62363
(217) 285–2129

PRINCETON
Comfort Inn,
2200 North Main, 61356
(815) 872–3300

Days Inn,
I–80 & Route 26, 61356
(815) 875–3371

QUINCY
Best Western
Rosewood Inn,
300 Gardner
Expressway, 62301
(217) 223–6780

Fairfield Inn by Marriott,
4315 Broadway, 62301
(217) 223–5922

Holiday Inn,
201 South 3rd Street, 62301
(217) 222–2666

Travelodge,
200 South 3rd Street, 62301
(217) 222–5620

ROCK ISLAND
Potter House B&B,
1906 7th Avenue, 61201
(309) 788–1906

Quality Hotel,
One Plaza Square, 61201
(800) 447–1297

**PLACES TO EAT IN
WESTERN ILLINOIS**

GALESBURG
Landmark Cafe,
62 South Seminary
Street, 61401
(309) 343–5376

Oogie's,
1721 North
Henderson, 61401
(309) 344–1259

Selected Visitors Bureaus and Chambers of Commerce

Illinois Bureau of Tourism-Travel Information,
(800) 2–CONNECT

Greater Alton/Twin Rivers Convention
and Visitors Bureau,
200 Piasa Street, 62002
(800) 258–6645

Galesburg Chamber of Commerce,
292 East Simmons Street, 61401
(309) 434–1194

Macomb Area Convention and Visitors Bureau,
804 West Jackson Street, 61455
(309) 833–1315

Peoria Area Convention and Visitors Bureau,
403 N.E. Jefferson Street, 61603
(800) 747–0302

Quad Cities Convention and Visitors Bureau,
2021 River Drive, 61201
(800) 747–7800

Quincy Convention and Visitors Bureau,
300 Civic Center Plaza, 62301
(800) 978–4748

Packinghouse,
441 Mulberry, 61401
(309) 342–6868

Risco's Italian Restaurant,
41 South Seminary, 61401
(309) 341–4141

The Steak House,
951 North
Henderson, 61401
(309) 343–9994

Tavern of the Pheasant,
260 South Soangetha
Road, 61401
(309) 343–7151

GRAFTON
Père Marquette Lodge,
Route 100, 62037
(618) 786–2331

MACOMB
Macomb Dining Company,
127 East Carroll
Street, 61455
(309) 833–3000

MOLINE
C'est Michele,
1514 5th Avenue, 61265
(309) 762–0585

NAUVOO
Hotel Nauvoo,
1290 Mullholland, 62354
(217) 453–2211

Grandpa John's,
1255 Mullholland
Street, 62354
(217) 453–2310

PEORIA
Carnegie's,
501 North Main
Street, 61610
(309) 637–6500

Jumer's,
117 North Western
Avenue, 61604
(309) 673–8181

Katie Hooper Pub & Grill,
1 Main Street, 61602
(309) 673–2628

Paparazzi,
4315 West Voss
Street, 61614
(309) 682–5205

River Station,
212 Constitution
Avenue, 61602
(309) 676–7100

The Grill,
456 Fulton, 61602
(309) 674–6870

**OTHER ATTRACTIONS
WORTH SEEING IN
WESTERN ILLINOIS**

Wyatt Earp Birthplace
Historic House Museum,
Monmouth

Old Carthage Jail
and Visitors Center,
Carthage

Central Congregational
Church,
Galesburg

Illinois Citizen
Soldier Museum,
Galesburg

Lake Storey
Recreational Area,
Galesburg

Seminary Street Historic
Commercial District,
Galesburg

Historic Barn Tours,
Macomb

Metamora Courthouse
State Historic Site,
Metamora

Pioneer Cemetery,
Monmouth

Baxter's Vineyards,
Nauvoo

African-American
Museum Hall of Fame,
Peoria

Glen Oak Zoo,
Peoria

Peoria Chiefs,
Peoria

St. Francis Monastery,
Peoria

Par-a-Dice Riverboat
Casino,
East Peoria

Channel Cat Water Taxi,
Rock Island

Hauberg Indian Museum
and Chief Black Hawk State
Historic Site,
Quad Cities

Southeastern Illinois

Red Hills Country

One mile northeast of Sumner in Lawrence County is **Red Hills State Park,** a 948-acre preserve of high wooded hills, deep ravines, meadows, and year-round springs. Hickory, oak, sycamore, maple, gum, crab, walnut, and apple trees grow in abundance in this area. Squirrels, doves, woodcock, quail, and rabbit live and multiply in this haven for nature lovers and sports enthusiasts.

U.S. Highway 50 divides the park into two sections, and the park itself is a historical crossroad, the westernmost edge being the first land in Illinois ceded by the Indians to the United States government. The borderline runs through the park from southwest to northeast and was set by a treaty made in 1795 at Greenville, Ohio, by Gen. Anthony Wayne and the Indians. The Indians relinquished all claims to the land northwest of the Ohio River and east of a specified line. The area was called the Vincennes Tract.

The name Red Hill comes from the peak by the same name, which is the highest point along the Baltimore and Ohio Railroad between Cincinnati and St. Louis. Red Hill is topped by a tower and cross, constructed and financed by residents cooperating in an interdenominational council.

> ### Southeastern Illinois Trivia
>
> *This section of Illinois is often called the "empty quarter," holding the state's least populous counties.*

The park has picnicking, fishing, boating, camping, and hunting facilities. A park interpreter conducts summer recreation programs. There is a trail through the woods, and other areas are suitable for hiking. Ice fishing and ice skating are permitted in season. The park is open from sunrise to 11:00 P.M. daily. For more details contact Red Hills State Park, R.R. 4, Sumner 62466; (618) 936–2469.

Lawrence County residents like to celebrate, and there are four festivals of note: **Bridgeport SummerFest,** the last weekend in June; **Sumner Fall**

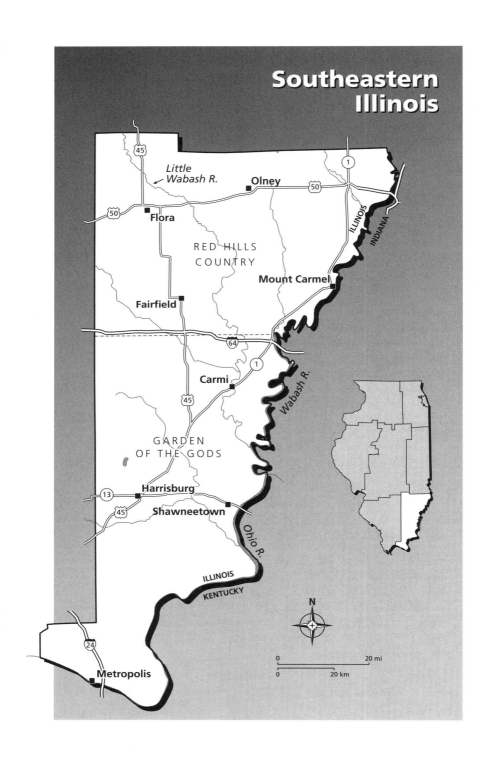

Southeastern Illinois

Little Wabash R.

Olney

45

50

50

Flora

1

ILLINOIS

INDIANA

RED HILLS COUNTRY

Mount Carmel

Fairfield

64

Carmi

1

45

Wabash R.

GARDEN OF THE GODS

Harrisburg

13

45

Shawneetown

Ohio R.

ILLINOIS

KENTUCKY

24

Metropolis

N

0   20 mi

0   20 km

SOUTHEASTERN ILLINOIS

Festival, the first weekend after Labor Day; *St. Francisville Chestnut Festival,* the first weekend in October; and the *Lawrenceville Fall Festival,* the third weekend in September. For exact dates and a list of activities contact the Lawrence County Chamber of Commerce, 1104 Jefferson Street, Lawrenceville 62349; (618) 943–3516.

For nature buffs *Beall Woods Nature Preserve and State Park,* 6 miles south of Mount Carmel in Wabash County, is the largest tract of original deciduous forest remaining in the United States and is relatively untouched by human beings. Sixty-four species of trees have been identified in the forest, and there is reason to believe that more will be discovered. Approximately 300 trees with trunks greater than 30 inches in circumference at chest height are in the park.

The tract of land that is now the park was under the ownership of the Beall family for more than 102 years. After the death of Laura Beall, the property was sold to a man who intended to clear the land and farm it. Conservation-minded individuals and groups helped to create the original acquisition by the state of Illinois in 1965 by invoking the law of eminent domain in order to preserve the virgin woodland for posterity.

Beall Woods is a registered landmark and is listed as the "Forest of the Wabash." The woods are made up of 270 acres of primeval woodland that borders the Wabash River, and the area was dedicated as an Illinois nature preserve to ensure that the forest will remain in its natural condition.

Beall Woods is sometimes referred to as the "University of the Trees" because it is a living forest community with a natural ecological system containing native plant and animal life. Hikers can view red fox, deer, raccoon, and pileated woodpeckers, and the forest floor supports a variety of interesting flowers.

There are plenty of hiking trails for those interested. The trails begin at the *Red Barn,* a remodeled barn that serves as a nature center. It has a display of seeds, native woods of Illinois, and Indian arrowheads. Hours are 7:00 A.M. to 4:00 P.M. daily.

There are also facilities for picnicking and a playground. The park is open year-round except for Christmas and New Year's Day. For information contact the Site Superintendent, Beall Woods Conservation Area, R.R. 2,

Mount Carmel 62863; (618) 298–2442. Beall Woods is near Keensburg off Route 1, about 6 miles south of Mount Carmel.

Edwards County is known as the Chowder Capital of the World. The aroma of this fragrant dish can be detected around the county anytime from June through September.

There is no exact information on when chowder became popular here, but records from the time of the Civil War indicate that it was enjoyed as early as the 1860s.

Southeastern Illinois Trivia

Marion's Illinois Centre Mall, spread over more than 200 acres, is Southern Illinois's largest shopping mall.

Chowder is generally cooked in large black kettles ranging in size from twenty to seventy gallons. A variety of ingredients, including tomatoes, are added to boiling water; chowder time traditionally starts when the tomatoes ripen and closes with the heavy frost.

The **Albion Pagoda** in Albion was erected in 1914 and is the town's pride. The first pagoda was built around the mineral-water well in 1890. The waters were said to cure rheumatism, kidney and urinary troubles, "derangements of the stomach and bowels," and many other afflictions. When the original pagoda deteriorated, a second one was built in the same location; then in 1906 the current two-story structure replaced the two previous ones. The third pagoda was designed by architect W. E. Felix of Fairfield and constructed as a community program by the Albion Women's Beautifying Club.

The pagoda is octagonal with eight brick columns. The roof is made of red clay, resembling the roofs of the pagodas in East Asia.

Bone Gap is a name that brings images of hunting and Indians to mind. The **Indian Hill Museum** in Bone Gap has exhibits of pioneer life and woodworking and blacksmith shops from early railroad days. Besides a collection of Indian artifacts, the museum has family heirlooms and historical items pertaining to the English settlements in the Wabash Valley.

Museum founders Norman and Sandy Reid's main objective is to educate the younger generation and create an air of reminiscence for others. You'll find a 1920 Keck-Gonnerman steam engine, which was used to power a sawmill and threshing machine; more than 10,000 Indian artifacts, including some dating back to the Archaic period 10,000 years ago; and a Regina music box with a cherrywood case and hand-painted view of the Midwest that dates to 1861. Norman Reid also has a collection of

TOP ANNUAL EVENTS

Annual Superman Celebration, Metropolis, mid-June, (800) 949–5740

Living History Weekend, May–November, Fort Massac State Park, Metropolis, mid-June, (800) 248–4373

Golconda Fall Festival, Golconda, mid-October, (618) 683–9702

Olney Community Christmas Light Display, Olney, late November–December, (618) 234–0600

Annual Tour of Homes, Metropolis, early December, (618) 524–7203

more than 300 guns, which includes handguns ranging from the Civil War period to the 1880 period, and an ancient buffalo skull that was found on the plains more than 107 years ago.

The museum is open Wednesday through Sunday from 9:00 A.M. to 5:00 P.M.; (618) 446–3277. Admission is by donation. The museum is on Route 3 in Bone Gap (from Albion take Route 130 to Route 3).

Olney is the home of the white albino squirrel. Local legend says that the white squirrel first appeared here in 1902. A hunter captured two squirrels, a male and a female, and put them on display in a town saloon.

Another townsman heard about the squirrels and sent his son over to get the animals and release them in the woods. As soon as the squirrels were freed, a large fox squirrel jumped down from a tree and killed the male. The son shot the fox squirrel as he tried to attack the female. Weeks later baby white albino squirrels were seen, and the population has increased to about 800 albino squirrels.

A city ordinance has been enacted to protect these special citizens. A white squirrel has the right of way on any street in Olney, and a motorist is fined $25 for running over one. Anyone caught taking one out of town will also be fined.

Olney residents are also protective of their bird population. At Bird Haven in **Robert Ridgway Memorial Arboretum and Bird Sanctuary,** you can walk and observe nature. Robert Ridgway, a naturalist, scientist, artist, and author, is famous for his books *Birds of Middle and North America* and *Color Stands and Color Nomenclature.* He was associated with the Smithsonian Institution and was a zoologist for the Survey of the Fortieth Parallel. He was also an authority in the field of ornithology.

Ridgway purchased the eighteen acres of Bird Haven in 1906. By the 1920s the arboretum and bird sanctuary was said to have had the second-largest number of plant species of any arboretum, second to a larger tract in Japan.

The Ridgway summer cottage once stood on the grounds, and a replica of the front porch has been reproduced on the cottage site. Dr. Ridgway's grave is on the grounds and is marked by a granite boulder with a bronze plaque with birds sculpted on it.

Believe It!

*I*t is worthwhile to visit West Salem (yes, it is located east of the town of Salem, and just south of Olney) to soak up a bit of both history and oddity. This little settlement was home to the only Moravian congregation in Illinois. These utopian pioneers, who believed in God, hard work, and communal living, first settled in Salem, North Carolina to escape religious persecution in nineteenth-century Europe.

Here in West Salem's little cemetery, you can see the only real remnants left of that historic community. Note that men and women are buried in separate plots. And a headstone reported to be the "smallest in the world" by Ripley's Believe It or Not is here, too. Can you find it? Call (618) 445–3612 for information.

Bird Haven's hours are from dusk to dawn. For more information contact Olney City Hall, 300 Whittle Avenue, Olney 62450; (618) 395–7302. Bird Haven is a half mile northeast of Olney on East Fork Lake Road.

Olney holds an annual *Arts and Crafts Festival* every fall. It is a performing arts showcase open to amateur and professional fine artists and craftspeople. Contact the Olney Arts Council, P.O. Box 291, Olney 62450, for specific dates and entry information.

Garden of the Gods

*I*n the southeast corner of the county, where it joins Gallatin and Hardin Counties, the *Garden of the Gods* is one of the state's most dramatic natural attractions. Created more than 200 million years ago from geologic uplifting, spectacular rock outcroppings have been formed through the action of water and wind. The unusual rock formations have been given names by imaginative explorers—Camel Rock, Noah's Ark, Mushroom Rock, Fat Man's Squeeze, and Tower of Babel are some of the more colorful ones.

One mile of well-maintained trails and 5 miles of semideveloped trails allow hikers to trek through the low mountainous region. Part of the Shawnee National Forest, which runs across the width of southern Illinois, the Garden of the Gods is a perfect spot for camping. For information on the Garden of the Gods, contact the Shawnee National Forest Headquarters, (618) 253–7114. Just north is the Saline County Conservation Area with its Glen O. Jones Lake.

Harrisburg, the county seat, was at one time a major center for tobacco growing and, later, coal mining. Here the **Saline County Area Museum,** 1600 Feazel Street, is a popular attraction. Set in a parklike setting are a handful of furnished historic buildings, moved here from around the area. You can visit a nineteenth-century one-room schoolhouse, an old Moravian church, a log cabin, general store, post office, and barn with its original threshing floor. The museum is open Tuesday through Saturday 9:00 A.M. to 4:00 P.M. and Sunday 1:00 to 4:00 P.M. Admission is $2.00 for adults, $1.00 for children. For information call (618) 253–7342.

The prize of McLeansboro, the Hamilton County seat, is the **McCoy Memorial Library,** on the west side of the public square. The Cloud Family built this handsome brick Victorian mansion, with a central tower and unique roofline, in 1884. It is listed in the National Register of Historic Places. Along with an 8,000-volume collection, the library boasts countless antiques on display for visitors. A central feature of the home is the number of noteworthy fireplaces throughout the structure. On the second floor, the **Hamilton County Historical Society Museum** exhibits souvenirs of the area's past. Open Monday, Wednesday, and Friday 1:00 to 4:00 P.M. Admission is $1.00 The library is open every day but Sunday.

Next to the library building and once a residence is the **People's National Bank,** built by the same family, the Clouds, and also listed in the National Register.

For a bite of something to eat, the hearty fare at **Pat's City and Country Cafe** on Route 14 East is some of the best in the county. Stop for shopping at **Southfork Antique Mall,** 105 East Broadway in McLeansboro.

Rocky Rim Rendezvous

*T*he last time I hiked through the Garden of the Gods region, I took the Rock Rim Trail into this rocky wonderland. It's perhaps the most unusual spot in the Shawnee—maybe all of Illinois.

I hiked over flagstone paths that meander through spectacular rock formations that have eroded and uplifted over more than 200 million years into a jumble of shapes and forms. But it

was on the way back to Golconda that I experienced my favorite southeastern Illinois moment. I stopped at Indian Kitchen, a tall rock shelf with a panoramic view of Lusk Creek Canyon. This is some of Illinois's most rugged (and unexpected) terrain.

And the narrow trail that leads up to the top of the precipice is a must for experienced trekkers.

Although today we can get in our cars and speed hundreds of miles over broad, smoothly paved interstate highways, travelers in the first part of the nineteenth century turned to rivers and riverboats for efficient travel. And of those rivers, the Ohio was one of the longest and most frequently chosen routes, an interstate expressway from Pennsylvania all the way to the Mississippi River. Thus, the importance of Gallatin County and its seat, Shawneetown, is clearly understood in terms of a river port. Today one of the world's longest span cantilever bridges crosses the Ohio at Shawneetown.

A New Illinois

Now that you have made it past the cornfields, past the sea of prairies, and past the glacier's drift, you'll discover a new kind of Illinois. One with dense forests, 200-million-year-old sandstone cliffs and outcroppings of spectacular shapes and sizes, deep ravines, and incredible river bluff vistas.

Your travels might be slower here due to the local geography. There are fewer big roads, but more backcountry beauty. Relax and enjoy, ease your pace. Follow the contours of the land to new adventures—the kind you never dreamed that you'd discover in Illinois.

Shawnee Indians had a village here in the mid-1700s, and burial mounds can be seen throughout the area. The earliest white settlers arrived around 1800. In 1810 the federal government laid out Shawneetown on the river, and it quickly became a major port and gateway for immigrants into the new frontier. In 1814 it became the first incorporated town in Illinois. A ferry service, crossing the river into Kentucky, was begun. Four years later the U.S. Land Office for southeastern Illinois opened at Shawneetown. Adding to the economic growth of the community were the nearby saltworks at Equality, which supplied an important pioneer commodity and shipped salt throughout the region. Thus, Shawneetown became an important financial center in the American westward movement. One early resident was Gen. Thomas Posey, a member of George Washington's staff who was present for the British surrender at Yorktown. He is buried 2 miles north of the town in **Westwood Cemetery.**

The first bank in the territory opened here in 1816. Known as the **John Marshall Bank** for the early merchant who began it in his house, the brick structure has been reconstructed by the local historical society and is open for tours by appointment. There are also walking tours available that take in a number of sites in the historic town.

A second bank, the 1839 **First State Bank,** is a handsome Greek Revival building with Doric columns supporting a portico. (It's now listed in the National Register of Historic Places.) For its construction, sandstone was floated down the Ohio by flatboat from quarries in the East. A favorite local story is of the time when businessmen from the tiny village of Chicago rode to Shawneetown to ask bankers there for a loan. They were refused on the grounds that Chicago was much too far from Shawneetown ever to prosper.

The Ohio River proved a blessing and a curse for the community. Major floods struck the town in 1884, 1898, 1913, and 1937. In 1937 residents rebuilt their community in the hills 3 miles inland. In Old Shawneetown, the original settlement, many of the old landmarks are part of **Shawneetown State Memorial Park,** on the banks of the river.

The most famous visitor of all to come to Shawneetown was Marquis de Lafayette. The Revolutionary War hero was honored here at a reception at the Rawlings' Hotel on May 7, 1825. Gov. Edward Coles greeted the soldier at the waterfront. The hotel burned in 1904 and was later rebuilt.

Equality, at the west side of the county near Route 142 and Route 13, was the site for the United States Salines, salty springs first discovered by the Indians. Later, French and American settlers made salt at the site. As an important early industry, the springs became the property of first the federal, then the state government. Andrew Jackson, before becoming president, attempted to lease these springs. Today only some crumbling foundations remain. A mural in the **Gallatin County Courthouse** depicts these salt-making operations.

At the northwest border of the county, at New Haven, once stood the mill of Jonathan Boone, who was the brother of Daniel Boone. Jonathan Boone died here in 1808. A state historical marker records the spot today.

Ridgway, in the center of the county, is the popcorn capital of the state and host to **Popcorn Days** each September. Call the Chamber of Commerce at (618) 272–7500 for more information. **National Oats Popcorn Factory** is located here.

Two miles off Route 1 and 11 miles south of Cave-in-Rock is Pounds Hollow, an especially scenic recreation area. A twenty-two-acre lake is nestled under steep bluffs. Follow Rim Rock Trail around the lake to the prehistoric **Pounds Wall,** a 7,000-year-old Indian structure. It is uncertain whether this Pounds Wall, once 8 to 10 feet high, was used as a fortification or for killing buffalo. Most experts guess the latter use, because a buffalo wallow is nearby. Buffalo would have been rounded up against the wall and slaughtered.

At the southeastern tip of Illinois, on the Ohio River, Hardin County has long been a stopping place for restless pioneers moving west. One of the first was Samuel Mason, an officer of the Continental Army and renegade son of an important Virginia family, who came to Illinois territory in 1797. Discovering a deep cavern on the bluff overlooking the river, Mason set himself up in business, advertising over the arched cavern opening, LIQUOR VAULT AND HOUSE OF ENTERTAINMENT. His business, though, was not innkeeping, but rather piracy, and he handily plundered gullible travelers and flatboat crews. When his notoriety caught up with him, he fled, leaving the cave to a long line of fellow thieves. It has gained further fame since being used as a locale for the movie *How the West Was Won* and the two television series about Davy Crockett and Daniel Boone.

Today **Cave-in-Rock** is part of a state park of the same name, with facilities for picnicking, hiking, boating, fishing, and camping (sixty sites, thirty-five with electric hookups). It's off Route 1 and open year-round, Box 338, Cave-in-Rock 62919; (618) 289–4325.

From the little town here runs the only ferry on the Ohio River that shuttles cars and passengers. It operates 6:00 A.M. to 6:00 P.M. daily. On the third weekend in July each year, Cave-in-Rock holds **Frontier Days** to commemorate its historic past. The event features a parade, beauty pageant, carnival, square dancing, and craft exhibits.

Four miles north of Rosiclare near the junction of Route 34 and Route 146 is the **Old Illinois Iron Furnace,** the first in Illinois. It began in 1837 on colorfully named Hog Thief Creek, eventually supporting one hundred

Cave-in-Rock Rocks

*L*et me set up the Cave-in-Rock scene for you in How the West Was Won, *a blockbuster movie starring a roll call of Hollywood stars of the 1960s, including John Wayne, Jimmy Stewart, Debbie Reynolds, and George Peppard. Debbie Reynolds's family is traveling down the Ohio on a river raft when they are lured to the shore by "merchants" advertising all kinds of needed goods from a perch in a cavern set high in a bluff overlooking the river.*

Of course, the "merchants" are nothing more than river pirates set on looting

the westward settlers, killing the men and stealing the women. And they would have, too, if not for the intervention of scout Jimmy Stewart, who comes to their rescue.

But go rent the movie at your nearest video store—not necessarily for the film itself (it's an okay flick). However, the photography at Cave-in-Rock, which was used for the location shoot for this segment of the movie, is spectacular. And once you get a glimpse of the beauty of southeastern Illinois country, you'll want to visit it even more.

Old Illinois Iron Furnace

families. Some of its production was used at the Mound City Naval Ship-yards to clad gunboats during the Civil War. The furnace was abandoned in 1883. There are two interpretive trails at the site along with an inviting "swimming hole" in Big Creek.

At Elizabethtown on Route 146 at the Ohio River is the *River Rose Inn,* (618) 287–8811, a bed-and-breakfast housed in a four-story Greek Revival building. The River Rose Inn specializes in gourmet breakfasts.

Seven miles west from Cave-in-Rock and about 4 miles south of Route 146 is *Tower Rock Park Recreation Area,* where the scenery is a fine example of that found throughout the Shawnee National Forest, which covers the county. The Ohio River runs along the southern edge of the park, providing opportunities for fishing and boating. Camping and picnicking are also available at Tower Rock. Ranger's Office: (618) 287–2201.

The people of Metropolis will swear to you that Superman really exists. Metropolis claims to be the hometown of the fictional movie and cartoon character Superman. A billboard of Superman welcoming visitors to Metropolis greets you as you enter the town, and another portrait of their hero adorns the water tower. The Chamber of Commerce boasts the only official Superman phone booth, where you can actually speak with the Man of Steel. And just for the sake of continuity, the local newspaper is called the *Daily Planet.*

An annual **Superman Celebration** usually falls on the second weekend in June, runs for two days, and includes a beauty pageant, style show, arts and crafts show, street dance, flea market, and Superman Run.

Metropolis also is the site of the **Curtis House Museum,** Fourth and Market Streets. This two-story brick house was restored to its original design and is open Sunday from 2:00 to 4:00 P.M. or by appointment. Call (618) 524–5120 for more information.

Massac County has a historical legend stemming from Fort Massac. One of five former French forts in the Illinois park system, it borders the Ohio River at the southern tip of the state. Indians were believed to have first used the site because of its strategic location on the river. In the early 1540s Spanish explorer Hernando de Soto and his soldiers constructed a fortification here for protection from hostile Indians.

Nerves of Steel

*S*o I was curious. Is that so wrong?

The first time I came across the tiny town of Metropolis, I was fascinated by its claim as Superman's hometown. I had been a huge Superman comics fan when I was a kid. And I always watched those old George Reeve Superman *reruns on Saturday morning television as well. That's why I kind of went goofy over the official Superman phone booth, the one where you can actually talk with the lost lad from Krypton.*

But my sense of journalistic curiosity got the better of me when I learned that the town's only newspaper was named the Daily Planet. *So I had to call the newsroom and ask the question that was on everybody's mind.*

"Pardon me," I harrumphed in my best reporter voice. "I'm doing a story on the town's Superman connection and I'd like to ask your help."

"Well, the Chamber (of Commerce) usually handles these kinds of inquiries," the newspaper's copydesk person told me. "But I'll do my best."

"Okay," I said. "Uh, your paper's called the Daily Planet, *right?"*

"That's right."

"And it's a real newspaper?"

"Of course," he answered.

"Superman, Daily Planet, *you know," I continued. "You don't happen to have a reporter on staff named Clark Kent, do you?"*

Apparently the desk person was stunned. "Sir, I said this was a real newspaper."

"No Mr. White as editor or publisher or anything like that?" I asked.

"Have a nice day," the desk person said. And hung up.

City of Festivals

*M*etropolis may be best known as the "home of the Man of Steel." Why not? It is the only town in the entire United States named Metropolis. And who's going to argue with Superman, anyway?

But Metropolis offers something much more for wanderers to this extreme southern outpost of Illinois. In fact, it might even be called a city of festivals, since it seems as if some kind of celebration is slated virtually every month.

So besides the annual Superman celebration in June, don't miss German Fest in April; the Rotary Car Show in June; Labor Day Celebration, Arts in the Parks, and Superman Jet Rally in September; the Fort Massac Encampment in October; the Home Town Christmas Light Display (at Fort Massac) in November and December; and the Old Tyme Christmas Celebration in December.

If you can't find something special to do in Metropolis, then you aren't trying. Call (800) 949–5740.

Legend tells us that during the first half of the eighteenth century, many soldiers were massacred here by Indians, thus the name Fort Massacre, later shortened to Massac.

Reconstruction of the fort and an accompanying museum was completed in 1973. Three of the buildings were originally used as living quarters for enlisted men and as means of defense, with loopholes for shooting muskets through.

The **Fort Massac Museum** houses a miniature replica of the fort, artifacts, and a history of the fort. It is open year-round Wednesday through Sunday 10:00 A.M. to 4:30 P.M. Guided tours are available. Call (618) 524–9321 for an appointment.

Fort Massac State Park is open daily. The replica of the fort is open 10:00 A.M. to 5:30 P.M. daily. The park offers picnicking, fishing, boating, and camping facilities, and two self-guided trails for hiking. Hunting is allowed in season. For information contact the Site Superintendent, Box 708, Metropolis 62960; (618) 542–9321.

The **Fort Massac Encampment** is an annual festival recreating the atmosphere of a military encampment in the Illinois country in the 1700s. It is traditionally held the third weekend in October. Contact the park office for events and times.

Fort Massac State Park is located 2¹/₂ miles west of Metropolis off I–24 on Route 45. The museum and encampment are on the grounds.

History Lesson

To discover an interesting slice of little-known southeastern Illinois history, put on your hiking boots—because you are going to need them. No doubt you'll have to slosh through some muck while visiting Miller Grove Cemetery in Golconda. It is said to be the last vestige of an early African-American settlement that some historians claim was the first "all-Negro" community in Illinois.

In fact the town of Miller Grove is thought to have been established before the Civil War began. Free black families came to live here in the 1830s, and some burial sites in the cemetery date back to 1865. However, people deserted the town by 1925. And the cemetery is all that is left of this historic locale.

Kitch-mus-ke-nee-be, or the Great Medicine Waters, was once the Indian name for the area known as **Dixon Springs State Park.** Part of the Illinois Shawnee Hills, the park sits on a giant block of rock, which dropped 200 feet along a fault line that extends northwesterly across Pope County.

The park is about 10 miles west of Golconda on Route 146 near the junction of Route 145. This spot was once occupied by the Algonquin Indians who, after the Shawnee tribe had been driven from Tennessee, settled near the mouth of the Wabash River.

The area was named for William Dixon, one of the first white men to build a home here. He obtained a school land warrant in 1848, and his cabin was a landmark for many years. A small community grew up at Dixon Springs, and in the nineteenth century it became a health spa, which attracted hundreds to the seven springs of mineral-enriched water. A bathhouse provided mineral or soft water baths.

The country is hilly, and during the rainy season rivulets cascade down the hills forming waterfalls.

Picnicking, camping, biking, and hiking are permitted. Enjoy the self-guided 1.7-mile nature trail or the modern swimming pool supplied by spring water, with lifeguard and bathhouse facilities. A concession stand is located near the pool as well as picnic shelters, playgrounds, and drinking water.

The park is open year-round except for holidays. For information contact the Site Superintendent, Dixon Springs State Park, R.R. 1, Brownfield 62911; (618) 949–3394.

The Mansion in Golconda is a Victorian-style house converted into a bed-and-breakfast and restaurant; several Illinois governors have enjoyed the home-cooked meals here; (618) 683–4400, P.O. Box 339, Golconda 62938. Full breakfast is included in the fare, and the restaurant is open to the public 11:00 A.M. to 2:00 P.M. and 5:00 to 9:00 P.M. daily except Monday, when it is open 11:00 A.M. to 2:00 P.M. only.

PLACES TO STAY IN SOUTHEASTERN ILLINOIS

ALBION
Albion Hotel,
Highway 15 West, 62806
(618) 445–2311

ELDORADO
Neal Motel,
1014 Highway 45
North, 62930
(618) 273–8146

GOLCONDA
Mansion of Golconda,
515 Columbus
Street, 62938
(618) 683–4400

San Domaino Retreat
Center, Route 1, 62938
(618) 285–3507

LAWRENCEVILLE
Gas Lite Motel,
Route 1, 62439
(618) 943–2374

METROPOLIS
American Inn,
1502 West 10th Street,
Highway 45 North, 62960
(618) 524–7431

Best Inns of America,
2055 Fifth Street, 62960
(800) 237–8466

Comfort Inn of Metropolis,
2118 East 5th Street, 62960
(618) 524–7227

Days Inn,
Routes 45 and 3, 62960
(618) 524–9341

Metropolis Inn,
Routes 45 and 24, 62960
(618) 524–3723

MT. CARMEL
Shamrock Hotel,
Route 1 North,
1303 North Cherry, 62863
(618) 262–4169

Town and Country Motel,
1515 West 3rd
Street, 62863
(618) 262–4171

Uptown Motel,
511 Market Street, 62863
(618) 262–4146

OLNEY
The Holiday,
Route 130 and
U.S. 50, 62450
(618) 395–2121

Royal Inn Motel,
1001 West Main
Street, 62450
(800) 433–5287

Super 8 Motel,
425 South West
Street, 62450
(618) 392–7888

Travelers Inn Motel,
1801 East Main
Street, 62450
(618) 393–2186

WEST SALEM
Thelma's Bed
and Breakfast,
201 South Broadway
Street, 62476
(618) 456–8401

PLACES TO EAT IN SOUTHEASTERN ILLINOIS

CAVE-IN-ROCK
Cave-in-Rock State Park
Lodge and Restaurant,
New State Park
Road, 62919
(618) 289–4325

GOLCONDA
Mansion of Golconda,
515 Columbus
Street, 62938
(618) 683–4400

METROPOLIS
Players Riverboat Casino,
Merv Griffin's
Landing, 62960
(800) 929–5905

Selected Visitors Bureaus and Chambers of Commerce

Southernmost Illinois Tourism
and Convention Bureau,
Ullin, 62992
(800) 248–4373

Illinois Bureau of Tourism–Travel,
(800) 2–CONNECT

**OTHER ATTRACTIONS
WORTH SEEING IN
SOUTHEASTERN ILLINOIS**

Albion Public Library,
Albion

Dixon Springs State Park,
Dixon Springs

The Chocolate Factory,
Dixon Springs

Lake Glendale Recreation
Area,
Dixon Springs

Jimmy Dean Marketplace,
Eldorado

Smithland Pool,
Golconda

Ohio River Recreation
Area,
Golconda

Lincoln Heritage Trail State
Monument,
Lawrenceville

Super Museum,
Metropolis

Major Elijah P. Curtis Home
and Museum,
Metropolis

Merv Griffin's Theater,
Metropolis

Players Riverboat Casino,
Metropolis

Beall Woods State Park,
Mt. Carmel

Olney Animal Sanctuary,
Olney

Lake Thunderhawk,
Ozark

Teutopolis Monastery
Museum,
Teutopolis

Moravian Church and
Cemetery,
West Salem

Southwestern Illinois

The Lake Region

Carlyle Lake, the largest inland lake in Illinois, lies primarily within the borders of Clinton County. Created in 1967 by damming the Kaskaskia River, its area covers some 24,580 acres with 83 miles of shoreline. The U.S. Army Corps of Engineers, which maintains the reservoir, estimates that more than 3½ million visitors enjoy the lake each year. Its primary attractions are fishing (for white bass, crappie, largemouth bass, channel catfish, and bluegill), sailing, boating, and hunting, in season. With two state parks on its shore—***Eldon Hazlet State Park*** and ***South Shore State Park***—camping is readily available. More than 400 sites (336 with electric hookup) can be found in the state parks alone. Additional campsites are available at lake recreation areas and at commercial campgrounds. Eldon Hazlet State Park is off Route 127, 6 miles north of Carlyle. South Shore State Park is off U.S. Highway 50, 2 miles east of Carlyle. The parks have the same phone number: (618) 594–3913.

A good place to begin a visit is the ***Carlyle Visitor Center,*** operated by the U.S. Army Corps of Engineers. The center displays a model of the lake and dam, showing how the reservoir was created. Exhibits of the area's natural history are especially informative. On weekends the center schedules worthwhile interpretive programs such as nature walks, discussions of area Indian history, and water safety seminars. Open Memorial Day through Labor Day 10:00 A.M. to 6:00 P.M. every day. Open weekends only in May and October; (618) 594–5253. The Carlyle Visitor Center is located at the Dam West recreation area, immediately west of the main dam 1 mile north of Carlyle off Route 127.

The ***West Access Marina*** supplies services to the lake's boaters—docking and fuel, motorboats, Hobie Cats, sailboards, and cabin sailboats for rent. The proprietor can be reached at (618) 594–2461. The marina is immediately west of the main dam, off Route 127 north of Carlyle.

Just south of the main dam, off Route 127, is a 1½-acre plot of natural prairie. In 1974 park rangers seeded the land with grasses and wild-

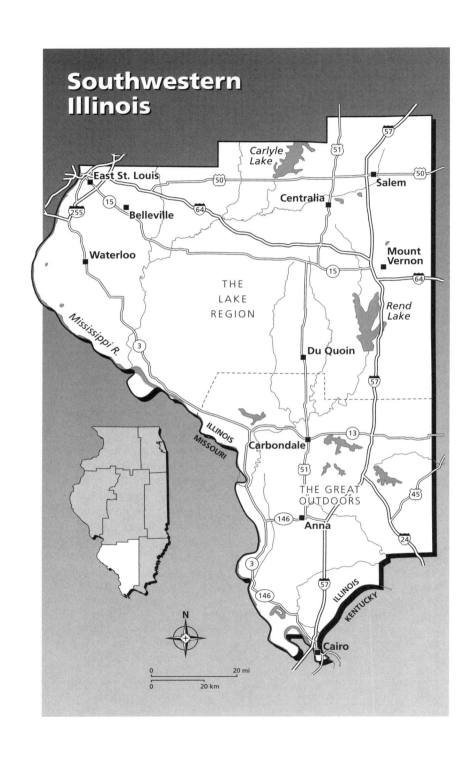

Southwestern Illinois

Carlyle Lake

East St. Louis

Belleville

Waterloo

Centralia

Salem

Mount Vernon

THE LAKE REGION

Rend Lake

Du Quoin

Mississippi R.

ILLINOIS

MISSOURI

Carbondale

THE GREAT OUTDOORS

Anna

ILLINOIS

KENTUCKY

Cairo

N

0   20 mi
0   20 km

AUTHOR'S TOP FIVE PICKS

1. *Giant City State Park and Lodge,*
   (618) 457–4836

2. *Fort de Chartres,*
   Prairie du Rocher,
   (618) 284–7230

3. *Du Quoin State Fair,*
   Du Quoin,
   (618) 542–9373

4. *Kaskaskia State Historic Site & Island,*
   Kaskaskia,
   (618) 859–3741

5. *Rend Lake, Whittington,*
   (618) 439–4321

flowers indigenous to the Illinois prairie of 150 years ago. A 1-mile trail leads through the prairie. Pick up a walking guide that explains the various plants at the Carlyle Visitor Center.

Carlyle even has its own entry in the National Register of Historic Places—the 1859 *General Dean suspension bridge,* the only suspension bridge in the state. Built to span the Kaskaskia River on the east side of town, the bridge was a link in the old St. Louis–Vincennes Trail. Stone towers 35 feet tall support a 280-foot span. The bridge was restored in 1977 for use as a pedestrian crossing. On the east side of the bridge is a recreation area with picnic tables and grills and a boat ramp. The bridge was named for William F. Dean, a Carlyle native and hero of the Korean War.

The Midwest has few stories about earthquakes, but Salem, surprisingly, was founded as a result of the New Madrid, Missouri, earthquake of 1811. The quake was so powerful that it caused the Mississippi River to flow backward and sent Capt. Samuel Young in search of a less shaky home. Young came to Marion County and found an abundance of game and tranquility. He even made his camp on what is now the courthouse square in Salem.

Salem became a stagecoach stop on the Vincennes Trail, and the arrival of the railroads from 1850 to 1860 produced Salem's first boom. In the early 1900s oil brought another boom to the town, and in 1939 Salem was the nation's second-largest oilfield.

Salem also has some prominent history in its veins. William Jennings Bryan, called the Silver-Tongued Orator and The Great Commoner, was born here. He was the United States secretary of state, 1913–15, and a three-time presidential candidate. *Bryan's birthplace* is now a museum located near the public library, which also bears his name.

Salem's American Legion Post was a pioneer in producing the GI Bill of Rights. It took seven months and eight days from the time the Salem Legionnaires collaborated on the plan before it was approved by Congress in 1944.

Salem is full of historic architecture, and the Chamber of Commerce, 210 West Main Street, Salem 62881, (618) 548–3010, has published a walking tour that highlights the sites. The tour begins at North Broadway and

Boone Streets and takes you through a *former stagecoach station, Max Corsset's Cafe* (home of Miracle Whip Salad Dressing, which was sold to Kraft Foods in 1931 for $300), past the *Marion County Courthouse,* a *statue of William Jennings Bryan* by Gutzon Borglum (famed sculptor of Mount Rushmore) in the park, and the *Silas Bryan Farm,* former home of William Jennings Bryan. A separate tour of the home is available. The tour continues on through several homes of the 1800s and 1900s and ends at Bryan's birthplace. Another illustrious native son was the late football great Jim Finks, recently inducted into the NFL Hall of Fame.

The *Halfway Tavern,* 10 miles east of Salem on U.S. Highway 50 East, was built in 1818 and served as a stagecoach stop until 1861. It was built on the trail across Illinois that Capt. George Rogers Clark had used in 1799, and Abraham Lincoln later used it as a stopover.

Oil was first discovered near Salem in 1909, but the oil boom came in 1938. The Salem Oilfield ranked seventeenth in the nation in volume of oil production. It currently produces more than 3,000,000 barrels a year. Pumps can be seen at the field 6 miles southwest of Salem.

Ingram's Log Cabin Village in Kinmundy, northeast of Salem, has thirteen authentic log buildings dating from 1818 to 1860. Ten of the buildings are authentically furnished and open to the public. The inn is a large,

The Town the Train Built

*I*llinois Central Gulf Railroad founded the town of Centralia, just southeast of Carlyle Lake. It's an interesting spot to visit for lots of reasons, but here are two:

The rail company had car shops on the south edge of town and at one time held deeds to almost all the land in the central business district. So this proud old railroad town displays one of the last great classic steam engines made here—Engine 2500, now located in Fairview Park. Volunteers had to lay more than 1 mile of temporary track to get this behemoth here from its former location.

Also in Centralia's central business district stands the Centralia Carillon, a huge tower boasting sixty-five bells, the largest of which weighs almost six tons. Local carilloneurs (that's what the musicians who play this instrument are called) must huff and puff up 173 steps (that's fourteen stories) to address a keyboard that's almost 8 feet long. The instrument can produce any kind of music, from pop and classical to marches and college fight songs. But music written specifically for the carillon is preferred by these specialized music wizards, who produce such dulcet tones from this mammoth instrument. Call (618) 532–6789.

Ingram's Log Cabin Village

two-story building, once a stagecoach stop. There are several homes, Millican's grocery store and post office, an apothecary, a cobbler's shop, and a church. The village is on sixty-five acres of land with a seven-acre lake.

Hours are by appointment. Contact Ingram's Log Cabin Village, Kinmundy 62854; (618) 547–7123.

The *Stephen A. Forbes State Fish and Wildlife Area,* 14 miles northeast of Salem, has outdoor recreation including fishing, hunting, boating, picnicking, water-skiing, swimming, camping, hiking, and horseback riding. A *Fisheries Research Center* conducts aquatic biology and fisheries experiments. The center is open to visitors Monday through Friday 7:00 A.M. to 4:00 P.M. Tours can be arranged by calling (618) 245–6348.

For information about the park, contact the Site Superintendent, Stephen A. Forbes State Fish and Wildlife Area, R.R. 1, Kinmundy 62865; (618) 547–3381.

Jefferson County is filled with southern hospitality brought over the state line from Dixie. Mount Vernon, the county seat, was settled by southerners and remains peopled by the descendants of southern families.

Mount Vernon is also known as "The King City" because it "crowns southern Illinois."

A variety of activities awaits tourists, ranging from cultural activities to historic sites, to sweet corn and watermelon festivals.

Top Annual Events

Riverboat Days, Cairo, early October,
(618) 734–2737

Birding in the Cache Wetlands,
Belknap, early October, (618) 634–2231

Oktoberfest, Maeystown, mid-October,
(618) 458–6660

Fort de Chartres Winter Rendezvous,
Prairie du Rocher, early November,
(618) 284–7230

Christmas Bird Count, Marion,
early December, (618) 997–3344

Bald Eagle Watch Tours, Marion, early to
mid-February, (618) 997–3344

Carlyle Lake Spring Cleanup,
Carlyle, mid-April, (618) 594–2484

Les Journees Pour Les Jeunes Gens,
Prairie du Rocher, early May,
(618) 284–7230

Herb, Gardening & Quilt Show,
Ellis Grove, early May, (618) 859–3031

Fruehlingfest (Springfest),
Maeystown, early May, (618) 458–6660

Heritage Days,
Okawville, mid-June, (618) 243–5694

Fort de Chartres Annual Rendezvous,
Prairie du Rocher, early June,
(618) 284–7230

Archeology Day, Kampsville, late July,
(618) 653–4316

Cobden Backyard BBQ,
Cobden, early July, (618) 893–2425

Annual Popeye Picnic, Chester, mid-
September, (618) 826–4567

Murphysboro Apple Festival,
Murphysboro, mid-September,
(800) 526–1500

**Traditional Music Festival & Craft
Show,** Kaskaskia, late September,
(618) 859–3741

The *Mitchell Museum,* on the grounds of *Cedarhurst,* an eighty-acre estate, features an 8,000-square-foot exhibit gallery, a smaller lecture gallery, and storage for its extensive collection of nineteenth- and twentieth-century American art acquired by the late John R. and Eleanor Mitchell.

Exhibits specially selected by the Mitchell Museum rotate monthly and include traveling exhibits and annually scheduled shows featuring southern Illinois artists.

To reach the museum, from Broadway turn north at Twenty-seventh Street and then go east on Richview Road to the museum entrance. Museum hours are Tuesday through Saturday 10:00 A.M. to 5:00 P.M. and Sunday 1:00 to 5:00 P.M.; closed Monday and national holidays. For information call (618) 242–1236.

Cedarhurst has several other attractions including hiking paths, a bird sanctuary, the Cedarhurst Arts Center, and a nineteenth-century restored village. The *Juniper Ridge Trail* is a half-mile path around Mitchell Pond, and the *Braille Trail* has been developed for the sight-impaired. A shelter for bird observation is on the Juniper Ridge Trail.

Visit the *Cedarhurst Arts Center,* which contains the county's first jail, a log structure built in 1820, and a log church dating from the 1870s. The Historical Society also has a small museum on the grounds, which is open for special occasions.

Cedarhurst is open Tuesday through Sunday from 8:00 A.M. to 4:00 P.M.; closed Monday and national holidays. The Arts Center is open Tuesday through Friday 8:00 A.M. to 4:00 P.M. Call (618) 244–6130.

The *Veterans Memorial Walkway* is a memorial to all Jefferson County soldiers killed in war. A special bronze plaque is mounted on granite for each soldier, and these granite stones border the County Courthouse at Route 37 and Main Street in downtown Mount Vernon. An 8-foot-tall black Carmelian granite monolith lists the wars in which Jefferson County citizens participated.

And the *Appellate Courthouse* has plenty of history within its walls. Abraham Lincoln successfully argued a famous tax case here in 1859, and Clara Barton used the building as a hospital in 1888. It is now the Fifth District Appellate Court and law library. Tours of the building are available when the court is not in session. It is located at Main and Fourteenth Streets. Hours are Monday through Friday 8:30 A.M. to 4:30 P.M. Call (618) 242–3120 for information.

The newly remodeled *Brehm Memorial Library* houses historical documents regarding local history and genealogy. It is located at 101 South Seventh Street, 62864, and its hours are Monday through Thursday 9:00 A.M. to 8:00 P.M., Friday 9:00 A.M. to 5:00 P.M., Saturday noon to 6:00 P.M., and Sunday 1:00 to 5:00 P.M.; (618) 242–6322.

> ## Southwestern Illinois Trivia
>
> *Steamboat pilots called the section of the Mississippi River between Cairo and St. Louis "the graveyard" because more than 300 boats had sunk in that stretch of water by 1867.*

The *Sweet Corn and Watermelon Festival* is held the third week in August. A week of activities includes free sweet corn and watermelon served in the town square. Contact the Mount Vernon Convention and Visitors Bureau, P.O. Box 2580, Mount Vernon 62864; (618) 242–3151.

As well as providing nine to eleven million gallons of water daily for the area, *Rend Lake* provides a recreational retreat. The lake is surrounded by rolling hill prairie country and has excellent crappie fishing. Waterfowl are hunted here as well as deer, rabbit, dove, quail, pheasant, and squirrel.

Picnic grounds for both small and large groups are adjacent to the lake, and *Sleepy Hollow Group Area* is designed for handicapped and disadvantaged youth groups. Advance reservations are necessary for that area.

Beaches are located at the **South Sandusky Recreation Area** and **North Marcum Recreation Area.** There are many boat launching facilities for sailboats and motorboats, and a marina is located on the west side of the lake. An eighteen-hole golf course, tennis courts, pro shop, trap shooting, restaurant, and meeting rooms are also available to tourists.

Observation of geese and ducks, eagles, osprey, loon, swans, heron, and songbirds on the Mississippi Flyway is a special treat for bird-watchers.

For information contact the U.S. Army Corps of Engineers, Rend Lake Management Office, R.R. 3, Benton 62812; (618) 724–2493; or Rend Lake Conservancy District, P.O. Box 497, Benton 62812; (618) 439–4321.

Franklin County shares its greatest natural resource, Rend Lake, with its neighbor, Jefferson County, to the north. Second largest in the state, the 18,900-acre lake has 162 miles of rugged shoreline, next to which is the 3,300-acre **Wayne Fitzgerrell State Park.** The park has 250 campsites, some with electric hookup, and offers a broad variety of recreational activities. For information contact the Site Superintendent, Wayne Fitzgerrell State Park, Route 154 and I–57, Benton 62812; (618) 629–2320. The park is open year-round.

The Rend Lake Reservoir was created by damming the Big Muddy and Casey Fork Rivers, giving it its unusual Y shape. The Army Corps of Engineers is responsible for the administration of the lake and its visitors center.

Crappie, bass, and catfish are the most-caught species here. In season, hunting is available for all types of waterfowl, quail, pheasant, rabbit, deer, and squirrel.

Families will enjoy the picnic areas scattered throughout the lake's recreation areas. Swimming beaches are located at the South Sandusky and North Marcum recreation areas. The one marina on the west side of the lake has boat rentals available.

On the east side of the lake, the **Rend Lake Golf Course** is a twenty-seven-hole PGA facility with especially scenic terrain. Tennis courts, a restaurant, and a championship trap-shooting range are part of the club. Bird-watching is excellent here, as the lake is situated on the Mississippi Flyway, allowing the observer to view great migrations of geese and ducks and offering sightings of eagles, ospreys, loons, herons, and other birds. In Wayne Fitzgerrell State Park, dog field-trial grounds are host to regional and national championships. For information contact the lake management office; (618) 724–2493. Located on the lake in the state park is **Rend Lake Resort;** (618) 629–2211. This new state facility has cabins and a "boat-el."

In mid-May each year the **Rend Lake Water Festival** features parades, a carnival, craft exhibits, and entertainment. Call (618) 438–2121.

For all of us who love days off, Franklin County's seat, Benton, is where Memorial Day was first established. Here John A. Logan, a Civil War major general, United States representative and senator, and candidate for vice-president in 1884, proposed the holiday in 1868, as commander of the Grand Army of the Republic. A historical marker designates his home site at 204 South Main Street.

At the southern edge of the county, West Frankfort boasts a fine **Area Historical Museum** on 2000 East St. Louis Street, 62896, with an old one-room schoolhouse, a mines and minerals display, and a program of events such as "Christmas on the Prairie" and "Brides Through the Decades."

Lodge Luxuries

*R*end Lake Resort is more than just your typical state-park overnight accommodation. This multigabled waterside getaway, which sits on the edge of the 18,900-acre Rend Lake, is one of the state's finest first-class resorts in one of the region's top recreational areas—Wayne Fitzgerrell State Park.

This stylish lodge creates an elegant atmosphere in the midst of natural wonders, with all ninety-one guest chambers (resort rooms and cabins) boasting balconies and decks. (Ask for one of the rooms featuring a lake-front view.) There are also full private baths, television for kids who can't live without it, telephone, and more.

Some special accommodations offer sleeping lofts and spas with whirlpools, too.

Let's not forget to mention the resort's premier restaurant, Windows on Rend. Whether you choose to dine inside or on the outdoor deck, you'll enjoy great food—including the restaurant's specialty: pork chops and catfish (though not necessarily together!).

And when you're ready to work off that meal, choose from a twenty-seven-hole golf course, fishing, pontoon boat rentals, hiking, swimming, tennis, even bird-watching (blue herons and bald eagles are plentiful here). Call (800) 633–3341.

Southwestern Illinois Trivia

The late Robert Pershing Wadlow, "the world's tallest man" at 8'11," was born in Alton.

Kaskaskia Island is the only part of Illinois that lies west of the Mississippi River.

There's also a branch in the old depot downtown housing veterans' memorabilia. Each September the museum puts on an *"Apple Butter Stir,"* in which the sweet stuff is made in huge copper kettles. It's usually all sold before it's finished cooking! The museum serves a tasty homestyle lunch on Wednesday and Thursday from 11:00 A.M. to 1:00 P.M. for less than $5.00! It's the best deal going! Museum hours are 9:00 A.M. to 4:00 P.M. Wednesday and Thursday and 1:30 to 4:00 P.M. on Sunday; closed January. Free admission; (618) 932–6159.

Du Quoin got its start as a stopping point on the old Shawneetown-to-Kaskaskia Road, where there was a crossing at the Little Muddy River. The town took its name from Kaskaskia Indian Chief Jean Baptiste Ducoigne, who came to the aid of George Rogers Clark after the fall of Kaskaskia and later served in the Revolutionary Army under Lafayette in Virginia. His tribe camped near the spot of the first white settlement, which took his name. When the railroad came to town in 1853, the town site moved a short distance to its present location.

Today the area is an important center for agriculture and mining and is the largest coal-producing county in Illinois. Numerous strip mines are found throughout the region. Du Quoin's major annual event is the *Du Quoin State Fair,* which begins ten days prior to Labor Day and runs through the holiday. Over 200,000 visitors are attracted to the more than-sixty-year-old event. Name entertainment, championship auto racing, and world-class harness racing headline the fair. The fairground's dirt track is called the "Magic Mile" for the number of speed records that have been set here. Tractor pulls and livestock shows round out the schedule. Throughout the year other events are staged at the fairgrounds, including camping rallies and a rodeo. Contact the Du Quoin State Fairgrounds at P.O. Box 191, Du Quoin 62832; (618) 542–9373.

Randolph is one of the most historically and geographically unique counties in all of Illinois. A tiny appendage protruding into the main body of Missouri, Kaskaskia Island is the only part of the state lying west of the Mississippi River.

Kaskaskia is the second-oldest settlement (after Cahokia) in the state, founded as a Jesuit mission in 1703. Thus, the area's French heritage is rich. Fort Kaskaskia was erected in the village and served as an outpost in the French and Indian War (1754–63). After the Treaty of Paris in 1763, the region came under British control. In 1778

George Rogers Clark captured the settlement for America, and it became a county of Virginia. It became part of the new Northwest Territory in 1787, part of the Indiana Territory in 1800, the capital of the Illinois Territory in 1809, and the first state capital in 1818 (until 1820 when the capital moved to Vandalia).

Kaskaskia declined in importance, and Mississippi floods around 1885 eventually destroyed the old settlement, cutting a new channel for the Mississippi through the heart of the town and creating Kaskaskia Island on the western side.

What remained on the eastern side of the river is now **Fort Kaskaskia State Historic Site** (618–859–3741). The park is an especially scenic area with places for picnicking among the trees. Situated on a hill, it overlooks the Mississippi River and Kaskaskia Island.

Just below the park, at the foot of the hill, between Chester and Ellis Grove, off Route 3, is the **Pierre Menard Home,** now a state memorial. Built in 1802 in French Colonial style, with a wide gallery porch and a low, hipped roof, this was the residence of the first lieutenant governor of Illinois, one of the most important men in the history of the territory. The house has been restored and furnished with pieces of the period. Open daily except major holidays; (618) 859–3031. The museum is free to the public, with hours from 9:00 A.M. to 5:00 P.M.

On **Kaskaskia Island** is the **Liberty Bell of the West.** A gift from Louis XV of France, the bell was towed upriver from New Orleans by men pulling it on a barge. Today it's a state memorial. To reach the island

Joyeux Noël!

*I*n Illinois, you always have one last chance to celebrate the Christmas season, and with a French accent at that! It's all thanks to the Twelfth Day of Christmas Celebration at the Pierre Menard Historic Site in Ellis Grove, held in early January. You'll enjoy a lively afternoon of French songs and dances, enjoy samples of colonial-style French pastries, and take tours of the vintage home led by guides dressed in period costumes.

But there is no Christmas tree in the French colonial holiday celebration. The French didn't raise trees for the Yuletide season. Rather, they saved their biggest celebration for the Twelfth Day of Christmas (the day the Three Wise Men are said to have come upon the Christ child in Bethlehem). So there is a nativity scene at the home.

Leave it to the French to be different.

cross the Chester toll bridge at Route 51 and travel 12 miles to St. Mary's, Missouri, then follow the directional signs to the island.

Chester, the county seat, is the site of **Greenwood Cemetery,** where Shadrach Bond, the first governor of the state (1818–22), is buried. A white granite monument erected by the state in 1883 marks the grave site.

Chester, too, is home to Popeye, the lovable sailorman. His creator, Elzie Crisler Segar, was born here in 1894. In 1977 a **statue of Popeye** was erected in Segar Memorial Park. A **Popeye Picnic and Parade** are usually held the first weekend in September.

North of Chester on Route 3, the Colvis and Gross families have large orchards with peaches, apples, and strawberries for sale. At the **Colvis Orchard,** you can view apple cider being pressed.

Seven miles east of Chester on Route 150 between Chester and Bremen is a **covered bridge** over Mary's River. One of the few such structures in the state, the 98-foot single-span bridge of hand-hewn native oak was erected in 1854.

North of Chester and Fort Kaskaskia are Prairie du Rocher (field of rock) and Fort de Chartres. No missionary is responsible for the settlement here. Instead credit goes to an early entrepreneur who set the stage for a long line of American land speculators to follow. John Law was a Scotch businessman who obtained a charter from the French government to colonize the region. His Company of the West brought in immigrants from France,

Covered Bridge over Mary's River

SOUTHWESTERN ILLINOIS

Italy, Switzerland, and Germany. Law promised speculators great profits, but his "Mississippi Bubble" burst in 1720, leaving the settlers stranded.

Most stayed, under the protection of Pierre Duque, Sieur de Boisbriant, commandant of the Illinois country. By 1720 he completed the construction of *Fort de Chartres,* named for the Duc de Chartres, son of the French regent. The fort was rebuilt three times, and its final form was considered one of the strongest in North America.

Today parts of the old fort have been reconstructed and are part of a state park. Each year in June the *Fort de Chartres Rendezvous* recreates life in the French era with volunteers in militia uniforms, a fife and drum corps, much firing of cannon, and French Colonial cooking. In early October there is an exciting *French and Indian War Encampment.* Fort de Chartres is open year-round, except major holidays, 9:00 A.M. to 5:00 P.M. Admission is free; (618) 284–7230.

In the northwest corner of the county, at Sparta, is the *Charter Oak School,* one of only a few octagonal schoolhouses remaining in the United States. Built in 1873, it served its public purpose until 1953.

From Chester, *U.S. Bicycle Route 76* leads east to Shiloh Hill and the county line, along scenic back roads. Also out in the country is *Kloth's Antiques,* one of the county's better collectible shops, located at the junction of Route 4 and Route 150, 2 miles west of Steeleville.

Perhaps one of the most unusual hotels in the state is the *Original Mineral Springs Hotel and Bath House* in Okawville, just off I–64 in the northwest part of the county. Built in 1892, the forty-room hostelry is listed in the National Register of Historic Places. For more than ninety years, guests have been coming for the relaxing mineral water baths. Book a Swedish massage and a therapeutic soak when you visit. Open year-round: rates for double $48.30 to $71.95, (618) 243–5458.

The *Okawville Heritage House and Museum* also is listed in the National Register and gives the visitor an idea of life in the last century. Open 1:00 to 4:00 P.M. Monday, Wednesday, and Friday, and noon to 4:00 P.M. Saturday and Sunday.

Magic Waters

I'm a lifelong Illinois resident, but it took me years to discover the Original Mineral Springs and Bath House in Okawville. It is the only place in the Land of Lincoln where you can find a genuine mineral springs. This one has been a "tourist haven" since Native Americans introduced white settlers to its soothing waters in 1867.

These waters, rich in mineral content, were once thought to cure all kinds of ailments, from neuralgia to arthritis. At any rate, it is a great way to get a good, relaxing therapeutic soak. And you can book a Swedish massage while you're here, too.

Nashville is the county seat, named after the hometown of the first settlers from Tennessee. In the northeast part of the city, on thirty-seven acres of rolling wooded land, **Nashville Memorial Park** is a center for outdoor recreational activity. A swimming complex with separate areas for diving, toddlers, and intermediate swimmers was completed in 1981. The pool can accommodate 371 on a busy summer day. The park's other facilities include four baseball diamonds, tennis courts, a playground, picnic areas, and even a challenging par 36 nine-hole municipal golf course.

In town the **First Presbyterian Church,** 300 West St. Louis Street, 62263, is one of the oldest churches in Illinois. Organized in 1832, the present church building dates from 1884.

The **Washington County Historical Society Museum,** 300 South Kaskaskia Street, 62263, houses artifacts and exhibits relative to the history of the area. The museum is open Sunday 1:30 to 3:30 P.M. or by appointment. The historical society also maintains the historic **McKelvey one-room schoolhouse** just west of town (open by appointment only).

Or plan a visit on the third week in September when Nashville holds its yearly **Fall Festival Days** on the courthouse square, complete with music, food, and crafts.

Four miles south of Nashville, off Route 127, is the **Washington County Conservation Area,** a 1,377-acre preserve set in rolling wooded hills. A central part of the area is a 248-acre lake with 13 miles of shoreline. Bass, bluegill, crappie, and catfish are the most frequently caught species. The lake, which has a ten-horsepower limit, has launch ramps and a marina that rents boats and motors and sells tackle, bait, and snacks. A 14-mile trail winds through the woods of the conservation area. Campers, too, can enjoy the habitat, with campsites for tent camping and others with electric hookups and showers. The park is accessible year-round.

More Surprises

Giant City, Fern Rocks, Buffalo Rock, Rainbow Arch . . . these names can't possibly describe stunning geographical features in the prairie state of Illinois, right?

Wrong. The surpassing terrain, at least surprising to visitors who haven't ventured to the far reaches of southern Illinois, is one of the great revelations of this region, one filled with rock formations and landforms that took more than 200 million years to develop into fantastical shapes. Then there's the Shawnee National Forest, another of Mother Nature's treasures. And what about those craggy, tree-studded bluffs hugging the shores of the Mississippi and Ohio rivers?

Surprises are endless for travelers here, so take your time (actually, you have no choice due to geography and resultant road patterns) and enjoy nature's handiwork.

The Great Outdoors

Civil War Memories

Once you stretch toward the southernmost points of Illinois, especially in the foothills-of-the-Ozarks country, you start to notice more mentions of the Civil War. When I'm in Carbondale, I like to take a brief sidetrip to Woodlawn Cemetery, which is listed on the National Register of Historic Places.

It was here in 1866 that the first official Memorial Day service was observed honoring our fighting men who died in battle. Wander the tranquil grounds and you'll discover more than sixty graves of Civil War soldiers.

arbondale, with a population of 26,000, is the largest city in Jackson County and home to **Southern Illinois University** (founded in 1869). The college, with 24,000 students, is known for its sports teams, the Salukis, especially in basketball, which is played at SIU Arena, and football, at McAndrew Stadium. If you're in town during the season, be sure to catch a game with all its Southern Illinois enthusiasm. For tickets contact Athletic Ticket Office, SIU, Carbondale 62901; (618) 453–5319. The university's **Faner Museum and Art Galleries** have changing exhibits and works of special interest to southern Illinois. Open daily Tuesday through Saturday 9:00 A.M. to 3:00 P.M., Sunday 1:30 to 4:30 P.M. Call (618) 453–5388.

With the city having a name like Carbondale, one might guess that a primary industry hereabouts is coal mining. On the banks of the Big Muddy River, which flows to the west of Carbondale, was the first coal-mining operation in Illinois. As early as 1810 the river bluffs supplied coal for local needs and to ship downriver to New Orleans. The beauty of the landscape, however, is largely undisturbed, with the Shawnee National Forest beginning just miles to the south and rivers and lakes all around.

Giant City State Park is located in the southeast corner of the county, 12 miles south of Carbondale off U.S. Highway 51 and Route 13 with 3,700 acres of recreational area. The park takes its name from the huge and dramatic sandstone formations here, such as the dramatic Devil's Stand-table, just west of the park's **Interpretive Center.** The center has trained staff who will explain the various natural features of the park and who present programs on its points of interest.

The **Robinson cabin** in the park is a reconstructed building that depicts life as it was in the area around 1880. An earlier structure, however, is the **Stone Fort,** a prehistoric stone wall at the top of an 80-foot sandstone cliff dating from A.D. 600–900. This is one of ten examples of such forts in southern Illinois, which may have been used for defense or ceremonial purposes.

Other evidence of prehistoric people in the region is found in rock shelters, whose roofs are presumably smoke-stained from campfires.

During the Civil War these shelters were used by deserters from both sides.

A surprisingly modern construction in the park is the award-winning design of the park's 100,000-gallon spherical water tank. Eighty-two feet high, the tower has an observation platform with excellent views of the park. Some 50 feet up, the platform is reached by a spiral steel staircase.

Within the park is the 100-acre **Fern Rocks Nature Preserve,** where such rare plants as French's shooting star and large flowering mint may be found. Hiking is allowed only on the preserve's well-marked trail. Spring may be the best time to visit the park, for it is abloom with more than 170 different types of ferns and flowering plants. Birds abound in the park as well, and they make for excellent bird-watching.

Fishing is offered at **Little Grassy Lake,** adjacent to the park, and picnicking and camping are available, too (161 sites, 117 with electric hookup). For information on Giant City State Park, contact the Site Superintendent, R.R. 1, Makanda 62958; (618) 457–4836. You will receive a brochure that includes a short discussion of Little Grassy Lake. For a complete list of regulations governing the use of boats on this lake, however, write: Refuge Manager, Crab Orchard National Wildlife Refuge, Marion 62958.

Noncampers will opt for the **Giant City Lodge and Cottages**—thirty-four rustic cabins built of native stone in the state park. The dining room serves hearty meals around a handsome fireplace. There's a swimming pool here, too. Open February to December; (618) 457–4921.

Land of the Giants

*T*his might be one of the most beautiful natural areas in the entire state. Giant City is nestled in the dense hills of the sprawling, 260,000-acre Shawnee National Forest. It got its name from early settlers who thought that the unusual sandstone rock formations, formed more than 200 million years ago, resembled the streets of a city built for a giant.

That's what I thought, too, the first time

I ventured down to this extreme southern portion of the state. But the long drive from Chicago was well worth it. And overnighting at the Giant City State Park Lodge was another good decision. Built in 1930 by members of the government's Civilian Conservation Corps, the Lodge is located in the midst of nearly 4,000 acres of sandstone bluffs and woods. Both the park and the lodge are listed on the National Registerof Historic Places.

Jackson County's second major city is Murphysboro, the county seat. The apple is king here, with more than thirty-one commercial orchards in the vicinity. In fact, mid-September ushers in the annual *Apple Festival,* with pie-baking, apple-peeling and apple-butter contests, a beauty pageant, and a parade led by Captain Applesauce. For dates and events, call the Chamber of Commerce at (618) 684–6421. Historically, Murphysboro is the birthplace of Gen. John A. Logan, Civil War leader and United States senator.

Lake Kincaid, northwest of Murphysboro, was created in 1972 by the state as a recreation area and water supply for the region. Its 2,750 acres, with 82 miles of timbered shoreline, serve those purposes admirably. Fishing, camping, boating, swimming, and hunting in season are offered. Bass fishing is best during the months of April and May in this deep reservoir, bottoming out at 68 feet near the dam. Lake Kincaid is bounded by Route 149, Route 3, and Route 151 and is located approximately 8 miles west of Murphysboro.

Two marinas service the boating public. One of them, *Kincaid Lake Marina,* not only sells bait and tackle but also has boat rentals, a restaurant, and campground; (618) 687–4914. To get there travel west from Murphysboro on Route 149 approximately 8 miles to a blacktop road marked Kincaid Lake.

Lake Murphysboro State Park is situated about 1 mile west of Murphysboro off Route 149. The 904-acre park offers a number of recreational possibilities, from fishing to woodland hikes. An unusual feature of the park is the patches of native wild orchids. Nine varieties grow here. Camping includes sites with electric hookups (seventy-seven sites total). Contact Site Superintendent, R.R. 4, Murphysboro 62966; (618) 684–2867.

Cedar Lake, in the southern part of the county, is a 1,750-acre body of water only 4 miles south of Carbondale on Route 127.

Crab Orchard National Wildlife Refuge was started in the 1930s when the government had rows of pine trees planted to provide work for the WPA (Works Project Administration) and the Civilian Conservation Corps. In 1947 the refuge was officially established by the Department of the Interior and now covers 43,000 acres. The area includes three lakes, twelve natural areas, and a 4,000-acre wilderness area.

Forest, prairie, and wetland plants and animals live harmoniously in Crab Orchard. Wildlife management is centered on providing winter feeding and resting areas for Canada geese, and the refuge's goose

Southwestern Illinois Trivia

Collinsville boasts the "world's tallest catsup bottle," which is actually a 170-foot water tank.

flock may build up to 200,000 birds by December. Many species of ducks and bald eagles can be seen in the trees overlooking the goose flock.

Spring brings most of the migratory waterfowl, and eagles, whitetail deer (common year-round), coyote, beaver, muskrat, opossum, and raccoon also inhabit the area. A bird list is available at the refuge headquarters.

Wildlife-oriented recreation is encouraged, and the opportunities for wildlife observation are excellent. For hikers there is the self-guided ***Chamnesstown School Trail.*** The trail explores a reconstructed schoolhouse and ventures out along old fire trails in open areas of the refuge. Observation towers are wonderful lookouts for watching geese, and there are picnicking areas by ***Crab Orchard Lake.***

Hunting and fishing are allowed, and there are a concession-operated campground and marina as well as swimming.

The refuge is located between Carbondale and Marion, accessible from I–57. Visitors are permitted only in designated areas. The visitors center is open 8:00 A.M. to 4:30 P.M. Monday through Friday. For information contact the Project Manager, Crab Orchard National Wildlife Refuge, P.O. Box J, Carterville 62918; (618) 997–3344.

Little Grassy Fish Hatchery, downstream of Little Grassy Lake, is a 115-acre hatchery with a visitors' observation area where you can view rearing, spawning, and egg incubation tanks.

The warm-water hatchery combines two methods of fish rearing: intensive and extensive culture. Intensive culture uses a high water exchange through a rearing unit for environmental control and allows rearing of large numbers of fish per unit. Extensive culture uses earthen ponds, an extension of nature, but with some control as to the number of fish per pond and the food organisms available.

The original hatchery was built in 1959, and expansion and modernization began in July 1979, as a result of a state study of projected demands for fish stocking. Largemouth bass, bluegill, redear sunfish, and channel catfish are reared here as well as some smallmouth bass, walleye, muskellunge, northern pike, and striped bass.

The hatchery is southeast of Carbondale and accessible via Little Grassy Road. It is within the boundaries of Crab Orchard Wildlife Refuge. Visitor tours are on a self-guided basis, though employee-guided tours can be scheduled for large groups. Hours are 8:00 A.M. to 3:30 P.M. daily; (618) 529–4100.

Nearby Marion has a quaint little shopping and dining house called *Collector's Choice,* 500 South Court Street; (618) 997–4883. Antiques, collectibles, and crafts fill this charmingly decorated Victorian home. A country store takes you back to the era of the well-stocked cracker barrel, and a tearoom features gourmet entrees. Hours for the stores are Monday through Saturday 10:00 A.M. to 5:00 P.M., closed on Sunday. Tearoom hours are 11:00 A.M. to 2:00 P.M. daily, closed on Sunday.

Johnson County is a paradise for those interested in Indian history and nature.

Buffalo Rock, 3 miles northeast of Simpson off Route 147 toward Reynoldsburg, has the outline of a buffalo etched into the side of a sandstone cliff. Indians are said to be the artists responsible for this drawing. The trail leading to the site is filled with lovely beech and sugar maple trees, and dozens of colorful wildflowers carpet the forest floor in spring.

The *Milestone Bluff,* north off Route 147 at Robbs, is an ancient Indian dwelling and burial site. The bluff has a prehistoric stone wall and Indian grave sites. The Mississippi Indians are believed to have inhabited the area from A.D. 1000 to 1500. The hiking trail to the bluff begins at the parking lot.

Rainbow Arch, less than 1 mile west of Cypress off Route 37, is a bridge of sandstone rock surrounded by beautiful white and red oak trees and wild black cherries. One of the largest natural bridges in southern Illinois, it is 66 feet long, 3 1/2 feet wide, and 7 feet high at its peak.

The *River-to-River Trail,* east off U.S. Highway 45, 3 1/2 miles north of I–24 at Vienna, is a dirt trail stretching nearly halfway around the entire southern tip of Illinois. Three connecting trails make it more than 23 miles long. Plans are being made to extend the trail over the entire southern end of Illinois.

And *Penn Central Tunnel,* 1 mile west off U.S. 45 and 6 miles north of I–24 at Vienna, is one of the oldest stretches of track still in operation. Original construction of the tunnel began in 1871–72 when a tunnel was blasted 800 feet through sandstone and shale. Speed on the track is restricted to 5 miles per hour in the tunnel, 8 miles per hour on the open track. Despite track conditions one train still makes a daily run.

Little Black Slough Natural Area, half a mile east of Route 37 and Route 146, boasts some of the most unusual and spectacular terrain in all of Illinois—and is one of its best-kept secrets. The area is a mixture of primeval tupelo and cypress swamps, rich floodplain forest, and upland woods, with small patches of limestone prairie glades. Some of the oldest living trees east of the Mississippi River are here, and a boardwalk allows access to the heart of the swamp. Nine miles of hiking trails wind through Little Black Slough, and the towering tupelo and cypress trees rising from the swamp make it a unique site in Illinois.

Ferne Clyffe State Park, 1 mile south of Goreville, is another natural eye-opener. It has more than 1,000 acres of the largest bluffs and caves in the area. A sixteen-acre fishing lake is within the park. The preserve has a central valley from which radiate gorges and canyons. Shady dells, natural cathedrals, domes, brooks, cascades, and rills have formed here. Several so-called caves are not really caves but great protruding ledges of rock that make an arched roof.

For information about both Ferne Clyffe State Park and Little Black Slough Natural Area, contact the Site Superintendent, Ferne Clyffe State Park, P.O. Box 120, Goreville 62939; (618) 995–2411.

Hawks Cave is a sheer cliff of stone so hewn by wind and water that an excavation has been made at its base at least 150 feet long and as many feet high. The cave has a natural pulpit and excellent acoustics.

Park facilities include picnicking, fishing, camping, and horseback-riding trails. Call (618) 995–2411 for more information.

Vienna can't live up to the expectations of its name, but it does have some attractions worth seeing. The *Vienna Times Building* is beautifully preserved. It was built around 1890 as a bank, and in 1915 the *Vienna Times* newspaper took it over. It is at the Vienna public square 4 blocks west of the junction of Route 146W and U.S. Highway 45 at the corner of East Main and Fourth Streets. It is open to the public during business hours.

The *Paul Powell Home,* also 4 blocks west of this junction at 404 Vine Street, 62995, is the home of former Illinois Secretary of State and Illinois Representative Paul Powell. Call (618) 658–4911 for hours. A historical museum is located in the basement of the house.

Cairo, the county seat of Alexander County, is where the magnolia vies with the mimosa. The southernmost city in Illinois, it stands on the tip of a narrow peninsula where the Mississippi and Ohio Rivers join on their journey to the Gulf of Mexico.

This area, known as Little Egypt, has many attractions for tourists to explore. *The Hewer,* Cairo's art treasure, is a heroic bronze nude by George Grey Barnard. It stands in Halliday Park between Ninth and Tenth Streets, presented to the city in 1906 by Mrs. W. P. Halliday and her children in memory of Capt. W. P. Halliday. The statue reads: A VISION OF MEN LABORING ON THE SHORE OF A FLOOD HEWING AND DRAGGING WOOD TO SAVE THE PEOPLE FROM DEATH AND DESTRUCTION. Lorado Taft said *The Hewer* was one of the two finest nudes produced in America.

The **Cairo Public Library** contains several fine works of art. The building itself is an example of Queen Anne architecture. The leaded stained-glass windows are original. In two niches at the entrance stand statues of *Clio,* the Greek muse, and *Concordia,* the Roman goddess of peace. A bronze fountain entitled **Fishing Boys** is the work of Janet Scudder, a famous American sculptor.

In the library reference room is a replica of the steamboat **City of Cairo** carved by a river pilot, Capt. Henry T. Ashton, in 1876. On the first landing is a rare *Tiffany grandfather's clock,* one of only four of its type made by Tiffany.

Other artifacts are a chandelier that originally hung in the Cairo Opera House, a desk belonging to President Andrew Jackson, Cybis porcelains, and a collection of fine paintings.

The library is open from 9:00 A.M. to 5:00 P.M. Monday through Saturday. It is located at 1609 Washington Avenue, 62914.

The **U.S. Customs House** at Washington Avenue and Fifteenth Street, is a rare example of a Palazzo or Commercial Italianate–style stone building. There are plans to reopen the building as a Civil War Museum and Cairo Tourism Office.

Southwestern Illinois Trivia

During the Revolutionary War, Illinois became part of Virginia when George Rogers Clark captured Kaskaskia and Cahokia from the English in 1778.

Magnolia Manor, 2700 Washington Avenue, 62914, is a Victorian mansion and museum. It is open Monday through Saturday 9:00 A.M. to 5:00 P.M. and Sunday from 1:00 to 5:00 P.M.; (618) 734–0201. The house is a four-story redbrick mansion of Italianate architecture. Large magnolia trees grace its lawn. There are fourteen rooms and a bed slept in by Gen. Ulysses S. Grant.

And the ***Magnolia Festival*** is an annual event that celebrates the blooming of the magnolia trees in Cairo. Dances, concerts, and other activities are held at the Magnolia Manor throughout the first week of May. Contact the Magnolia Manor for information.

Now a park, Fort Defiance, at Cairo Point, was a strategic site for settlement and fortification as early as 1673, when it was first sighted by explorers Jacques Marquette and Robert La Salle.

Where the Mississippi and Ohio Rivers meet, there is a single piece of mounted artillery. Starting in 1848 the cannon was used to greet arriving boats.

Fort Defiance State Park has facilities for picnicking and fishing on its thirty-eight acres. The ***Riverboat Memorial*** is a triple-decked cement building resembling a square boat. The first deck is a sheltered picnic area with tables. The second and third decks provide outlooks; the second also supports the flagpole. For information contact Park Ranger, Box 77, Miller City 62962; (618) 776–5281.

Mound City National Cemetery, 4 miles from the park, is a Civil War cemetery with twenty-seven identified Confederate soldiers and 2,441 unknown ones.

Also interesting is the ***Thebes Historical Courthouse*** in Thebes, west of Route 3 at Thebes Spur. It is a brick and stone courthouse set precariously near the edge of a limestone bluff overlooking the town of Thebes and the Mississippi River. The courthouse was known as the "Courthouse on the Bluff." Here Dred Scott was imprisoned and Abraham Lincoln practiced law. It is an example of Greek Revival architecture and made of local materials. The courthouse is open 10:00 A.M. to 4:00 P.M. daily; (618) 764–2600.

Between mid-December of 1838 and early March 1839, 10,000 Cherokee Indians were forced to travel 800 miles from their home in the Great Smoky Mountains to a reservation in present-day Oklahoma. The exiled Cherokees stopped in southern Illinois because of floating ice on the Mississippi and made camp. The camp provided little shelter against the unusually severe winter that year, and many died. The Cherokee's westward journey became known as the "Trail of Tears."

Trail of Tears State Forest, formerly Union State Forest, is northwest of Jonesboro near the Mississippi River. It lies within the beautiful Shawnee Hill country and is a preserve to protect native tree species of Illinois.

Approximately sixty acres are devoted to the Union State Tree Nursery, and nearly all species of trees in southern Illinois are found here.

The park has picnicking facilities, approximately forty-four trails totaling more than 36 miles, hunting, and tent camping. You can reach the park by taking Route 3 to Wolf Lake; then drive east for 5 miles. For information call (618) 833–4910.

The *Union County Conservation Area* is in the Lower Mississippi River Bottomlands Division of Illinois. It is a haven for wildlife; most prominent for five months of the year is the flock of Canada geese and other waterfowl that winter in the area. No hunting is allowed, and there are no overnight facilities. This conservation area is southwest of Jonesboro off Route 3 near Reynoldsville. For information contact the Union County Conservation Area, R.R. 2, Jonesboro 62952; (618) 833–5175.

Finally, the *Cobden Museum* in Cobden, affectionately known as the Appleknocker Town, was opened by three amateur archaeologists who spent more than thirty years searching for Indian artifacts in the southern Illinois area. They stored their finds in a basement and soon outgrew the space. Apparently the wives of the amateurs did not like having Indian skeletons and grave goods in their basements and told their husbands to move the stuff. The men decided to open a museum.

Museum hours are weekends only from 12:30 to 4:30 P.M. March through November; (618) 893–2067. It is advisable for visitors to call to make sure the museum is open. It usually closes for the winter in late November and reopens in March. Admission is free, but donations are welcome.

PLACES TO STAY IN SOUTHWESTERN ILLINOIS

CARBONDALE
Best Inns of America,
1345 East Main
Street, 62901
(618) 529–4801

Comfort Inn,
1415 East Main
Street, 62901
(618) 549–4244

Holiday Inn/Holidome,
800 East Main
Street, 62901
(618) 529–1100

Ramada Inn,
3000 West Main
Street, 62901
(800) 2–RAMADA

Touch of Nature Environmental Center Lodge
at Southern Illinois
University,
Giant City Blacktop, 62901
(618) 453–1121

DU QUOIN
Budget Inn,
Route 51 South, 62832
(618) 542–5014

St. Nicholas Hotel,
12 South Oak, 62832
(618) 542–2183

FAIRVIEW HEIGHTS
Best Western Camelot Inn,
300 Salem Place, 62208
(618) 624–3636

Drury Inn,
12 Ludwig Drive, 62208
(618) 398–8530

French Village Motel,
1344 North 94th
Street, 62208
(618) 397–7943

Hampton Inn,
150 Ludwig Drive, 62208
(618) 397–9705

MARION
Comfort Suites,
2608 West Main
Street, 62959
(618) 997–9133

Holiday Inn/Holidome,
I–57 and Route 13, 62959
(618) 997–2326

Red Lion Days Inn
I–57 and Route 13, 62959
(618) 997–1351

OKAWVILLE
Original Mineral
Springs Hotel,
506 Hanover, 62271
(618) 243–5458

**PLACES TO EAT IN
SOUTHWESTERN ILLINOIS**

CARBONDALE
Mary Lou's Grill,
114 South Illinois
Avenue, 62901
(618) 457–5084

Tres Hombres,
119 North
Washington Street, 62901
(618) 457–3308

Selected Visitors Bureaus and Chambers of Commerce

Southwestern Illinois Tourism and Convention Bureau,
10950 Lincoln Trail, Fairview Heights, 62208
(800) 442–1488

Carbondale Convention & Visitors Bureau,
1245 East Main Street, Carbondale, 62901
(800) 526–1500

Williamson County Tourism Bureau,
8588 Route 148 South, Marion, 62959
(800) 433–7399

Booby's,
406 South Illinois
Avenue, 62901
(618) 549–3366

DU QUOIN
To Perfection,
US 51 and Ill. 14, 62832
(618) 542–2002

MARION
The Pioneer's Cabin,
1325 Main Street,
(Carterville), 62959
(618) 985–8290

20s Hideout Steakhouse,
2606 West Main
Street, 62959
(618) 997–8325

**OTHER ATTRACTIONS
WORTH SEEING IN
SOUTHWESTERN ILLINOIS**

Cairo Custom House,
Cairo

Southern Illinois University
Touch of Nature
Environment Center,
Carbondale

University Museum,
Carbondale

West Walnut
Historic District,
Cairo

Hundley House,
Cairo

Chester Riverfront Mural,
Chester

Owl Creek Vineyard
and Winery,
Cobden

St. Clair Square,
Fairview Heights

Maeystown National
Historic Site,
Maeystown

Little Grand Canyon,
Murphysboro

Poos Museum,
Okawville

General Index

Entries for Festivals and Museums appear in the special indexes on pages 207–9.

GENERAL INDEX

GENERAL INDEX

Mount Pulaski Courthouse, 116
Mount Vernon, 177
Murphysboro, 189

N

Nachusa Hotel, 62
Naperville, 29
Nashville Memorial Park, 186
National Oats Popcorn Factory, 165
Nauvoo, 137
Nauvoo Restoration
    Visitor Center, 137
Nauvoo State Park, 139
Nettle Creek, 42
New Lenox, 42
New Salem State Historic Site, 147
Niabi Zoo, 82
Nike Town Chicago, 3
Normal, 119
North and South Island Parks, 42
Northern Illinois University, 71
North Marcum Recreation Area, 180
Norway, 77

O

Oak Brook, 30
Oak Brook Center, 33
Oak Brook Polo Club, 32
Oak Hill Cemetery, 145
Oakland Cemetery, 148
Ogle County Courthouse, 64
Oglesby Mansion, 123
Old Bagdad Town, 95
Old Bailey House, 136
Old Cemetery and
    Chambers Cemetery, 99
Old Graue Mill, 30
Old Grist Mill, 66
Old Illinois Iron Furnace, 166
Old Main, 142
Old Market House, 54
Old Naper Settlement, 29

Old St. Charles, 36
Old Settler's Memorial Log
    Cabin, 62
Old Shab-a-nee, 43
Old Stockade Refuge, 55
Old Waukegan, 24
Olivet Nazarene University, 45
Olney, 161
Onstot Cooper Shop, 147
Oregon, 64
Original Mineral Springs Hotel
    and Bath House, 185
Original Three Happiness, 8
Osage Orangerie Gift Shop, 127
Ottawa, 71
Ottawa Avenue Memorial
    Columns, 73

P

Paramount Arts Centre, 33
Paris, 101
Pat Crane Memorial Playhouse, 136
Pat's City and Country Cafe, 163
Patton Cabin, 122
Paul Powell Home, 192
Paul Sargent Art Gallery, 98
Pekin, 117
Penn Central Tunnel, 191
People's National Bank, 163
Peoria, 148
Peoria Historical Society, 150
Père Marquette Lodge, 151
Père Marquette State Park, 150
Perry Mastodon, 31
Peter Stewart House, 42
Pettengill-Morton House, 150
Pettit Memorial Chapel, 69
Pheasant Run, 37
Phelps Store, 145
Pierre Menard Home, 183
Pike County Courthouse, 133
Pike Marsh Nature Trail, 29

Pine Lakes Camping and
  Fishing Resort, 134
Pioneer Cemetery, 143
Pioneer Farm, 34
Pioneer Settlement, 41
Pirate Bob, 13
Pittsfield, 132
Pittsfield Theatre Guild, 133
Polar Dome Ice Rink, 38
Popeye statue, 184
Postville Courthouse, 116
Pottery Barn, The, 144
Pounds Wall, 165
Prairie Settler Day, 102
President Ronald Reagan
  Boyhood Home, 61
Princeton, 77
Printer's Row, 10
Prophetstown, 66
Prophetstown State Park, 66
Purple Martin Junction, 133

Q

Quad Cities, 80
Quad Cities Downs, 82
Quality Gardens, 60
Quincy, 127
Quincy Art Center, 129
Quincy Levee, 131

R

Rails to the River, 81
Rainbow Arch, 191
Rainey Memorial Park, 152
Ramsey Lake State Fish and
  Wildlife Area, 107
Raven's Grin Inn, 58
Ravinia Park, 23
Red Barn, 159
Red Hills State Park, 157
Reddick Mansion, 72
Reed's Canoe Trips, 44

Remembrance Rock, 141
Rend Lake, 179
Rend Lake Golf Course, 180
Rend Lake Resort, 181
Resurrection Cemetery, 11
Rialto Square Theatre, 39
Richard's Farm Restaurant, 101
Richmond, 28
River-to-River Trail, 191
Riverboat Memorial, 194
River North, 11
River Rose Inn, 167
Riverview Park, 131
Robert Ridgway Memorial
  Arboretum and Bird
  Sanctuary, 161
Robinson Cabin, 187
Rock Creek Canyon, 45
Rock Cut State Park, 68
Rock Island, 80
Rock Island Arsenal, 81
Rockford, 66
Rockome Family Style Restaurant, 95
Rockome Gardens, 95
Roodhouse Reservoir, 152
Rosa's, 15
Rosebud Cafe, 9
Ross Hotel, 145
Ross Mansion, 145
Rossville, 89
Rushville, 134
Rutledge Tavern, 147

S

St. Charles, 35
St. Charles Belle, 36
St. Louis Street Historic District, 113
Salem, 175
Salt Fork River Forest Preserve, 93
Sandwich Antiques Market, 72
Santa's Village, 38
Saturday Night Auction, 101

Festivals

Museums

About the Author

Bob Puhala is an award-winning writer and travel expert who has authored more than 30 books; he also wrote a syndicated travel column for the *Chicago Sun-Times* for 15 years. His work has appeared in several national magazines and he is a frequent expert guest on television and radio talk shows. Bob's travels have taken him extensively through America's heartland, as well as the rest of North America. Internationally, he has written on his adventures that have included everything from sliding down Alpine glaciers and trekking the Russian steppe to exploring the tropical beaches of the South Pacific and riding with a camel caravan in the Middle East.